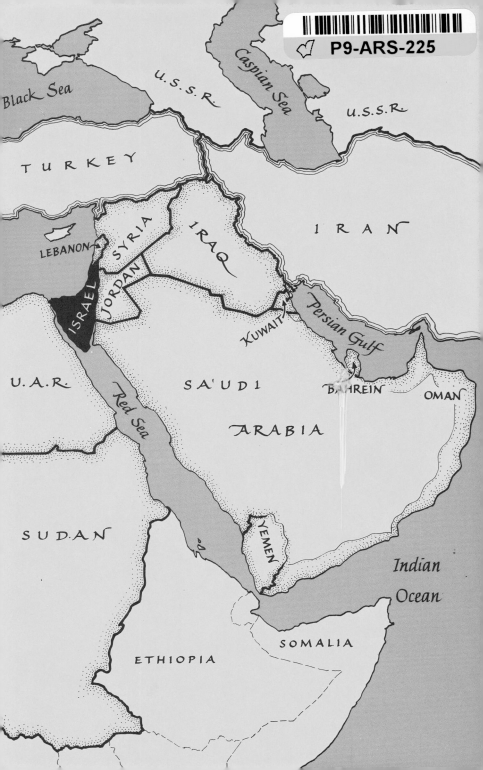

CROSSCURRENTS
IN THE
MIDDLE EAST

BY JAMES P. WARBURG

BOOKS

RECENT PAMPHLETS

JAMES P. WARBURG

CROSSCURRENTS IN THE MIDDLE EAST

A PRIMER FOR THE GENERAL READER,
INCLUDING A HISTORY OF THE REGION,
A SURVEY OF RECENT DEVELOPMENTS,
AN APPRAISAL OF
WESTERN RESPONSIBILITY
AND THE PROSPECTS FOR PEACE

ATHENEUM *NEW YORK*

1968

WI

FOREWORD

Three times within the last twenty years, the Arab states and Israel have been at war. Twice—in 1956 and 1967—the conflict has threatened to engulf the entire world in flames, for behind the two protagonists loom the two great superpowers of our time, who dare not fight each other except by proxy, be it in Southeast Asia or the Middle East.

This book attempts to provide a primer for those who are not especially familiar with the Middle East but who have become concerned about the threat to peace posed by its unstable condition.

My work—for ten years as an international banker, then as an adviser to President Roosevelt on international affairs and, finally, as a writer—has been concerned chiefly with the role of the United States in a rapidly changing world environment in which the abolition of war as an instrument of national policy has become increasingly imperative. However, as the

American official who was charged, during most of World War II, with the direction of American propaganda warfare in the European Theater and its coordination with that of our British ally, I became directly concerned with the Middle East at a time when its defense was of crucial importance. Egypt, North Africa and the whole of the Arab world required intensive study by those of us who were concerned with creating a climate of opinion favorable to the Allied cause.

The primary targets of our psychological warfare were, of course, Germany, Italy and the enemy-occupied countries. My wartime assignment was largely due to my long familiarity with Europe and, especially, with Germany.

My father, Paul Warburg, belonged to the twelfth generation of a Jewish banking family, long established in Hamburg. He and his younger brother Felix emigrated to the United States at about the turn of the century, married American wives and became partners in the New York banking house founded by my mother's father, Solomon Loeb. My father's parents and three other brothers remained in Germany, and the welfare of his German relatives remained a matter of great concern to my father throughout his life.

Because of his contribution to the much-needed reform of the American banking system, Paul Warburg was appointed by President Wilson in 1914 to the Vice-Governorship of the first Federal Reserve Board, on which he served during World War I. In 1921 he founded the International Acceptance Bank of New York in cooperation with M. M. Warburg & Co. of Hamburg and leading banks and bankers in England, France, Switzerland, Holland and the Scandinavian countries. The chief purpose of this novel institution was to promote the economic reconstruction of Europe and the world trade of the United States. In this work I was privileged to participate for over ten years. Prior to founding the International Acceptance Bank, my father had labored unsuccessfully with the economist John Maynard Keynes for a modification of the reparations clauses in the Versailles Treaty. Had he and Keynes succeeded, history might have taken a different course, as I have indicated in Chapters 6 and 7 of this study.

My uncle Felix Warburg was more interested in philanthropy

than in finance. He organized the Federation of Jewish Charities in New York and, shortly after World War I, founded the American Joint Distribution Committee for the relief of oppressed Jews in other countries—a work which assumed major importance after the rise of Hitler. To what extent he sympathized with the Zionist cause prior to Hitler's advent I do not know. My father, who died shortly before Hitler came to power, was definitely not a Zionist.

My parents belonged to a reform congregation—Temple Emanu-El—but rarely attended services. At my own request, because I wanted to know what it meant to be a Jew, I studied under Rabbi Judah L. Magnes and was *Bar Mitzvah* (confirmed) at the traditional age of thirteen. I was fascinated by the Hebrew language and by Jewish history and ethics, but not by Judaism as a religion. As a thoroughly assimilated, non-religious Jew, educated in New England and married to a Christian, I have always remained respectful of and grateful for my Jewish cultural heritage. Believing in the universalism of all the great prophets and religious teachers, though not in their theology, I abhor racial, religious or extremely nationalistic particularism; and, being an internationalist, I could see no reason for the creation of a Jewish nation in Palestine until Hitler made its creation a desperate necessity.

I have stated these facts because a Jew writing about the Middle East in these troubled days owes the reader a statement of his attitude toward the area and of the factors that have shaped it.

From my point of view as an American concerned for the future of his country and the peace of the world, Israel is one of a number of foreign states whose policies and actions I endeavor to appraise—as I appraise the policies and actions of my own country—on the basis of whether or not they seem to me conducive to the creation of a world so appealingly described by the Prophet Micah as one in which "every man shall sit under his vine and under his fig tree, and none shall make them afraid."

I apply the same criterion to the policies and actions of the Arab states.

This study is neither a defense nor an indictment of either

side in the present tragic conflict. As I see it, there have been right and wrong—justice and injustice—on both sides of a confrontation for the existence of which neither the Arabs nor the Jews were originally responsible.

The indictment in this study is against religious bigotry, against arrogant imperialism and against European greed and quarrelsomeness. It is against my own country's irresponsibility in the years between the two World Wars, against its connivance at Anglo-French "appeasement" of the fascist dictators, against its blundering, oil-tainted postwar diplomacy and against the obsession with communism which has made the United States unfriendly if not openly hostile to all revolutionary change. Above all, the indictment is against the savage inhumanity let loose upon the world by Adolf Hitler and those supposedly civilized Germans who carried out his orders.

The numerous authors to whose works on the Middle East I am indebted are listed in the bibliography; the text contains frequent footnotes citing sources upon which I have specifically relied. I am most grateful to my friend Joseph Barnes for suggesting a number of works which I have found most useful and also for his helpful, sharp-eyed criticism upon which I have relied for many years. My sister Dr. Bettina Warburg, who has devoted many years to the work of the Iran Foundation, has provided me with valuable information about that country. A. G. Mezerik, editor of the *International Review Service*, has furnished me with invaluable chronological records of the work of the United Nations in the Middle East and has also given the whole manuscript a careful reading, as has my friend and neighbor Frances Schuman. Finally, I am indebted to my talented publisher Simon Michael Bessie for numerous helpful suggestions concerning the organization of this attempt to bring together the essential facts concerning the past, the present and a speculative look into the future of this turbulent part of the world. For the opinions expressed, I alone am responsible.

To my wife Joan I owe—among many other things—the peace of mind required for intensive study.

J.P.W.

CONTENTS

PART THREE

MAPS

Designed by Ava Morgan

PART ONE

1

Introduction

Broadly speaking, the peoples of the West are only dimly aware of their responsibility for the tragic conflict between Jews and Arabs—two peoples that had for centuries lived peacefully together in the Middle East. Both of the major ingredients of the present hostility were created by the West.

The activation of Zionism as a political force demanding the creation of a Jewish state in Palestine was the product of centuries of ill-treatment and persecution, by professedly Christian European nations, of the Jews scattered throughout their lands in the diaspora. These centuries reached back into Roman times, continuing throughout the Middle Ages, the Spanish Inquisition, the expulsions of German Jews into eastern Europe and the murderous pogroms in Tsarist Russia, eventually culminating in the genocidal barbarism practiced by Nazi Germany.

The second ingredient of conflict—Arab anti-Western nationalism and hostility toward the Jews—was created fifty years ago, when the Arabs were liberated from three centuries of Turkish rule by the West and then betrayed by Western imperialism.

Apart from Western responsibility for the Arab-Israel confrontation, relatively few Westerners are familiar with the history of the Middle East and the extent to which this area has been exploited—first, by old-fashioned Western imperialism and then, more recently, by a neo-imperialist struggle for supremacy between the Western powers and the Soviet Union in an area of great strategic and economic interest.

In attempting to provide some of the background essential to an understanding of the existing explosive state of affairs in the Middle East, a few definitions may be useful.

1. The term *Middle East* is commonly applied to the area reaching from the western frontier of Egypt to the Indus Valley in India. For the purposes of this study, this definition is both too broad and too narrow. It is too broad because it includes Afghanistan and Pakistan, two Moslem countries which belong more to Asia than to the much-fought-over land bridge between Asia, Africa and Europe. It is too narrow because it does not include that part of the Arabized Moslem world—the *Maghreb,* meaning the West—which stretches from Egypt's western frontier along the North African coast to the Atlantic Ocean.

As used in this study, *Middle East* comprises the area from Morocco in the west to the eastern border of Iran. It includes the Moslem but non-Arab flank countries, Turkey and Iran. It includes the Maghreb (Morocco, Algeria, Mauretania, Tunisia and Libya), as well as all the modern Arab states in Western Asia plus Egypt and the Sudan. It includes Israel, a non-Moslem, non-Arab splinter recently intruded into the Arab heartland—a foreign body which Arab flesh has sought to expel.

2. *The West* is a term used for brevity and convenience in this study. Prior to the nineteenth century, it is used almost as a synonym for Christendom. Thereafter, it applies to the imperialist nations of Europe, including half-European Tsarist Russia, but should be understood to exclude those European countries, notably the Scandinavian nations and Switzerland, that did not participate in the competition for colonial empires. In the twentieth century, the term applies primarily to Britain, France, Germany, Italy, the Soviet Union and the United States.

3. The terms *Semite* and *Semitic* are often mistakenly used in the West to denote race. There is no Semitic race. Neither the Jews nor the Arabs are a race. Properly used, the term *Semitic* denotes a group of languages, including Hebrew, Aramaic, Arabic and Syriac, distinguishing them from the *Hamitic* languages of North Africa, such as Berber or pre-Arabic Egyptian,

and from the Indo-European languages of the Middle East, such as the Farsi language of Persia.

Both Jews and Arabs were originally tribal people. Both claim descent from Abraham, who, because of the legend of the Great Flood, is thought to have led a migration from some part of the Tigris-Euphrates Valley. The time of this migration is not known, but it is established that for some time prior to 1200 B.C. the Jewish tribes were in captivity in Egypt, from which they were led out into the desert by Moses between 1200 and 1100 B.C., ultimately settling in Canaan, a part of Palestine which is described in the Hebrew Bible as "The Promised Land." Seventeen centuries later the prophet Mohammed declared that the Bedouin tribes who then inhabited the Arabian peninsula were likewise descended from Abraham, through his son Ishmael. There is, however, no recorded history of the Bedouin tribes prior to the time of Mohammed.

Among both Jews and Arabs there are people of widely varying physical characteristics, some whose skins are white and others of various shades of dark pigmentation. Jews and Arabs are distinguishable from each other by their history, their culture, their language and, of course, by their religion.

4. The term *Jew* is applied in this study to the people whom Moses led into Palestine and who, after a thousand years of nationhood in the Middle East, were driven out and dispersed by the Romans in the first century A.D. The citizens of Israel, including the Arab minority, are referred to as *Israelis*. The Jewish settlers in Palestine prior to the creation of Israel are generally referred to as *Zionists;* the Hebrew *Yishuv* is occasionally used to denote the Palestinian Jewish community. The *Jewish Agency* was the governing body of the *Yishuv* before Israel became a state; its Executive Council was the *Va'ad Leumi*. The Israeli parliament is called the *Knesset*. Other terms, such as *Haganah*, are explained in the text as they occur.

5. The term *Arab World* is used in this study to signify collectively the various Arab states both before and after the breakup of the Ottoman Empire. In some of these states pure Arab (i.e., Bedouin) blood is predominant; in others the infusion of Bedouin stock into the populations that existed before the Arab conquest varies in degree. There is no *Arab Nation*

that unites the Arab states. They are united only by the Arabic tongue and the Moslem faith and—since 1947—by hostility toward Israel. Indeed, there is strong rivalry among the more important Arab states for leadership of the *Arab World*. In part, these rivalries spring from tribal or dynastic roots; in part, they are caused by differences in political and social outlook, in economic conditions and in the unequal distribution of natural resources. To a considerable extent, the Arab states were artificially created by the Western powers in furtherance of their imperialistic ambitions.

Although this study is primarily concerned with that part of Middle East history which began with the nineteenth-century intrusion of the West, the next chapter will outline at least briefly the long history which preceded that period, emphasizing particularly the nature and the impact of the Arab and Turkish conquests.

In subsequent chapters the reader will encounter a number of digressions from strictly Middle East history. These have been deliberately designed to provide insight into the causes of Western behavior in the Middle East and elsewhere. Thus, Chapter 4 will discuss the origins of political Zionism. Chapters 6 and 7 show how the fear engendered in the West by the Russian revolutions of March and October 1917 affected Western aims and policies, especially with respect to Germany. Surely, in any study of the Middle East it is essential to outline, even if only briefly, the major conditions which caused the Weimar Republic to turn into the savage Third Reich of Adolf Hitler. And again, after World War II, it is important to understand how Western postwar aims and ideas were once more distorted by fear—this time, by fear of what appeared to be a worldwide communist conspiracy serving the interests of Soviet expansionism under Josef Stalin.

Although what appeared to be a menacing communist monolith has since partially disintegrated, the Middle East remains today one of the major areas of confrontation between non-Middle Eastern contenders for world hegemony. The recurring crises in the area are not due solely to the Arab-Israeli conflict created by Western bigotry and imperialistic greed.

They are a part of the difficult and painful process by which a radically changed world is groping toward some sort of stable order; they are part of an incomplete anti-colonial revolution and of an increasingly dangerous antithesis between the world's rich and poor nations.

In many ways the Middle East is a laboratory in which most of the problems of the twentieth-century world may be observed and in which solutions to these problems may be tested.

2

Early Background

Some three thousand years before the beginnings of Biblical history, civilized life began in the valley of the Nile and in the Fertile Crescent that is watered by the Tigris and Euphrates Rivers of Mesopotamia (the land between the rivers). Here, and in the Indus Valley in India and the Yellow River Valley in China, man first ceased to be a wandering tribal hunter and settled down to cultivate the soil, to build villages, towns and cities and, eventually, to create city-states and kingdoms.

Egypt was probably the first nation-state founded by man.

From about 4000 B.C. until 2700 B.C. there existed what is known as the Old Empire of Egypt, with its capital at Memphis in the Nile Delta. The Pharaohs of the Old Empire built the Great Pyramids at Gizeh and the inscrutable Sphinx, demonstrating remarkable skill in architectural design and in the use of slave labor to execute it.

The later Middle Kingdom (2700–1670 B.C.) had its capital at Thebes and then at Tanis, both in the upper part of the Nile Valley. During this period a feudal system developed under which Egypt achieved a high degree of civilization and prosperity. Reservoirs and canals were built to carry the fructifying waters of the Nile beyond the natural boundaries of its annual overflow. Handicrafts flourished and a rich culture found expression in painting and remarkably fine sculpture, often of gigantic dimensions. Papyrus, ink and the art of writing were developed, at first in hieroglyphs and then in a phonetic language. Egyptian ships sailed into the Red Sea and explored the shores of the Mediterranean.

In 1670 B.C. Egypt was for the first time conquered by invaders from the north. The Hyksos, warlike tribesmen who used horse-drawn war chariots, defeated the Egyptian foot soldiers and established the dynasty of the Shepherd Kings. This was one of the earliest examples of a phenomenon that was frequently to occur in the history of the Middle East: namely, the conquest of a settled area by homeless nomads.

In 1501 B.C. the Hyksos were expelled by a "modernized" Egyptian army led by King Thutmose III, sometimes referred to as "the Napoleon of Egypt." This able warrior not only freed Egypt but pursued his enemy into Western Asia, welding together an empire that endured for almost one thousand years and included not only parts of Western Asia but the northern half of the Sudan. The warships of Thutmose III dominated the eastern Mediterranean and ranged as far north as the islands of the Aegean Sea. This was the high-water mark of Egyptian glory, maintained until the Persians, under Cyrus the Great, conquered Egypt in 525–500 B.C.

Prior to their conquest of Egypt, the Persians had also overrun the last of a long line of Mesopotamian civilizations: namely, that of the Second Babylonian Empire (600–525 B.C.). The earliest of these Mesopotamian civilizations had been founded by the Sumerians, probably at about the same time as the founding of the Old Empire of Egypt. The Sumerians invented the wheel, were the first people to divide the circle into degrees and developed a cuneiform art of writing on clay tablets or stone with a wedge-shaped stylus. In 2450 B.C. the Sumerians were conquered by the Akkadians under King Sargon. Then came the Babylonians (1900–1600 B.C.), the Kassites (1600–1150), the Assyrians (*ca.* 900–600 B.C.) and, finally, the Second Babylonian Empire.

During the latter part of the tri-millennial span of Mesopotamian civilizations there existed a number of smaller kingdoms west of the Fertile Crescent and along the Mediterranean coast. The Hebrew settlements in Palestine were probably founded during the rule of the Kassites in Mesopotamia, the Age of Judges being commonly dated from about 1100 B.C. to 1000 B.C. Then followed the reigns of Saul, Solomon and David. Sol-

omon's domain extended from the Sea of Galilee in the north
to his gold mines at the head of the Gulf of Aqaba. After David's reign the Jews split into two kingdoms, Israel in the north
and Judea in the south. In 800 B.C. Israel was conquered by the
Assyrians, and about two hundred years later Judea fell to the
Babylonians, who destroyed Jerusalem and carried off the Jews
into captivity. A century later the all-conquering Persians liberated the Jews, most of whom returned to Palestine to re-
establish a Jewish state and to rebuild Jerusalem.

After Alexander the Great's conquest of Persia, the Jews had
almost continuously to defend themselves against the surrounding pagans; under the leadership of the Maccabees, they beat
off the Syriac Greeks led by Antiochus, who had succeeded to
the West Asian part of Alexander's empire. Then, when the
Romans conquered the Greeks, the Jews fiercely defended
their kingdom against the imposition of Roman rule until, in
the first century A.D., they succumbed to Vespasian's legions
and were driven out of their lands. A last remnant of about
one thousand brave Zealots under Eleazar Ben Ya'ir held out
for some months on the summit of Masada overlooking the
Dead Sea and, when their defenses were breached, killed themselves rather than surrender.*

Thus the Jews, who now appear as foreign intruders into the
Middle East, actually lived intermittently as a nation in Palestine (or as captives in Babylon) for more than a millennium
and a half before the Arabs erupted from the desert to conquer
the entire area.

Three thousand years ago, in the midst of a polytheistic pagan world, the Jews gave birth to the first lasting monotheistic
religion, building upon it a highly developed civilization and a
rich literature which survives to this day. More than one thousand years after Moses descended from Sinai with the Ten
Commandments, Judaism gave birth to Christianity. The pagan
Romans crucified Jesus, but within three centuries adopted and
to a large extent distorted the modified Judaism that he had

* The story of this heroic remnant has only recently come to light
through the excavations conducted by Yigel Yadin, who commanded the
Israeli forces in their war of liberation 1948-1949. For a fascinating
account, see Moshe Pearlman, *The Zealots of Masada: The Story of a
Dig.*

taught; and because the Jews would not submit to Roman rule, the still pagan Romans destroyed the Temple at Jerusalem and dispersed the Jews from their kingdom. This was some six hundred years before the Bedouin nomads adopted Islam, the third great monotheistic religion that sprang from both Judaism and Christianity.

The history of the periods of Greek and Roman supremacy is well known to every Western schoolchild. The Greeks were halted in the west but penetrated eastward as far as the Indus River in India. The Roman conquests, on the other hand, stretched westward and northward from Italy but were halted in the east by the Parthians who had overthrown the Seleucid Greeks in Persia. (Seleucus was one of Alexander the Great's generals, who inherited the eastern portion of his empire.) At its height, the Roman Empire reached eastward through Greece and Macedonia across West Asia until it encountered the Parthians in Persia. Southward, it reached into Egypt and along the northern shore of Africa. The Mediterranean Sea was *Mare Nostrum*, a Roman lake with both of its shores settled as Roman provinces or dependencies, from the Pillars of Hercules to the Hellespont. Northwestward, the Roman legions had conquered Spain, Gaul, Switzerland, the German tribes west of the Rhine and England, though not Scotland or Wales.

After some six centuries of ascendancy, the Roman Empire weakened and split into two parts, one still centered at Rome and the other Eastern or Byzantine Empire centered at Constantinople. The split caused a permanent schism in the Christian church between Roman and Greek Orthodox Christianity.

In the fifth century A.D. the Western Roman Empire succumbed to successive waves of barbarians from the north. Goths and Visigoths were followed by Vandals who sacked Rome and occupied both shores of the Mediterranean. The Byzantine Empire survived but was gradually confined to the Anatolian peninsula (modern Turkey). In Western Europe, little remained of the Christian Roman civilization. Towns and cities were abandoned. Roads fell into disrepair. Only the Pope at Rome and the widely scattered priests and monks kept Christianity alive in an area that in general had reverted to semi-barbarism. The decay was less pronounced in the Visigoth

kingdom of Spain, partly because a considerable number of
Jews had settled there and helped to keep alive the light of
civilization.

East of the Mediterranean the only civilization that survived,
besides that of Greek Byzantium, was that of Persia. Under the
Sassanian dynasty Persia had freed itself once more and was
enjoying a cultural revival that very nearly equaled the earlier
great Achaemenid period in which Persia, under Cyrus the
Great and Darius I, had conquered a vast empire.

The Arab Eruption

Into the vacuum created by the fall of Rome and the weakening power of Byzantium there now flowed a new and hitherto unsuspected stream of vigorous power.

For an unknown period of time, Bedouin nomad tribes had
inhabited the arid and partly mountainous area that lay south
and southeast of Mesopotamia between the Persian Gulf and
the Red Sea. The ancestral Arab lands comprised the Nejd,
Shammar, 'Asir and the Hejaz, now constituting the kingdom
of Sa'udi Arabia, as well as the ancient kingdom of Yemen and
the various coastal sheikhdoms. Little is known of the early
history of Arabia because the tribes were illiterate and left no
written records. Some of the Arabic poetry was, however,
orally transmitted from father to son, most of it consisting of a
kind of verbal warfare in which one tribe would glorify its
ancestors and their deeds while heaping scorn upon the ancestors of another. Also handed down were poems which exalted
the pleasures of the flesh. The intra-tribal organization was
democratic to the extent that the headmen, or sheikhs, were
chosen by the elders, with great store apparently being laid on
illustrious male ancestry, prowess in war and excellence in the
breeding of camels. There were some towns or cities of unknown antiquity in the Yemen and in the Hejaz where certain
tribes adopted a sedentary life, but little is known of them
prior to the time of Mohammed.

The Prophet was born in Mecca in 570 A.D. or perhaps in the
following decade. At this time, urban life in South Arabia and

the Hejaz was well developed. South Arabia was the center of a flourishing spice trade and was known to the Romans as *Arabia Felix*. Mecca was a center of trade ruled by a business aristocracy known as the Quraysh, to the lower fringe of which Mohammed himself apparently belonged. In Yemen there was a large settlement of Jews that had existed for at least a century. Yathrib (later Medina) was a town inhabited chiefly by Jews and a few Christians. Apparently there were also Jewish agricultural settlements between Mecca and Medina.*

From contact with Jews and Christians, Mohammed became familiar with their monotheistic religions. Authorities differ as to whether Mohammed could or actually did read the Hebrew scriptures or whether he absorbed their contents at second hand. In any case, at the age of about forty he became convinced of the existence of a single divine being and felt a call to convert his neighbors to a new monotheistic faith which he named Islam, meaning "submission to Allah." The Qoran, which he then wrote (or perhaps dictated to a scribe), was in many respects a modified version of the Old Testament and prescribed a simplified ritual and a strictly defined way of life devoted to the service of Allah, whose will determined all things. Man himself was not responsible. If good or evil fortune befell him, it was the will of Allah. Entry into Paradise was assured to all who obeyed the laws laid down by the Qoran, and these were not essentially different from the laws laid down by the Old and New Testaments. Mohammed proclaimed himself the "Seal of the Prophets," claiming direct descent from Abraham and Moses. He referred to Christians and Jews as "the People of the Book," but as discrepancies appeared between Islamic and Judeo-Christian theology, he attributed these to error on the part of the Jews.

The remarkable success which Mohammed's efforts at conversion achieved made him unpopular with the Quraysh of Mecca, although his chief concern seems to have been the conversion to Islam of the Bedouin tribes rather than the townspeople. Mohammed's flight from Mecca to Medina (the

* For an interesting though necessarily somewhat speculative account of this period and of Mohammed's career, see Joel Carmichael, *The Shaping of the Arabs*.

Hegira) in 622 A.D. is the first firm date in Arab history and the start of the Moslem calendar. In Medina, Mohammed became a statesman as well as a prophet, organizing his followers into what he called the *Umma*, a sort of universal Islamic state which was destined later to develop into a Moslem empire. The conquest of Mecca became the first objective of the *Umma*, and this was accomplished by armed force in 630 A.D. At about this time Mohammed broke with both the Jews and Christians because of their refusal to adopt Islam; some of them were killed, some fled, while others remained in isolated enclaves.

Prior to Mohammed's advent, some of the Bedouin tribes had already moved out of the peninsula into Syria and Mesopotamia, where they had begun, in the fourth century A.D., to establish small kingdoms. One such kingdom, in Mesopotamia, was subsidized by the Persians. Another, in Syria, became a satellite of the decaying Byzantine Empire. With the conversion to Islam of the desert Bedouin tribes in the seventh century, these outlying settled areas became the first targets of the amazing march of conquest which, within a single century, was to create an Arab empire reaching from the Atlantic Ocean to the borders of India and to spread the Moslem faith far beyond India into Asia.

The eruption of the desert tribes was fired partly by the fanatical religious zeal inspired by Mohammed but also, in large measure, by the desire for booty derived from the plunder of settled civilizations. In Syria the desert raiders were welcomed as liberators from Byzantine rule by the partly Arab, partly Aramaic inhabitants, many of whom joined the invading raiders in defeating the forces of the Emperor Heraclias. From Syria the Arab armies moved northward until they were halted in Anatolia and southward through Palestine into Egypt where, for the first time, they discovered the need for sea power. In an incredibly short time the Arabs constructed a navy and soon mastered the warships of Byzantium. Their rapidly acquired skill at sea, derived perhaps from the similarity of the open sea to the trackless desert, enabled them to move rapidly from Egypt along the coast of North Africa and across the Mediterranean to Sicily and Spain. In moving from Morocco into Spain and southern France, the Arabs were joined by the native Berbers, whom they had defeated but not subdued. In their westward march of conquest, the Arabs carried out two historical processes: conversion of the pagan native populations to Islam; and the imposition of the Arabic language. Islamization left the Jewish and Christian communities free to practice their respective religions but imposed a tax upon them somewhat heavier than that levied upon the converted pagans. As a rule, the Arabs did not move into the cities which they conquered, preferring to build armed camps of their own. These were usually divided into tribal quarters. The armed camps soon developed into towns and cities in which dwelt an Arab aristocracy that held supreme power. Since the native populations needed to communicate and trade with their Arab overlords, they rather rapidly adopted the Arab language. Thus conquest, Islamization and Arabization went hand in hand. In due course, Arab blood mingled with that of the indigenous peoples, the extent to which this occurred decreasing the farther the Arabs moved from their homeland.

In Mesopotamia, as in Syria, the Arabs first overran the Arab settlements which had been founded in the fourth century and had become satellites of the Persian state. Here, too, they were welcomed as liberators, but when they attempted to conquer Persia, they encountered stiff resistance. The Persian armies were eventually defeated, but the Persian people were neither Arabized nor did they wholly adopt the Sunni Moslem religion of their conquerors. They became Moslems, but created a Shi'ite sect which claimed descent from the Prophet via 'Ali, his son-in-law. From Persia, Shi'ite Islam spread into Asia and also into parts of modern Syria and Iraq. The Persians retained their Indo-European language and sustained only a negligible infusion of Arab blood. In fact, they exercised a strong influence upon the Abbassid dynasty of Arab Caliphs who were to rule over the eastern portion of the Arab Empire.

The most remarkable feature of the Arab conquest and of some eight centuries of subsequent Arab rule was the ability of these originally primitive tribesmen to settle down and establish a highly developed civilization. One of the three major centers of this civilization was in Baghdad, where the Abbassid Caliphs ruled from 750 to 1100 A.D. Among them were al-

Mansur (754–775), Harun al-Rashid, the Caliph of the *Arabian Nights* (786–804) and Masmun (813–833). In the western part of the Arab Empire, Abd-er Rahman established in 756 an Omayyad dynasty of Caliphs whose capital was situated in Cordova, Spain. The third, Fatimid, dynasty ruled in Egypt and founded Cairo as a seat of learning and government administration. In all three centers the arts and sciences flourished to a degree then unknown in Western Christendom.

Industry, commerce and agriculture prospered under Arab rule, although in some parts of the Arab homeland a deterioration began as camels and goats destroyed vegetation. The Arab heartland produced rugs, textiles, glass and steel. Paper, introduced from China, was manufactured in quantity. Flowers were grown commercially for the manufacture of perfumes and unguents. Trade with India and China was carried on both by overland caravan and by sea. In North Africa and Spain the Arabs stimulated the growing of sugar cane and introduced fruits and vegetables, such as artichokes, unknown to the West.

Unlike most previous conquerors, except the Persians, the Arabs were tolerant of diversity among their subject peoples. The numerous Jews who had settled in Western Asia, Egypt and along the North African coast after their eviction from Palestine were treated with consideration. Many of them attained high posts in government and at the Arab universities. Some, like Maimonides, were responsible for the translation of the literature of Greece into Arabic and, in later years, for recording the works of Arab scholars, astronomers, physicists and mathematicians. The fact that the Jews had at one time conquered Palestine and had there maintained their own kingdoms for a thousand years left no resentment on the part of the Arabs since they themselves had been latecomers to Palestine and felt no bond of consanguinity with the Aramaic Canaanites whom the Jews had dispossessed. During the eight centuries in which the Arabs dominated the Mediterranean world, from Spain to the Persian Gulf, Arabs and Jews lived peacefully side by side, while the Jews scattered throughout Christian Western Europe were persecuted and confined in ghettos.

In the end, the Arabs left strangely little cultural heritage of their own. They left as monuments magnificent mosques and fortifications, but theirs was essentially a civilization of the spoken word that left few written records. Their great contribution to the progress of civilization was that they preserved and passed on to the West the culture of the Greeks and the literature of the Jews.

In the eleventh and twelfth centuries, the great Arab Empire was weakened by internal dissension. This opened the door for a slowly reviving Western Christendom, in alliance with the Byzantines, to attempt a recapture of the Holy Land and, incidentally, to regain control of the eastern Mediterranean. Harun al-Rashid had voluntarily recognized an informal Frankish protectorate over the sites sacred to Christians during the reign of Charlemagne as Holy Roman Emperor, but this agreement had lapsed in 1010. In 1071 the Arabs lost Jerusalem and the Holy Land to the Seljuk Turks, a Central Asian tribe that had been dislodged by the westward migration of Asian peoples. It was against these non-Arab invaders, the so-called Saracens, that Christian knights from the West launched their first crusade in 1096. From 1100 until 1145 the Crusaders were able to establish and maintain a foothold in what is now Lebanon and the northern part of Israel. Then they were dislodged by a second wave of Turks, the Osmanlis or Ottomans, who were pressing in upon Byzantium. The second and third crusades failed to regain a foothold. The fourth and last had very little to do with an attempt to regain the Holy Land; urged on by Venetian and Genoese mercantile interests and escorted by their fleets, the Western Crusaders occupied Constantinople.

While the Ottoman Turks began to push northwestward into Europe, the Seljuks turned eastward, overran Mesopotamia and attacked Persia, whose brief prosperity under Moslem Caliphs had been cut short by the Mongol invasions. In 1515 the Seljuks under Selim I finally conquered and subdued Persia. A year later, as the Seljuk dynasty disintegrated, the Ottoman Turks overran Mesopotamia, Syria and Egypt. Under Suleiman the Magnificent, the Turkish Empire expanded until it reached from Aleppo in Anatolia to the Indian Ocean, and embraced all of what had been the Arab Empire except Morocco and Spain. (The Arab-Berber tide, halted by Charles Martel at the battle of Tours, in 732, had already receded from southern France,

but below the Pyrenees the Iberian peninsula remained in
Moorish hands, while Morocco itself became an almost entirely
independent little empire.) Constantinople had fallen to the
Turks in 1453; what remained of the Byzantine Empire, plus
Persia and all of the Arab-conquered lands, now fell under the
blighting rule of the Turks and would so remain for the next
three centuries. Somewhat like the Mongol conquerors, the
Turks did not bring in a new civilization; they merely imposed
their rule by military force, exploiting the poeples whom they
conquered and all but extinguishing their civilizations. Unlike
the Mongols, however, they did not recede back into Asia. The
Ottoman Turks pressed forward from Constantinople into the
Balkans and up the valley of the Danube where they encountered fierce resistance from the Hungarians under the latter's
great leader, Hunyadi. Our concern in this study is, however,
less with the Turkish threat to Europe than with the effect of
Turkish rule upon what had been the Arab-dominated Middle
East.

The Turkish armies consisted largely of enslaved prisoners
of war, many of them Christians. Their officers were either
Turks or recruits from the Balkans. A succession of Turkish
Sultans, served by subservient Moslem Caliphs, governed what
amounted to a far-flung police state, replete with sycophants
and informers. The privilege of collecting taxes to sustain this
regressive rule was auctioned off to the highest bidders among
the wealthy landowning families who, in turn, farmed out the
privilege to lesser agents scattered throughout the realm. The
mass of the subject population was mercilessly exploited.

In Syria and Mesopotamia, farmers, who had for centuries
carefully cultivated terraced or irrigated land, were reduced to
serfs living upon a subsistence diet of the coarsest foodstuffs. A
tax was imposed upon every tree and vine until few trees or
vines remained. Canals and irrigation systems silted up. Ter-
races crumbled. Cities were abandoned. Many of the former
farmers and city-dwellers reverted to nomadic life; their goats
and camels devoured the remaining vegetation. The population
rapidly decreased. What was left of it became a slave population ruled by a few rich landowners and money-lending
effendis.

In Roman times Western Asia had been the economically most advanced part of the empire, exchanging its manufactured goods for the raw materials of the West. The "fine linen of Beth Shaan" is mentioned in the Hebrew Talmud. The English word "gauze" is derived from Gaza, where dyed silks and cotton were manufactured in the town which, in our time, has become the barren home of Palestinian refugees. From Gaza to Aqaba, and all through Mesopotamia, there are ruins of once densely populated cities. In Roman and Arab times it is estimated that 25 million people prospered on the fertile soil of the Tigris-Euphrates Valleys where now, after Turkish rule, some 5 million Iraqis eke out a meager living. In Palestine 5 million people lived in the fertile valleys and wooded hills before the Turkish occupation reduced the once beautiful land to swamp and desert, inhabited by perhaps 200,000 impoverished Arabs.

The impact of the Turkish conquest upon Egypt and the more distant Maghreb was less drastic. While the history of Western Asia had been one of the rise and fall of successive civilizations, Egypt's history had been less disrupted in spite of repeated conquest by invaders. Throughout its long history, Egypt had been able to absorb its conquerors, often being strongly influenced by them but never wholly destroyed. After the Persian conquerors had come the Greeks and, after the Greeks, the Romans. From each, Egypt had acquired new cultural wealth. Under Grecian influence, Alexandria had become one of the cultural centers of the Mediterranean world. After the fall of Greece and Rome, the Arab tide had flowed over Egypt, bringing with it a new religion, a new way of life and a new language. Yet Egypt was not Arabized to the same extent as those countries which received a greater infusion of Arab blood. The Egyptian fellah retained much of his age-old Pharaonic characteristics and the upper crust of Egypt's population retained a sense of "Egyptianness" only partly submerged by Arab Islamization.

Under Turkish rule, Egypt was not depopulated as were the Arab countries. Blessed with the annual flooding of the Nile Valley, Egypt was less dependent upon irrigation and less vulnerable to deforestation and erosion. Its problem became and has remained one of overpopulation, with its rapidly increasing people crowding the available arable land. The upper, wealthier strata of the Egyptian population received a strong infusion of Turkish, Circassian and Albanian blood, traces of which are clearly visible in the present-day ruling class. Some of the Mameluke slaves to whom the Turks delegated the rule of Egypt became landowners and have left their imprint upon some segments of the fellahin, but Egypt remained essentially Egyptian in spite of eight centuries of subjugation to the Arabs and three centuries of Turkish rule.

The Arab Maghreb, too, suffered less under Turkish rule than the Arab heartland. The Turks never conquered Morocco and gained possession of parts of North Africa only after a protracted struggle with Austria and Spain after Spain had expelled the Moors from its own soil. Even then, the Turks never really fastened their grip upon Algeria, Tunisia and Libya, although all three countries came under a loose sort of Turkish suzerainty.

Such, then, very briefly, was the condition of the Middle East in the early eighteenth century when the Europeans first began to be interested in it. What aroused this interest was not the Middle East itself but the Turkish threat to Europe's own security.

Throughout the sixteenth and most of the seventeenth centuries, Europe had been preoccupied with its own internal quarrels: with wars of dynastic succession involving chiefly France, Austria and Spain; with a long power struggle for European hegemony between Britain and France; with competition for overseas possessions; and with the Thirty Years' War between the Catholic Holy Roman (Austrian) Empire and the Protestant states of northern Germany. It was only after the Thirty Years' War was over that the Turkish invaders were finally defeated at the gates of Vienna in 1683.

Turkish pressure from the southeast had been in part responsible for Europe's turning westward. The voyages of the early sixteenth-century explorers not only opened up a new world across the Atlantic; they also established a cheaper and more rapid means of communication and trade with East Asia than had been provided by the Moslem-controlled routes through the Middle East. This new access to East Asia by sea brought about an Anglo-French struggle for the control of India, and it was this contest that, for the first time, made the Middle East important in the eyes of the West European contenders for colonial empire and world supremacy.

3

The Beginning of the
Western Intrusion

In the early decades of the eighteenth century, a few British explorers penetrated into the Arabian peninsula, but these were archaeologists and Arabist scholars rather than outriders of empire. Actually, it was Tsarist Russia which, under Peter the Great, began the Western intrusion into the Middle East by its seizure, in 1722, of the southern and western shores of the Caspian Sea. Although this conquest was later yielded, Russia had, by about 1800, established something like a protectorate over the weak Qajar dynasty in Persia. By this time Britian had acquired an empire in India, while France, though driven out of India by Britain, had by no means lost her imperial ambitions; Napoleon was eyeing both Persia and Egypt as possible gateways to the East. Both Britain and France were determined to keep Russia out of the Middle East.

When Napoleon attempted to seize Egypt in 1800, he met defeat at the hands of Britain and Turkey. This occasioned the first Arab revolt against Turkish rule—a strange sort of revolt that was led by an Albanian Turk and frustrated by an English diplomat.

The First Arab Revolt

The Sultan of Turkey had sent Mehemed Ali, an Albanian general, to fight with the British against Napoleon in Egypt. After Napoleon's defeat and withdrawal in 1801, Mehemed Ali turned his well-trained army against the Sultan's Mameluke rulers of Egypt, conquered them and declared himself Pasha of Egypt.

Calling upon the Arabs in the Hejaz to revolt against Turkish rule, Mehemed Ali conquered the Arabian peninsula with its holy places and from there moved into Syria to overthrow Turkish rule. Next he built a navy and fought a successful naval war against the Greeks. In 1820 Mehemed Ali conquered the northern part of the Sudan.

Had it not been for British intervention, this remarkable Albanian Turk might have established a second Arab Empire under Egyptian leadership.

France favored the rebellion because its success would endanger the British lifeline through the Middle East. But Napoleon was by this time an exile on St. Helena and France, after Waterloo, was in no position to intervene. Britain's Lord Palmerston feared the success of the rebellion and preferred to have Egypt remain under flaccid Turkish control. Under Palmerston's leadership, Anglo-Russian intervention destroyed Mehemed Ali's naval power. Mehemed's son, Ibrahim, likewise an able general, remained for a time in Syria but was forced to withdraw in 1841 when the European Concert of Powers imposed a Middle East settlement under which Mehemed Ali was forced to give up most of his conquests, although he was conceded the hereditary title of Viceroy of Egypt under re-established Turkish suzerainty.

Ibrahim's short rule in Syria had one effect of lasting importance; namely, it opened Syria to Western Christian missionaries. The rather limited spread of Christianity by these missions was less important than the fact that they established schools and reawakened the Arabs' long-dormant pride in their own language and literature. During this period (1847–1868) two great Arab scholars and teachers, Yazeji and Bustani, were outstanding in reawakening the Arab spirit.* At the same time, through the missionaries the Western world acquired its first insights into the submerged Arab culture.

Although Britain had cooperated with Russia in quelling the Arab revolt of Mehemed Ali, she remained in conflict with Russia with respect to Turkey and Persia.

* See George Antonius, *The Arab Awakening*, pp. 22–34.

The Crimean War

In 1852 Lord Palmerston suspected that Russia was about to attempt the seizure of Constantinople and the Dardanelles. Together with France and Turkey, Britain organized an expeditionary force which encamped at Varna on the Black Sea to await attack by the Tsar's forces. When no such attack materialized, the allied commanders became impatient and decided, although they had no knowledge whatever of the lands across the Black Sea, to launch an attack upon the Crimea. The campaign was ill prepared and the troops were inadequately equipped. Losses from malnutrition and disease eventually exceeded those suffered in combat. Nevertheless, the invaders finally succeeded in surrounding and laying siege to Sevastopol. The Tsar's forces, equally ill equipped, resisted heroically and suffered huge casualties, but eventually the Black Sea fortress fell, and the expeditionary force retired, having eliminated the Russian threat to Constantinople. The Crimean War of 1853–1854 is known to history chiefly as the scene of the famous, brave and futile charge of the British Light Brigade at the mismanaged battle of Balaklava. Its true significance lay in proving the value of combined naval and military operations by powers that controlled the sea.

Rivalry Over Egypt

Although Britain and France cooperated against Russia, Anglo-French rivalry for control of Egypt reached another acute stage during the 1850's. The French engineer Ferdinand de Lesseps obtained a concession from the Egyptian Khedive, authorizing his company, jointly owned by Egyptian and French interests, to construct the Suez Canal for ocean-going vessels. For several years Turkish confirmation of this concession was blocked by Palmerston's influence at Constantinople. Eventually, however, Turkish consent was obtained by the French and the Canal was completed in 1869. The French diplomatic triumph was short-lived. In 1875 Disraeli, then Prime

Minister of Britain, succeeded in buying out the holdings of the bankrupt Egyptian government. Four years later, Anglo-French control was established over Egypt's finances; and when this failed to assure the payment of Egypt's debts, the British moved in with military force. Thus began, in 1882, a British occuption of Egypt which, though announced as temporary, was to last for three-quarters of a century, arousing strong Egyptian resentment.

Anglo-French rivalry in Egypt continued until 1904, when the rapid rise of Imperial Germany as a would-be colonial power brought about the Anglo-French *Entente Cordiale*—an agreement in which France conceded to Britain a free hand in Egypt in exchange for French freedom of action in Morocco and Tunisia.

The "Liberation" of the Maghreb

France had already annexed Algeria. During the late eighteenth and early nineteenth centuries, the pirates of the Barbary Coast, whose main strongholds were in Algeria, Tunisia and Tripoli (now Libya), harassed Mediterranean shipping. The young United States Navy had put an end to their depredations upon American shipping in the wars of 1805 and 1815, but the Dey of Algiers continued to prey upon European trade. In 1830 Maréchal de Bourmont, Minister of War for Charles X of France, sailed with 350 ships and 37,000 soldiers to occupy the Algerian capital and begin a century of French occupation. During the reigns of Louis Philippe and Napoleon III, sporadic resistance continued. French occupation on a major scale began under the Third Republic, with the organized settlement of European immigrants accompanied by massive efforts at development. Roads and harbor installations were built and agricultural development was undertaken in the belief that these activities would result in the "assimilation" of the native Arabs and Khabyles that would transform them into contented and useful second-class French citizens. This colonial exploitation, organized under the fiction of granting the native Algerians the rights of French citizenship when actually very few such rights were conferred upon them, lasted for 84 years without producing any major rebellion.

In neighboring Tunisia, the Husseinite Arab dynasty had striven since 1705 to assert its autonomy under Turkish rule. A succession of native rulers succeeded in instituting a number of reforms but incurred such heavy indebtedness to France and Italy that an international control commisson was appointed in 1869. Italian rivalry for control of Tunisia incited the French to intervene and to conclude with the Bey of Tunisia the Bardo Treaty of 1881, under which Tunisia became a French protectorate. French colonization and exploitation similar to that which took place in Algeria dated from this period. The Tunisian nationalist reaction did not set in until after the First World War.

The Sherifian Empire of Morocco had never fallen under the rule of the Turks; it had long been an independent Arab-Berber nation when the United States achieved its independence. (One of George Washington's first official communications as President had been addressed to "His Majesty, the Emperor of Morocco.") European rivalry for colonial possessions brought about a collision of imperial interests over Morocco in the early twentieth century. So far as Britain was concerned, any conflict with France over Morocco had been eliminated by the *Entente Cordiale* of 1904, but there remained a conflict between France, Spain and Johnny-come-lately Imperial Germany. The swashbuckling German Kaiser William II twice provoked a crisis. The Algeciras settlement of 1911, mediated by President Theodore Roosevelt, averted war and resulted in the establishment of a French protectorate over all of Morocco except for a small area placed under Spanish protection and an internationalized enclave at Tangiers.

Libya, the only other country in the Maghreb, became in part (Tripoli) an Italian protectorate in 1904 and was later liberated altogether from Turkish rule by the Italo-Turkish war of 1911.

Britain and Russia in Persia

The decaying Ottoman Empire was shrinking in Europe as well as in the Middle East; it had been propped up by Britain until Britain had seized Cyprus in 1878 and decided to occupy Egypt in 1882. Marked by Balkan wars, the slow retreat of Turkey from Europe, which had begun with defeat of the Turks at Vienna in 1683, now created a vacuum which both Austria-Hungary and Tsarist Russia endeavored to fill.

On the eastern flank of the Middle East, Britain and Russia continued their competition for control of Persia. Each obtained concessions from weak Persian governments only to be elbowed out by the other. In 1905–1906 there was a revolution in Persia against the absolute monarchy. A parliament, the Majlis, was created under a new constitution reluctantly granted by the Shah, who promptly violated it and called in Russia troops to aid in supressing the subsequent rebellion. A year later, alarmed by the rising influence of Imperial Germany with its dream of a Berlin-to-Baghdad railway, Britain and Russia set up a Russian sphere of influence in the north and a British sphere in the south of Persia. The Persians were bitterly resentful of this dual occupation but were powerless to prevent it. (One reason for Britain's determined interest in Persia was that oil had been discovered there in 1908.)

4

Zionism—An Ancient Hope Becomes a Political Force

Ever since the Jews were driven from their thousand-year-old home in Palestine by the Romans at the beginning of the Christian era, they have cherished a hope, or a belief inspired by their religion, that some day they or their children would be able to return to Zion, the land of their forefathers. Among the devout Orthodox Jews, this hope is based upon the belief in the coming of a Messiah who would lead the children of Israel back to Jerusalem and the lands once ruled by Hebrew kings.

Throughout most of the nineteen centuries of the diaspora, this hope has been a passive expectation rather than an aim to be accomplished through action. It became more than a patient expectation of fulfillment only within the last century, when the accumulation of long and bitter experience gave rise to the conviction that fulfillment could be attained only through action.

The bitter experience which energized passivity into thoughts of action was acquired by those Jews who were scattered throughout the half-Christian and half-pagan Roman Empire when they were driven from their homeland and who were later joined by the Sephardic Jews who had lived in reasonable happiness in Portugal and Spain prior to the Spanish Inquisition. Driven from Spain and Portugal in the fifteenth century, these Sephardim moved into Africa, the Near East and Western Europe—chiefly into Holland, France, Germany and Austria-Hungary—where there were already the Ashkenasim groups of Jews that had moved directly into Western Europe from Palestine. They found these Ashkenasim settled in ghettos and joined them there, to be treated along with them as unwelcome intruders into a still semi-barbaric, nominally Christian Europe.

There were a number of reasons for this ill-treatment, some religious and some secular, some having to do with the nature of European society, others deriving from the behavior of the Jews within that society.

One important reason for Christian hatred of the Jews was the belief, assiduously spread by the Church of Rome, that the Jews—not the Romans—had crucified Jesus. (It is only in our day that Rome has officially repudiated that falsehood.)

Another reason for European dislike of the Jews was the prevalent dislike and fear of all foreigners. This affected not only the attitude toward Jews in the various European countries but also the attitudes of the peoples of these countries toward each other. The English distrusted the French, and the French disliked the English, as well as the Germans whom they disliked most of all. The northern blonds looked down upon the darker-skinned Mediterranean peoples, and the Mediterranean Latins looked down upon the blond northerners as barbarians. The Jews were in this sense quite simply the victims of an almost universal xenophobia; wherever they might go, they were identifiable foreigners.

The behavior of the Jews added to their "foreignness." They wore different clothes, ate different food, kept the Sabbath on Saturday instead of Sunday, and spoke a different language among themselves. In a sense, the Jews were self-isolated.

To say this does not excuse the barbarously cruel treatment to which the Jews were subjected, but it may partially explain why they were unwelcome.

The more the Jews were segregated into ghettos, the more "foreign" they became. Denied the right to own land, they became urbanized at a time when the majority of the European population consisted of farmers or, more accurately, of serfs working the land for their feudal overlords. The more the

Jews became urbanized, the more they turned their talents to mercantilism—to shopkeeping and money-lending. They became the people who had what others needed and who made a profit out of supplying the necessities of existence. They became the modest capitalists in primitive agricultural economies, supplying the farmers with seed and their landowning feudal lords with money with which to pay for their retinues of mercenaries. This did not endear them to the peoples among whom they lived.

What else were they to do? The belief grew current that all Jews were rich. The truth was that many of them were extremely poor, but unlike their Christian neighbors, the Jews took care of their own poor. One of their laws of life prescribed that every individual in the Jewish community must give at least 10 percent of his earnings to support those of the community who were in need. Thus Jewish scholars, philosophers, writers and musicians were supported by the community—by those who engaged in profitable business—while Christian artists and scholars received no such support, except from a few feudal potentates who, likely as not, borrowed money from Jewish money-lenders. A few of these Jewish money-lenders became *Hofjuden* (court Jews), semi-officially recognized as servants of some of the many German princelings and kings, of which there were something like 300 at the time of the Protestant Reformation.

The Reformation divided Christianity against itself and added a new dimension to the religious issue. Catholics and Protestants now hated each other, while both continued to hate the Jews. The feudal rulers of the little German kingdoms and principalities adopted the doctrine of *cuius rex ejus religio,* which meant that the people of each feudal entity were expected to adopt the religion of its ruler. Prior to and during the Thirty Years' War between Roman Catholic Austria and the Protestant states in northern Germany, Catholics commonly fled from a state ruled by a Protestant, while Protestants emigrated from Catholic-ruled states to live under Protestant rulers. The Jews, being neither Roman Catholic nor Protestant, were despised outcasts throughout Germany and Austria and, to a slightly lesser extent, in France. England tried to exclude them altogether. At about this time, large numbers of Jewish people moved out of Germany and Austria into Poland and Russia, especially into the Ukraine, while others moved into Romania. In these East European countries, the lot which befell the Jews was no better; here, too, they were soon confined in Pales of Settlement and in ghettos. Even worse was to befall them later.

In Western Europe the French Revolution, with its proclamation of the "Rights of Man," inaugurated a new era and, for the Jews, brought a considerable amount of relief from long centuries of ill-treatment. Napoleon's artillery knocked down the walls of the ghettos of Western Europe. England began to admit Jews to equal citizenship. France granted them full political and economic freedom, based, to be sure, upon the expectation that the Jews in France would rapidly become "assimilated Frenchmen," even though they might continue to practice their own religion. Even in Germany the ghettos were opened and Jews were for the first time permitted to own land, to attend schools and, in limited numbers, to enter universities and some of the professions. On the other hand, Jews were, with very few exceptions, excluded from the official bureacracy and, though subject to military service, were not permitted to become commissioned officers. This situation prevailed in Germany throughout most of the nineteenth century.*

Holland was by far the most liberal of the West European countries in its treatment of the Jews, until England opened its doors, allowing Jews to become members of Parliament and even permitting a baptized Jew, Disraeli, to become Prime Minister. France permitted Jews to become commissioned officers, but it was in the French army that an event occurred which triggered the development of political Zionism. This event was, of course, the famous Dreyfus case, in which a Jewish captain was unjustly accused, convicted and sent to Devil's Island for alleged treason. The story is worth a brief retelling because of its profound effects.

France had been defeated and humiliated by Prussia-

---

* For example, in the Hanseatic City of Hamburg, one of the most liberal of the German states, it was not until 1900 that Paul Warburg became the first Jew elected to the lower house of Parliament.

Germany in the war of 1870–1871. The defeat rankled and the French General Staff was only too willing to have someone develop the theory that France had been stabbed in the back. Shortly, a book appeared—*La France Juive* by Edouard Drumont—which undertook to prove that France had been betrayed, that the French Jews were in the pay of Germany, and that the Jews had been responsible for the defeat, for the downfall of Napoleon III and for the creation of the Third Republic, *"la République Juive."*

Alfred Dreyfus was a wealthy Jew who had become a captain in the French army and a member of the General Staff. In December 1894 he was accused of having sold military secrets to the Germans, dragged before a summary court-martial, accused without evidence, degraded and marched around the court of the *Ecole Militaire* while his fellow officers shouted, "Jew! Judas! Traitor!" and a mob outside screamed, *"A bas les Juifs!"**

In a supposedly civilized and liberal France, one hundred years after the Declaration of the Rights of Man, large numbers of Frenchmen were still unwilling to extend these rights to a Jew. Dreyfus, protesting his innocence, was sent off to prison in exile.

In 1896 Colonel Picquart, Chief of Intelligence, discovered the true culprit, a Major Esterhazy. He informed his superior, a General Gonse, of what he had learned and asked for a retrial of Dreyfus. "Why," asked the General, "are you interested in his release?" Picquart replied, "Because he is innocent." The General said, "That makes no difference. The affair must not be reopened. Two generals are deeply involved in it."

"But what about his family?" Picquart asked. "Suppose they discover the facts—"

"Colonel, if you keep your mouth shut, no one will ever discover the truth."

But Colonel Picquart did not keep silent. Although he was at once sent "on a mission to the East," he and his friends in the ministry succeeded in 1898 in putting Esterhazy on trial. He was acquitted because the army refused to produce the evidence of his guilt.

* For a full account, see Nicholas Halasz, *Captain Dreyfus.*

The great novelist Emile Zola wrote his famous *J'Accuse* in protest and was sentenced to a year's imprisonment. Picquart, too, was sent to jail. Then Georges Clemenceau, later the war-time Premier of France, took up the cause, and because of his efforts a Colonel Henri, who had been Esterhazy's accomplice, confessed his guilt and committed suicide.

Esterhazy fled the country, and in 1900 Dreyfus was granted a new trial, at which, in spite of all the revelations, he was again condemned to ten years' imprisonment by an army court, although he was also pardoned. The General Staff could not admit that it had been wrong. Zola died in 1902. It took Clemenceau until 1906 to accomplish the complete exoneration of Dreyfus. The affair rocked France and drew worldwide attention.

The whole Dreyfus case from beginning to end was witnessed by a young Jewish correspondent of the Vienna newspaper *Neue Freie Presse*. His name was Theodor Herzl. In May 1895 he published a pamphlet entitled *Der Judenstaat* (The Jewish State) in which he wrote of a "promised land where we can live at last as free men on our own soil, where we can die peacefully in our own fatherland . . . where the offensive cry of 'Jew!' may become an honorable appellation."

Herzl was not the first advocate of a Jewish state. Moses Hess, a German Socialist, had written in 1840 that the Jews would always be strangers among the nations. Leo Pinsker, a Russian physician, had written in his *Auto-Emancipation*, published in 1882, that it was a tragic illusion of the Jews in Europe to think that they could ever achieve identification with the life of the Europeans among whom they lived. There were Russian-Jewish students who felt that life in Eastern Europe was intolerable and who urged the Jews to found their own state. But it was Herzl's work which energized the Zionist movement and led to the first International Zionist Congress which met at Basel, Switzerland, in August 1897, and to which Herzl addressed the words:

"We are here to lay the foundation-stone of the house which is to shelter the Jewish nation. . . . "

That was the beginning of political Zionism as an active force.

For the next two decades there were many arguments among the Jews of Europe and the United States. By no means all of them agreed that the hope of achieving full equality and assimilation among the Western peoples was an illusion. Some Jews, especially in England and in America, had achieved something very close to full recognition of equality. In the English-speaking world, anti-Semitism was rapidly becoming little more than a social prejudice no longer seriously affecting education, employment or the enjoyment of a full life. In England a Rothschild sat in the House of Lords and Ernest Cassel, a Jewish financier who conceived of building the first Aswan Dam, had become the intimate friend and advisor of King Edward VII. Even in Germany Albert Ballin, founder of the great Hamburg-American Steamship Line, had become a member of the Kaiser's inner circle.

All this was true, but so was the fact that in Poland and Russia millions of Jews still lived in ghettos, were denied all semblance of citizenship and were periodically exposed to mass murders, especially when the Tsarist government needed a scapegoat to maintain itself in power, as it did during the revolutionary discontent which followed upon the Russian defeat at the hands of Japan in 1905.

Throughout the nineteenth century millions of Europeans had emigrated to the United States to escape from poverty and varying degrees of oppression. Among the great waves of Irish and Italian immigrants there had been thousand of Jews, at first mostly from Germany but later also from Russia and Eastern Europe. Many of them had become prosperous and more or less assimilated. "Reform Judaism" had eliminated for many the demands of strict Orthodoxy which tended toward self-isolation. These Jews, especially in their second and third generations, had become sufficiently Americanized so that they no longer felt themselves to be foreigners. Few of them felt that there was a need for a Jewish state in Palestine or elsewhere. On the other hand, these American Jews were by no means indifferent to the fate of their co-religionists in Eastern Europe. More than any other people, Jews have always felt a responsibility for each other and a bond which ties them together. The American Jews regularly contributed large sums of money to the relief of suffering and to the escape from bondage of their European brethren. Many Polish and Russian Jews were thus helped to emigrate into the United States. Similar efforts were made by a few wealthy French Jews to resettle emigrants from Eastern Europe in Argentina.

However, in the period between the first Zionist Congress and the outbreak of World War I, Zionism found relatively few adherents among the assimilated or semi-assimilated Jews in England or the United States, and even fewer among the relatively free and prosperous Jews in Western Europe. The soil in which Zionism flourished was that of the East. The idea took root among the Jews in Russia and Poland and among those who had only recently escaped from the fearful conditions that existed there. Chaim Weizmann, born in Pinsk and a recent immigrant into England, was one of the latter.

During the last decade before the outbreak of World War I, Zionism remained more or less latent. A relatively small number of Jews, mostly from Russia and Poland and financed by American subsidy, settled in Palestine where they founded settlements on land purchased from the Arabs. In these early settlements urbanized, ghetto Jews learned to become farmers and to organize their lives not as individuals but as members of a community, developing a high degree of solidarity and communal self-reliance. They were welcomed by the Palestinian Arabs because they paid high prices for land and provided employment. Generally speaking, these early Jewish settlers in Palestine were not thinking of founding a Jewish state. Nor were the wealthy American Jews who aided them with financial subsidies and, later, built the Hebrew University in Jerusalem. However, these charitable efforts were grist to the mill of a growing group of ardent Zionists in England among whom Chaim Weizmann became the leader. They found support in the United States from a certain number of Jewish leaders, among whom the most prominent were Louis Marshall, Supreme Court Justice Louis Brandeis, Felix Frankfurter and several labor leaders.

In Germany a group of Zionists urged an apparently friendly Emperor William II to negotiate with the Turks for the acquisition of part of Palestine. This, in turn, fired the competitive zeal of the English Zionists.

Such, briefly, was the condition of the Zionist movement when war broke out in Europe in August 1914. When Turkey and Bulgaria joined the Central Powers—Germany and Austria —the situation changed. From the point of view of the Allies, Palestine was now enemy territory, while Tsarist Russia, the perpetrator of repeated pogroms against the Jews, had become an ally.

Note

This chapter has touched only briefly upon the causes of anti-Semitism, a subject about which much has been written. The emphasis here has been upon anti-Semitism *as a cause of political Zionism*, rather than upon the origin of the prejudice. As to the latter, two excellent works are recommended: the first by James Parkes, an English parson, entitled *The Jew and His Neighbors* (Student Christian Movement Press, London, 1930); the second by Rabbi Milton Steinberg, entitled *A Partisan Guide to the Jewish Problem* (Bobbs-Merrill, New York, 1945).

5

World War I in the Middle East

World War I was fought chiefly on two fronts, both remote from the Middle East. When more or less of a stalemate was reached on the bloody battlefields of Belgium and France, while Russian offensives against Germany and Austria in the East met with small success, the British, under the urging of Winston Churchill, launched a diversionary naval attack upon Turkey, hoping to force the Dardanelles and thus to link up with their Russian ally in the Black Sea. This brilliantly conceived effort failed, although it might have succeeded had the British known, as they did not know until after the war, how close they had come to victory. When the first naval attack failed to open the Straits, it was followed by landings of troops, but these were delayed long enough to permit the Turks and Germans to reinforce the defenses. These were ably conducted by the German General Liman von Sanders but were actually on the point of collapse for want of supplies and ammunition, when one of the last remaining floating mines struck and sank the British battleship *Queen Elizabeth* and caused the British to give up the adventure.

A second Allied campaign, based on the Greek port of Salonika, was aimed at rescuing Serbia and splitting Turkey from Bulgaria, while another British force under General Allenby moved out of Egypt across the Sinai Peninsula to attack Arabia. This campaign, aided by an Arab revolt about which more will be said presently, eventually broke the back of Turkish resistance and led to Turkey's surrender.

A third campaign by Anglo-Indian forces was launched in 1915 from the Persian Gulf with the object of capturing Baghdad. The initial effort was ill prepared and resulted in General Townshend's force being halted, besieged and ultimately forced to surrender at Kut-el-Amara. A second effort, launched two years later with stronger forces led by General Maude, succeeded in capturing Baghdad and driving the Turks out of most of Iraq.

In 1916, when the British advance out of Egypt upon the Arabian peninsula was being planned, formal negotiations were opened between the British government and the Zionist leadership which, largely inspired by Dr. Weizmann, had drawn up a "Program for the Jewish Resettlement in Palestine in Accordance with the Aspirations of the Zionist Movement." In essence, this was Herzl's project for the creation of a Jewish state, although Weizmann denied that such a state was contemplated in the near future. On the other hand, Nahum Sokolov, leader of the German Zionists and Weizmann's closest associate, made no secret of the fact that the plan did involve the creation of a Jewish nation. This ambiguity with regard to Zionist intentions was in part the cause of later misunderstandings.

The Balfour Declaration

On November 2, 1917, the British government published a letter from Arthur Balfour, then Foreign Secretary, to Lord Rothschild, whom Weizmann had suggested as the proper addressee. The letter read:

I have much pleasure in conveying to you on behalf of His Majesty's Government the following declaration of sympathy with the Jewish Zionist aspirations, which has been submitted to and approved by the Cabinet:

His Majesty's Government view with favor the establishment in Palestine of a National Home for the Jewish people, and will use their best endeavors to facilitate the achievement of this object, it being clearly understood that nothing shall be done which may prejudice the civil and religious right of existing non-Jewish communities in Palestine, or the rights and political status enjoyed by Jews in any other country.

I should be grateful if you would bring this declaration to the knowledge of the Zionist Federation.

More than a year prior to the issuance of the Balfour Declaration, the British government, through its High Commissioner in Egypt, Sir Henry McMahon, had given to Sherif Hussein of the Hejaz a promise of future Arab independence if Hussein would lead an Arab revolt and help Britain to overthrow the Turks. Hussein's domain lay along the shore of the Red Sea and was important not only because it contained the two holy cities of Mecca and Medina but because it was traversed by the chief Turkish line of communications, the railway from Damascus to Medina. Hussein was Sherif of Mecca as head of the Hashemite family which claimed direct descent from the Prophet. Negotiations with him were begun by Ronald Storrs, a former governor of Jerusalem, and concluded by a series of letters from Sir Henry McMahon. The promise of independence was hedged by certain rather vague reservations concerning the territory within which the Arabs were to be given self-rule. Excluded were Aden and those parts of South Arabia where the British and Indian governments had already established protectorates, as well as those parts of Syria which Britain had secretly promised to France in the Sykes-Picot Agreement. The letters made no mention whatever of Palestine, leaving the possible inference that it, too, would become a self-governing Arab land.*

Hussein and his sons, Abdullah and Feisal, raised a revolt, cut the railroad and in a campaign largely inspired and directed by a young British intelligence officer, T. E. Lawrence (the later

* For the most clearly stated Arab interpretation, see George Antonius, *The Arab Awakening.* For an objective statement of the British view, see Christopher Sykes, *Crossroads to Israel.* Both are recommended as extremely helpful in understanding the origin of the Arab-Israel conflict and have been extensively used as source material by the writer.

famous Lawrence of Arabia), reached and captured Aqaba.
Moving north from there, Feisal's Arabs formed the right flank
of General Allenby's advance to Jerusalem and Damascus.*

Two shocks awaited the Arabs in 1917, after they had fulfilled their side of the bargain with McMahon.

The first shock came as the result of the Balfour Declaration
and was partly allayed by a visit to Hussein on the part of a
British emissary, the distinguished Arabist, D. G. Hogarth.
Hogarth explained the importance which the British attached
to Jewish influence in the world and pointed out the benefits
which a certain amount of Jewish settlement would bring to
Palestine. Hussein agreed that Palestine had not been specifically mentioned in the McMahon correspondence and evinced
no proprietory interest in the area about which, indeed, he
knew very little. He expressed no hostility whatever toward
the Jews and agreed that a certain amount of Jewish immigration and settlement might be desirable but made it quite clear
that "he would not stand for a Jewish state." Had this interview been published, it would have gone far toward refuting
the charge later leveled against the British of having "twice
promised the Promised Land." The interview was kept secret
by both sides—by Hussein because his position with the Arabs
was delicate, having led a revolt against the Caliph and aided
the infidel British, and by the British perhaps out of respect for
Hussein's position or perhaps just because of the British predi-
lection for secret diplomacy.†

The second and even greater shock to the Arabs was occasioned by the publication of the secret treaty which the British
had signed in April-May 1916 with France and Tsarist Russia
for the dismemberment of the Ottoman Empire into spheres of
influence. This so-called Sykes-Picot Agreement was published
by the Bolshevik government after the Tsar's regime had been
overthrown. The British intention in making this agreement
had not been wholly inconsistent with the later promise of independence for the Arabs. Sir Mark Sykes (father of Christopher Sykes, whose work has been cited above) and the French

* For a fascinating account of these operations, see T. E. Lawrence,
The Seven Pillars of Wisdom.
† See Sykes, *Crossroads to Israel*, pp. 29–33.

negotiator, Picot, had in mind the creation of British and French temporary protectorates over their allotted spheres of influence—that of Britain in Iraq and that of France in Greater Syria. However, the French government, under the influence of the later notorious Pierre-Etienne Flandin, refused to go along with Picot's liberal views; the French government wanted outright colonial possession of Syria and Lebanon, as well as part of Iraq. At the time when the agreement was published in Moscow, the British could not explain this without risking a head-on collision with France.

It is not difficult to understand why the disclosure of the secret treaty, plus the Balfour Declaration, gave the Arabs the feeling that they had been betrayed.

To this day it remains somewhat of a mystery why the British government decided to issue the Balfour Declaration when it did. Lloyd George probably stated the truth when he frankly told Parliament later that the Declaration had been decided upon as an act of wartime propaganda strategy in order to win the support of Jews throughout the world for the Allied cause. (The United States had only recently entered the war and the British attributed to the Jews a probably exaggerated influence upon American policy; there was a powerful Zionist movement in Germany,* and Jews were prominent members of the Bolshevik Party in Russia.) Weizmann undoubtedly had a certain amount of influence upon Churchill, who was, in any case, sympathetic to the Zionist cause. It is difficult to come to any conclusion as to what motivated the inscrutable Balfour. Some have attributed to him purely imperialist motives, while others have expressed the view that his action was inspired by sympathy for the Jewish people whom he regarded as victims of an historic injustice.

To the extent that Balfour and other members of the War Cabinet may have been motivated by a desire to atone for past injustice, the expiation which this ambiguous declaration sought to achieve was designed to be accomplished at the expense of the Arab peoples who had had no part in the ill-treatment of the Jews and who, on the contrary, had treated

* The Kaiser was rumored to be negotiating with the Turks for the sale of land to provide a Jewish home in Palestine.

the Jews under their rule during some eight centuries far more fairly than had the Christian nations of Europe. What the Balfour Declaration proposed was, in effect, something like a British assertion of the right of eminent domain over a portion of the Arab lands for the purpose of establishing a "national home" for the Jews.

Whatever was meant by the phrase, "a national home in Palestine," was obscured by the ambiguous meaning of the expressed intention to "fulfill Jewish Zionist aspirations," since these aspirations were at the time far from clearly defined. Vincent Sheean's astringent comment on what he called "the rubbery phrases of the Declaration" seems worth quoting:

> The Declaration seemed to promise the Jews everything and to reserve everything for the Arabs, at one and the same time and with one twist of the pen. I was to learn in Palestine that it had actually given the Jews little, had reserved little for the Arabs, and had achieved one certain purpose only: the installation of the British as the governing power in the country.*

The state of confusion was further compounded by the far from clear relationship between Sherif Hussein and the Arab leadership outside of the Hejaz.

Neither Hussein nor his son, the Emir Feisal, had any real authority over the Arabs in Palestine and Syria. Hussein had become "King of Arabia" in name only. Even his rule in the Hejaz was constantly threatened by the Sa'udi Arabian dynasty which had gained control of Shammar, the Nejd and 'Asir north of the Hejaz in the Arabian desert. Feisal was a man of distinguished bearing and indubitably good intentions. Weizmann went to see him at Aqaba in 1918, and a little later the two men met in London. In these talks Feisal was friendly throughout. He and Weizmann signed an agreement in the autumn of 1918 which read in part:

> All necessary measures shall be taken to encourage and stimulate the immigration of Jews into Palestine on a large scale and, as quickly as possible to settle Jewish immigrants upon the land through closer settlement and intensive cul-

* *Personal History*, p. 341.

tivation of the soil. In taking such measures the Arab peas-
ant and tenant farmers shall be protected in their rights and
shall be assisted in forwarding their economic development . . .

The Zionist Organization proposes to send to Palestine a
commission of experts to make a survey of the economic
possibilities of the country and to report upon the best
means for its development. . . . The Zionist Organization
will . . . assist the Arab state in providing the means for
developing the natural resources and the economic possibilities thereof.

Feisal added a codicil in his own writing which was signed
also by Weizmann:

Provided the Arabs obtain their independence as demanded . . . I shall concur in the above articles. But, if
the slightest modification or departure were to be made, I
shall then not be bound by a single word of the present
agreement.

What Feisal meant by "the Arab state" was an independent
Greater Syria that included Palestine. By allying himself with
Weizmann, he hoped to force the British to insist that such a
state be created. But this could not be done without a betrayal
of the Balfour Declaration and a head-on collision with France.
The British did not want a conflict with France even though
they cordially disliked the crude colonial ideas of empire prevalent at Paris. They compromised by making Feisal King of
Syria, excluding Palestine from his domain. Neither the French
nor the Syrians liked this solution. The Syrians did not wish to
be ruled by either France or a Hashemite king. They considered Feisal a foreign intruder and accused him of being in the
pay of the French. To counter this suspicion, Feisal allied himself with the radical Syrian independence movement and
thereby infuriated both the conservative Syrian leaders and,
above all, the French. In July 1920 the French extinguished the
independent Syrian kingdom by direct and ruthless military
action and forced Feisal into exile.

Because of the overthrow of the Tsarist government in Russia, the Western Allies were unable to put into effect the Sèvres

Treaty of 1920, by which they had planned to accomplish the dismemberment of the Ottoman Empire. At a conference held at San Remo, they decided to deal at least with the Arab parts of the empire. Here it was agreed that France would be given a mandate under the newly formed League of Nations over Syria (including modern Lebanon), while Britain was given the mandate over Palestine and Iraq. (The French gave up their claim to the Mosul oilfields in Iraq in exchange for a share in their exploitation.) Thus, Sa'udi Arabia and Yemen were the only Arab countries to be given immediate and complete independence.

The League mandates were conceived by President Wilson as a form of temporary trusteeship to be liquidated as soon as the native populations might be able to set up viable independent governments. Had this been the result, the McMahon promises would have been fulfilled, for both Hussein and Feisal had agreed to and even expressed the desire for temporary tutelage. But neither the French nor the British shared Wilson's views. The French had no intention of ever withdrawing. The British intended to set up native governments which, though nominally independent, would be client states of the Empire. In Iraq they could proceed to set up a client kingdom, but in Palestine they faced a dilemma, for here they could not set up an independent Arab state without violating their promise to the Zionists. In Palestine their mandate and their commitments were self-contradictory.

While not as flagrantly imperialistic as France, the British were by no means solely concerned with resolving their Arab-Jewish dilemma. They were equally if not more concerned with their own imperial interests. Middle East oil had assumed great importance, not only for the Royal Navy and the Royal Air Force but for Britain's whole economic life. Egypt was growing restless under the protracted British occupation, and Palestine appeared to offer a more secure British base for the protection of the Suez Canal and the lifeline to India.

While the British War Cabinet was sympathetic to the Zionist cause, the management of the Palestinian mandate fell into the hands of the "Office of Occupied Enemy Territory," known as OETA. The occupation forces were concerned, as such forces inevitably are, with the preservation of "law and order." Whitehall was imbued with the Imperial tradition; it was accustomed to dealing with "natives" by playing the game of divide-and-conquer with indigenous potentates as the pawns. The British administration in Palestine tried to play this game by "being fair to both sides," with very little understanding of the conflicting British commitments to Arabs and Jews and the feelings which these engendered. In its attempts to be neutral, the administration alienated both Arabs and Jews. The Zionists, whose ultimate aim was the establishment of a Jewish state, feared that the administration's neutral policy would frustrate their desires; while the Arabs, correctly suspecting the true Zionist aim, feared that they would eventually be outnumbered in Palestine and become a minority in a Jewish-controlled state.

There was a possible answer to the dilemma. Judah L. Magnes, later the first president of the Hebrew University in Jerusalem, visualized the creation of a binational Arab-Jewish state in which both elements of the population would be equally represented. He foresaw that in such a state a renewed Arab-Jewish symbiosis might develop, with vastly beneficial effects upon the whole politically and economically backward Middle East area. But this imaginative concept did not appeal to the Zionists; they had their hearts set upon the creation of a Jewish nation.

The Arabs, originally friendly to the Jews and to their limited settlement in Palestine, found the Westernized settlers difficult to understand. They were clearly not the "Semitic cousins" with whom their ancestors had lived in peace and whom Hussein and Feisal had welcomed. They were Westerners, alien to the Middle East and implanted in the Arabs' midst by a Western power which, as the Arabs saw it, had betrayed them. Through no fault of their own, the Zionists became the surrogates of the Western imperialism which the Arabs had learned to distrust and hate.

What was more, the Jewish immigrants turned out to be the carriers of ideas, such as socialism and democracy, that were wholly foreign to the feudal order of Arab society. Many of them came from Poland and Russia and were, hence, suspected of being infected with the virus of atheistic communism—an ideology wholly abhorrent to devout Moslems. (Actually, there was among the settlers a tiny minority of communists, whom the majority intensely disliked; and, ironically, an outburst of violence by the majority against the little communist [Mopsi] organization was misunderstood by the Arabs and led, in Jaffa, to the first violent encounter between Arabs and Jews.) Today, when Arab nations are asking for and receiving aid from communist countries, and when Israel is condemned as a capitalist outpost in a would-be socialist Arab world, it is interesting to recall this earlier Arab attitude.

The British administration also found the Westernized Jewish settlers somewhat difficult; they did not fit into the pattern of "natives" whom the Colonial Office was accustomed to rule. It was much easier to deal with the Arabs, who were used to authoritarian government. The idea of a Palestinian state controlled by self-willed, social-revolutionary Jewish immigrants from Eastern Europe did not greatly appeal to the proconsuls of His Majesty's Empire.

Actually, Arab fears of being outnumbered and Colonial Office apprehension concerning an unruly Jewish state were scarcely warranted in the early days of the mandate. Much to the dismay of the Zionist leadership, only a relatively small number of Jews sought admission to Palestine. This was due to the fact that the defeat of the Central Powers seemed to have inaugurated a new era in which all people would be entitled to self-determination. Poland had been liberated. The Pale of Settlement had been eliminated. Russian Jews had been released from their ghettos. The reactionary Hapsburg Empire had been dismembered; Germany had become a democratic republic, as had also what was left of Austria. For those European Jews who did not share the prevailing optimistic view of Europe's future, the doors of the United States remained wide open into a life that, to many, seemed more attractive than settlement in Palestine.

Nevertheless, Arab fears persisted—and not without reason, for the Zionists were dismayed but not discouraged. Judah Magnes and his followers still saw some hope for their dream of an Arab-Jewish reconciliation in a binational state.

6

The Peace That Brought No Peace

We must digress at this point in order to review briefly certain aspects of the so-called peace settlements concluded by the warring Western powers.

The facts concerning the Versailles and Trianon Treaties with the Central Powers are well known and need not be reviewed here. The peace terms imposed upon Germany were harsh, but far less so than those imposed by Germany upon Russia in the Treaty of Brest-Litovsk or those which probably would have been imposed by Germany upon France and Britain if Germany had won the war. But that is not the point. Nor will it serve any useful purpose to speculate upon what might have been the course of European history if President Wilson had been able to persuade Britain and France to make a "peace without victory."

In a later chapter we shall have occasion to note the consequences of one fatal aspect of the Versailles Treaty, namely, the delusion that it created in Western minds concerning the defrayment of the costs of the war. At this point, however, we should note certain things which happened before the peace treaties were signed and which affected the future of the West at least as much as, if not more than, the treaties themselves.

The one single factor which, more than any other, caused the peace to become merely a twenty-one-year armistice was the impact of the Russian Revolution. One may doubt whether the Allies or even the United States fought the war "to make the world safe for democracy." But there is no doubt that the fear inspired by the Russian Revolution caused the Allied war aim to become one of making the world safe against revolutionary change.

When the Tsarist regime was overthrown, in March 1917, the new constitutional government headed by Prince Lvov in many ways resembled the moderate regime which overturned the Bourbons in the first stages of the French Revolution. Later in the summer Alexander Kerensky became head of the new government. These events were welcomed by President Wilson and by most Americans. However, the British and French governments took quite a different view. For various reasons they considered their vital interests threatened by the overthrow of the Tsar and almost immediately began to intrigue with reactionary Russian restorationists. Although the Lvov-Kerensky government remained faithful to the alliance against the Central Powers, British and French support was secretly given to both General Kornilov and Admiral Kolchak, the two outstanding Tsarist leaders who were trying to overthrow it. Little was known about this at the time, but it remains a fact that the new democratic government in Russia was undermined from the start, not merely by the Germans who smuggled Lenin into Russia in order to get Russia out of the war, but by the governments of Britain and France.

Both London and Paris were frightened by the Tsar's overthrow. Had this fear been merely one of losing a much-needed ally, Anglo-French diplomacy would have exerted itself to strengthen a regime which had pledged itself to continue the war and which might be expected to win greater popular support for the war effort than its predecessor.

The conclusion seems inescapable: the democratic revolution frightened the British and French governments *precisely because it was democratic*—because it threatened a change in the social structure of Europe which might alter the status quo and endanger the privileges of the ruling elites. This would explain why the people of Britain and France did not share the apprehensions of their governments and were as little alarmed by the March Revolution as were the people of the United States.

The Bolshevik Revolution of October-November 1917 was a wholly different matter, frightening the entire Western world by its ruthlessness and also by the Marxist doctrines it proclaimed, for these doctrines were a challenge to the fundamental social, religious and economic concepts of Western society. The Allies, including the United States, made no attempt to win the Bolsheviks to a continued participation in the war. Britain and France quite deliberately decided that the Bolshevik government must be overthrown and continued their assistance to Kornilov (and, later, to Denikin) in the south and to Kolchak in Siberia. Once the Germans surrendered, the United States joined in this effort. A British-American expeditionary force was sent to Archangel and Murmansk. Japanese and American troops landed in Siberia. The efforts failed and the forces were withdrawn after a little over a year of bloody civil war from which the Bolsheviks emerged victorious. But the effect of this Allied attempt to overthrow the young Soviet regime did more than prejudice future relations between Russia and the West; it profoundly influenced Allied policy with respect to Germany.

In the confusion of the defeat of the German armies, the abdication of the Kaiser and the collapse of all authority, only the German Social Democrats were capable of assuming the responsibilities of government. Their party comprised the majority of German workers and had the support of many of the soldiers in the defeated army. The Social Democrats knew what they wanted but were caught unprepared to carry their program into effect in the new Weimar Republic. What they wanted to do was to break up the great Junker estates into small farms, to socialize the heavy industries controlled by the industrial barons and to create a people's defense force free from domination by the hitherto all-powerful officer caste.

However, the Social Democrats were confronted by a highly articulate minority of Spartakists, who were outspoken followers of Lenin, and a group of "Independent Socialists," who were early prototypes of the later "fellow travelers." To control this radical minority, the Social Democrats needed the support of the army, but the army leadership could not be won to any program which would destroy the power of the officer class. Friedrich Ebert, the first president of the Weimar Republic, managed to make an alliance with General Wilhelm Groener, the only high-ranking officer at Ludendorff's headquarters who had preserved cool-headed calm in the disaster of defeat. Groener undertook to bring the army home in good order and to help establish lawful government on condition that the honor of the army would be upheld. This agreement, while undermining the democratic revolution and ultimately making the army once more the arbiter of German affairs, need not have had such disastrous consequences had it not been for the policy pursued by the Allied Armies of Occupation.

Before the armistice was signed Soldiers' and Sailors' Councils had sprung up in various parts of Germany and a number of "People's Governments" had been set up in towns and cities. These revolutionary organizations were by no means controlled by the extremists and could quite easily have been weeded out so as to become nuclei of spontaneous democratic government. However, on November 10, 1918—the day before the signing of the armistice—the Supreme Allied Command decreed that it would deal with none but the local authorities of the ex-Kaiser's Imperial Government. The occupation forces then proceeded to insist upon the reinstatement of these old officials in place of the revolutionary groups.

The Allies welcomed a German "revolution" insofar as it meant the substitution of a formal republic for the Kaiser's Imperial rule, but they feared and objected to any change in the basic socio-economic structure of Germany, refusing to permit the displacement of the bureaucracy which had served the dominant Junker-military-industrial cliques of Imperial Germany.

Formal democracy was established with adoption of the Weimar constitution, but social and economic democracy were strangled at birth by Allied governments so frightened of Bolshevism that they had become hostile to any basic change.

One may legitimately question whether, even without Allied intervention, the traditions of a long authoritarian past would not eventually have reasserted themselves and subverted the

Weimar Republic, but the fact remains that a democratic revolution was aborted by the victorious Allies. The result of the status-quo reorientation of Allied policy—as the succeeding years would soon show—was not to make the world safe from revolution but to make it safe for counterrevolution and antidemocratic reaction.

The alteration in the climate of Western opinion between March 1917, when a war to overthrow "autocracy" had almost universal appeal, and Wilson's return from Paris in the summer of 1919 may have had as much to do with Wilson's repudiation as partisan hostility, political ineptitude and the defects in the proposals which Wilson submitted to the American people.

Be that as it may, in the following year the American people, disillusioned with the peace and the disavowal of the ideals for which they thought they had gone to war, turned their backs upon Europe and voted overwhelmingly for what Warren G. Harding promised them—"a return to normalcy."

The United States had become the most powerful nation in the world but realized neither its power nor its responsibility. The war had greatly stimulated the economic growth of the United States while weakening the economies of the European powers. It had shifted the center of gravity of the Western world from London, Paris and Berlin to New York and Washington. Most important of all, it had transformed the United States from a debtor to a creditor nation and so radically changed its international balance of payments that its high protective tariff had become a menace both to world trade and to its own vastly expanded economy. Neither Harding nor the Congress elected in 1920 were aware of what these changes implied.

At this point, a word of explanation may be in order to answer the question:

"What has all this to do with the Middle East?"

This study is concerned with the impact of the West upon the Middle East. The profound change in the political orientation of the West, which we have just noted, inevitably bore consequences in almost every part of the world. It laid the foundation for fascist counterrevolution in Italy, Spain and, most important of all, in Germany, where counterrevolution nourished and was nourished by the most vicious and brutal form of anti-Semitism the world had yet known. From Germany, the virus spread through most of Central and Eastern Europe, eventually seeping even into France. It is hardly necessary to point out what the Nazi persecution of the Jews had to do with postwar developments in the Middle East: it created the major problem in that area; and the manner in which the Western powers reacted to that problem was profoundly influenced by their fear of Bolshevism.

However, as we shall see in the next chapter, it was not only the bungled peace settlement after World War I that caused counterrevolution in Germany to assume its peculiarly vicious form. It was also the postwar behavior of the West, and especially the irresponsibility of the United States, that shaped the future of Germany.

7

Self-Delusion and Irresponsibility Lead to Disaster

The war left a spirit of pacifism in both Britain and the United States and, for a short time, in Germany. A partial Naval Disarmament Treaty was signed in 1921 by the United States, Britain, Japan, France and Italy. In 1928 the major powers of the world renounced war as an instrument of national policy in the Paris Pact (the Kellogg-Briand Treaty). However, the spirit of pacifism did not extend from the political into the economic area of international relations in which selfish nationalism and the irresponsibility of the United States led the world into disaster.

War Debts and Reparations

During the war the United States had loaned over $10.5 billion to the Allies—about $4 billion to Britain, slightly less to France and the remainder scattered. (Britain had loaned to the other Allies more than she had borrowed from the United States; France alone owed Britain $3.5 billion.)

President Wilson had regarded and caused the American people to regard these war loans as ordinary borrowings to be repaid at the end of the war. (They could more properly have been regarded as a partial offset to Anglo-French sacrifices made before the United States entered the war.) Because Wilson expected repayment, he had been powerless to combat the Anglo-French demand at Paris that the entire cost of the war should be extracted from Germany in the form of reparations. Nor was he able to set a global limit to the reparations that Germany would be expected to pay, nor to set a schedule for repayment nor to limit the time during which Germany would be compelled to continue payments. (This was the fatal mistake made at Versailles alluded to in the preceding chapter.)

Thanks largely to J. Maynard (later Lord) Keynes, the British were quick to realize the danger created by the dual fiction of war debts and reparations. Just before Wilson left office, they suggested that the Allies and the United States cooperate in the economic reconstruction of Germany in order to avoid the creation of a dangerously explosive situation in that country. Wilson replied: "How can your experts and ours be expected to work out a *new* plan to furnish working capital to Germany, when we deliberately start by taking away all Germany's *present* capital? How can anyone expect America to turn over to Germany . . . new capital to take the place of that which the European nations have determined to take from her?"

It was a good question. The American business interests that dominated the Harding administration and insisted that wartime controls be abolished and that government should "get out of business" thought they had the answer. In effect, American businessmen and bankers undertook to make the fiction of war debts and reparations come true. They were ably assisted by a multimillionaire Secretary of the Treasury who reduced taxes and created easy money.

Meanwhile, however, conditions in Europe grew steadily worse. Poland invaded Russia and captured Kiev. Then a Russian counteroffensive carried to the gates of Warsaw. Russia and Germany were developing a common interest in suppressing the newly independent Republic of Poland. The German Foreign Minister Walter Rathenau startled the West by his Treaty of Rapallo with the Soviet Union (1921). A large credit granted by Germany to Russia ostensibly to promote

Russo-German business cloaked a secret agreement for the building of airplane and tank factories in Russia and the training of cadres for an illegally enlarged German *Reichswehr*.

Toward the West, Germany pursued a "policy of fulfillment" while at the same time frantically seeking a reduction of the reparations clause in the Versailles Treaty. France refused to consider any reduction.

In Italy mass unemployment and severe suffering created a revolutionary atmosphere. Fearing Bolshevism and unwilling to undertake the needed reform of an outmoded social-economic structure, the ruling clique of industrialists, large landowners and courtiers connived with the king in the establishment of Mussolini's fascist dictatorship. The "March on Rome" set the pattern of unconstitutional seizure of power by an illegally armed minority, soon to be followed in Germany, Austria and Spain. Counterrevolution from the right caused no alarm in Britain or the United States.

But Britain was alarmed by what was happening in Germany, where the flight of capital was causing a rapid depreciation in the value of the German currency. In 1922 the British government offered to cancel all debts owed to it by the other Allies if the United States would cancel its war loans. President Harding and his Secretary of the Treasury Andrew Mellon bluntly refused this suggestion. They were far too busy reducing taxes and retiring the public debt on the pleasant assumption that the war debts were "good assets."

By the end of 1923 the German mark had become practically worthless and the savings of the German workers and of the middle class had been wiped out. (Actually, German savings had already been largely destroyed by the huge costs of the war, but this became apparent only when the currency panic was precipitated.)

The German government now declared that it could no longer meet its schedule of "payments in kind." (These consisted for the most part in deliveries of coal.) Thereupon, France and Belgium sent troops to occupy the coal-producing German Ruhr. The occupation lasted until 1925 and produced disastrous results. The French discovered that coal could not be "mined with bayonets," and a sullen spirit of resentment was kindled in Germany.

Before Harding suddenly died on August 2, 1923, his administration undertook a series of moves with regard to the Far East which, taken together, alienated Japan and weakened the position of both Britain and the United States in that area. These need not concern us here; they have elsewhere been discussed in some detail by the writer.*

What does concern us here is the onset of a worldwide economic depression that grew out of French intransigence, British euphoria, German weakness and, above all, out of American irresponsibility.

With the taciturn but complacent Calvin Coolidge in the White House and Andrew Mellon continuing as Secretary of the Treasury, far more thought was given in Washington to reducing the national debt and to making things easy for business than to the affairs of Europe. Coolidge's attitude toward the Allied war debts was even simpler than that of Wilson; he expressed it in the well-known sentence: "They hired the money, didn't they?" To be sure, the war debts were funded and the accumulated interest was "generously" scaled down, but the fiction was maintained that the principal would be repaid out of German reparations.

As to the latter, General Charles G. Dawes was assigned the mission of working out a method by which reparation payments might be continued. Under the Dawes Plan of 1924 Germany was given a large loan secured by a lien on German railways and factories and reparation payments were reduced to a series of annual installments. This lightened the immediate burden but left the Germans without knowledge of what their ultimate liability would be. The chief benefit of the plan was that it made possible the reorganization and stabilization of the German currency. On the other hand, its effect was to create an apparent German prosperity which served not only to maintain the fiction of the ultimate collectibility of reparations and war debts but also to open the way to an ultimately disastrous flow of foreign loans to German industries, states and municipalities.

* See J. P. Warburg, *Western Intruders: America's Role in the Far East* (Atheneum, New York, 1967), pp. 132–134.

Having done what they could to help the Allies repay by sending Dawes to "straighten out" German affairs, Coolidge and Mellon sat back and waited for American bankers to make loans and investments that would rebuild Germany's productive power.

This scheme of things was helped along by the vastly improved atmosphere created in Europe by the Locarno Treaties of 1925 in which Germany voluntarily agreed to a permanent settlement of its relations with its western neighbors, even though the Germans refused to recognize as permanent the settlement of their eastern frontier with Poland. The "spirit of Locarno" was only slightly disturbed when Stresemann next signed a friendship pact with Russia (the Treaty of Berlin). The West did not suspect that the Rapallo Treaty of 1921 had already laid the foundations for the secret training of German cadres in Russia and that Stresemann's Berlin Treaty foreshadowed Soviet-German cooperation against Poland. (One of Stresemann's most influential advisors in working out his policy of playing off the West against the East and vice versa was Konrad Adenauer, then president of the Prussian State Council.)

It was at about this time, when the American bankers were embarking upon an orgy of investment in Germany, that the preconditions for the National Socialist counterrevolution were being created. Inflation had destroyed the stable lower middle class and a new group of inflation profiteers had come into being. Most of the big industrialists and bankers had managed to preserve and even to augment their wealth and power, while the little people had been powerless to prevent the destruction of what wealth they had possessed. This produced two major ingredients of fascist counterrevolution—strong anti-capitalist sentiment among the masses and fear of revolution among the privileged few. The harsh Versailles Treaty and the occupation of the Ruhr united all kinds and classes of Germans in a common sense of outraged nationalism and played into the hands of the militarists and nationalist leaders who were already thinking of the next war. Thus, both the socialist and the nationalist ingredients of what was soon to become National Socialism were latent in the Germany which

Americans were so anxious to rebuild in order that the war
debts might remain a "sound asset" on Mr. Mellon's books.

In the United States, the reduction of taxes and the plentiful
supply of money created a runaway business boom which soon
developed into a wild inflation of security prices and a nation-
wide speculative mania. In an atmosphere of irresponsible
financial anarchy, the opportunity to float German and other
foreign loans represented to many bankers nothing more than
an opportunity to make money by selling an ever greater quantity of securities to an insatiable public. (As a matter of fact,
the German loans were for the most part better secured than
many of the pyramided domestic issues sold to the public at the
time.) Soon there was a scramble among bankers on both sides
of the Atlantic to see who could offer the most attractive terms
to German steel manufacturers and other industrial concerns.
In this respect, the Coolidge-Mellon scheme worked quite
nicely.

But if Germany was to keep up her reparation payments, she
needed not only to produce but to export her products in
order to acquire foreign exchange. Above all, Germany needed
access to the American market, as, indeed, did all the European
industrial producers. This, however, did not suit Washington
at all. In the Harding-Coolidge era the idea was to keep all of
the domestic market for American producers and, so far as possible, to capture world markets from the British. In 1922 the
relatively liberal Underwood Tariff of 1913 was repealed and
the much more restrictive Fordney-McCumber Tariff was enacted. This was only a foretaste of what was yet to come.
Thus, while American and British loans were helping to build
up Germany's industrial capacity, Anglo-American trade policies were making it impossible for Germany to sell its goods
for foreign exchange.

It did not take the Germans long to discover that the eager
American bankers might supply them with the foreign exchange that the American manufacturers were unwilling to let
them earn by exporting their products. Accordingly, the German government encouraged not only the German industries
but every conceivable governmental agency, including provin-
cial and municipal governments, to contract loans in Britain or

the United States.

When President Hoover took office in 1928, these processes of financial anarchy were already in full swing, but firm action might have arrested the domestic boom and put a stop to excessive foreign lending. Far from taking such action, the Hoover administration continued the complacent course of its predecessor. In April 1929 the Dawes Plan was supplanted by the Young Plan which again revised German reparations downward and provided for another large international loan to the German government. This created even greater confidence in German recovery and increased the flow of loans and investments.

At least one American banker* warned in the spring of 1929 that a collapse of the inflated security markets was imminent, but nothing was done to arrest speculation and overexpansion. In October the stock market collapsed, bringing ruin to a large part of the investing public. Even then, the Hoover administration did not seem to realize what was happening. Hoover himself issued a number of reassuring statements. There was no cause for alarm, he said. Prosperity, he said, was "just around the corner."

So little did the Congress and the administration understand the basic falacies upon which the boom had been created that they proceeded to enact a new tariff act (the Smoot-Hawley Act) that raised import restrictions to the highest point in American history. It was worldwide disaster—not prosperity—that now waited around the corner.

It is not necessary to recall here how the Great Depression spread, at first throughout the American economy and then throughout the Western world. What we have tried to do here is to analyze the causes of the disaster.

In 1931 banks began to crash in Austria and Germany as they had earlier in the United States. No one wanted to lend or invest money; everyone wanted to borrow. Great Britain was forced to abandon the gold standard, unable any longer to settle her accounts by shipping gold. All the gold in the world was being sucked into the United States. In country after country, currencies depreciated and desperate measures were taken to

* The writer's father, Paul M. Warburg.

cut down imports, force up exports and control the flight of
capital. Economic nationalism—the pattern which the United
States had set in its selfish irresponsibility—became by sheer
necessity the guiding principle for all nations. World trade
dried up. Some countries approached starvation while others
were smothered in surplus foodstuffs for which no market
could be found.

The political effects of the economic collapse were calami-
tous in Asia as well as in Europe, and especially in Germany
and Japan.

In Germany five years of false prosperity had merely put off
the evil day. With the collapse of foreign borrowing, business
came to a standstill and mass unemployment set in. Once more
the German people were desperate and disillusioned. The weak
government of the senile President von Hindenburg and his
irresolute Chancellor, Heinrich Bruening, became more and
more of a dictatorship—a flabby, indicisive dictatorship which
discredited democracy but failed to solve the economic problem. Indeed, there seemed to be no solution for the economic
problem except a wholesale repudiation of reparations and
debts. In October 1930 Hitler's National Socialists gained their
first big bloc of seats in the Reichstag. In the presidential election that followed, von Hindenburg was barely able to defeat
the Nazi Fuehrer because the dominant Nationalists under
Hugenberg were not yet ready to accept the Austrian up-
start. In 1932 the intrigues of General von Schleicher and
Franz von Papen forced Bruening's resignation. The ambitious
general and the bumbling Junker diplomat then proceeded to
write the last pages of the tragic history of the Weimar Republic. When von Papen induced Hitler to accept the Chan-
cellorship, the Nationalist clique thought that it had captured Hitler, only to find within a short time that Hitler had
captured them and, along with them, the control of Germany.
From that moment it became certain that Europe would either
have to accept the hegemony of Nazi Germany or fight for its
independence.

In Japan, too, unemployment and distress were caused by
the worldwide depression and the drying up of markets and
the flow of capital. Dissatisfaction with the moderate demo-

cratic regime brought the militarists into power. At the same time, the emergence of what appeared to be a strong Kuomintang government in China threatened Japan's interests on the mainland. In 1931, with the Western world gripped by depression and near-panic, the Japanese military leaders felt safe in launching an invasion of the long-coveted Chinese province of Manchuria.

President Hoover's far-seeing and courageous Secretary of State, Henry L. Stimson, issued a forceful protest but received little backing at home or abroad. The League of Nations appointed an investigatory commission under the chairmanship of Lord Lytton. The League itself possessed no military or naval power; without strong British support, it was impotent to halt Japanese aggression, but Britain was no more ready than the United States to go to war in order to preserve the integrity of China. London rebuffed Stimson's protest and President Hoover—much to Stimson's chagrin—refused to take any further action. Thus the first overt challenge to the League of Nations, the Paris Pact against war and the Nine-Power Treaty with respect to China* went unanswered. The precedent for aggression was set. The curtain was rising upon another world war.

In November 1932 the American people overwhelmingly rejected the eight-year record of Republican irresponsibility and elected a Democratic President and a Congress in which both houses were controlled by the Democratic Party. Perhaps even more than a vote against the Republican Party or President Hoover, it was a vote against the business leadership which had been permitted by three Republican Presidents to dominate United States policy. But this was true only with respect to domestic affairs; it was not a vote against isolationist foreign policy. Indeed, foreign policy was scarcely debated during the presidential election campaign. The American people were almost solely concerned with the domestic disaster that had befallen them, the full extent of which they had not yet experienced.

If the governments and peoples of Europe cherished any

* Treaty of 1922 guaranteeing Chinese integrity. See Warburg, *Western Intruders*, pp. 132–134.

hope that Franklin D. Roosevelt would bring the United States
out of isolationism and cause it to be more helpful in world
affairs, they were due for a sad disappointment, at least so far as
the immediate future was concerned.

During the first three months of the Roosevelt administration, the world watched with admiration and wonder
the manner in which the new President tackled the stupendous
task of restoring the confidence of a frightened people, of
clearing away the wreckage and of enacting the reforms of the
New Deal. "The First Hundred Days" seemed like a miracle.
They restored hope not only in the United States but throughout the world. In large measure these hopes were focused upon
the World Economic Conference, to be held at London, at
which the miracle that had been worked in America might be
extended to the shattered economy of the whole Western
world.

The sad awakening came when, during this conference, the
President suddenly reached the decision that the economic recovery of the United States must remain his primary concern,
if necessary at the cost of a further deterioration of world sta-
bility. The decision, announced by cable to the conference
while it was in session, took the form of a repudiation of the
attempt being made to stabilize the world's major currencies
and an announcement that the United States intended to exper-
iment with a medium of exchange based not upon gold but
upon commodity prices.*

From 1933 until 1937 the United States was to all intents and
purposes an absentee member of the world community. Eu-
rope, Asia and the Middle East were left to their own devices.
The United States did establish diplomatic relations with the
Soviet Union; it did establish a "Good Neighbor" policy with
Latin America, in place of "Dollar Diplomacy" and interven-

---

* The writer, who had been appointed as financial advisor to the
United States delegation to the Conference and resigned as a consequence
of the President's message, has written extensively about this episode and
its impact upon later developments in *The Money Muddle* (Knopf,
New York, 1934) and *The Long Road Home* (Doubleday, New York,
1961). He has also deposited with the Oral History Department of Co-
lumbia University a diary covering the "hundred days" and the World
Economic Conference which is open to students but has not been published.

tionism; and it did, in 1936, adopt a policy of reciprocal tariff reduction that was later to bear fruit. In 1936 a bill was passed by Congress promising independence to the Philippines within ten years.

During these years the only people in the United States who were seriously interested in the Middle East were the American oil companies, the supporters of missions and colleges in the Middle East, a handful of Zionists and the American Joint Distribution Committee.

The writer cannot recall that Palestine was ever mentioned during Prime Minister MacDonald's visit to Washington in the spring of 1933. At the Word Economic Conference at London, shortly thereafter, the sole Middle East matter to be brought up was the question of a loan to Iraq.

8

The Middle East in the 1920's

President Wilson had endorsed the Balfour Declaration and had sponsored the League Mandate scheme at the Paris Peace Conference. However, when it came to the Middle East, he realized that both France and Britain regarded the mandates as cover for imperialist designs. He proposed that an Anglo-French-American commission be sent to the Middle East to ascertain the wishes of the Arab peoples. France and Britain at first agreed and then declined to participate. Wilson thereupon sent his own two-man mission, the King-Crane Mission, to investigate. Its report, backed by the testimony of President Bliss of the American University at Beirut, convinced him that Arab sentiment was opposed to the mandate idea, especially if either Britain or France were to be the mandatory powers. Asked whether the United States would undertake the Palestine mandate, Wilson wisely declined, recognizing that the position had been hopelessly compromised by conflicting promises and secret treaties.

After the American people had repudiated the League and returned to isolationism, the affairs of the Middle East were left almost entirely in the hands of Britain and France.

France, having ousted Feisal from Syria, had considerable difficulty in suppressing a series of nationalist uprisings. The British were alarmed by the sudden threat of Feisal's older brother, the Emir Abdullah, to march on Damascus with a Jordanian army in order to oust the French and restore Hashemite rule. This would have brought Britain and France into direct conflict.

In 1921 Winston Churchill became Colonial Secretary and immediately called a conference at Cairo of all Britain's representatives in the Middle East. These representatives were a curious collection of Arabist scholars, career diplomats and individualists, such as T. E. Lawrence and Alexander Kirkbride, who had acquired a deep affection for the Arab people. Churchill himself seems to have been fascinated by the Egyptian scenery and held many of the meetings in the desert, where he could indulge in his hobby of painting as he listened to the ideas of his advisors.

Two extremely important decisions emerged from this conference:

1. It was decided to install Feisal as King of Iraq. This was chiefly the idea of Miss Gertrude Bell, an enthusiastic Arabist, and Sir Percy Cox, the British High Commissioner at Baghdad.

2. It was decided—and here T. E. Lawrence seems to have been the moving spirit along with Alexander Kirkbride, the British-installed "King" of the tiny Jordanian country of Moab —to pacify Abdullah by lopping off Transjordan from Palestine in order to create a separate state with Abdullah as its king.

Thus, out in the desert, with Churchill painting pictures of the pyramids and the Sphinx as his advisors talked, began an Anglo-Hashemite alliance by means of which the British hoped to creat two client kingdoms which could be induced by subsidy and protection to serve Britain's imperial interests in the Middle East.

Feisal, at first not over-eager to go to the run-down capital of a strife-torn backward country, agreed to the proposal and was duly installed at Baghdad by means of a "popular election" skillfully prepared and rigged by Gertrude Bell and Sir Percy Cox. By nature a man of the desert, he soon gained the friendship of the Bedouin and embarked upon the difficult task of reconciling the warring tribes.

Abdullah, more ebullient than his brother, eagerly moved with his warriors to Amman. Kirkbride became his political advisor and a British-financed and British-officered Arab Legion

under the command of the Irishman John Glubb became the
guardian of his kingdom. A wild attack by Sa'udi Arabian
tribesmen was beaten off with the help of a few British armored vehicles.*

Churchill's two actions were approved without much enthusiasm by Parliament in 1922.

By creating the separate state of Transjordan, Britain all but
killed what hope there had been of developing a binational
Arab-Jewish state, not because the Zionists, except for a
Revisionist minority, had any plans for settling in Transjordan,
but because the truncation of Palestine reduced the area within
which Jewish and Arab claims would have to be reconciled.

Neither the Zionists nor the Palestinian Arabs were pleased,
the Zionists because they rightly foresaw a limitation of land
purchase and immigration, the Arabs because they feared that
they could be more easily outnumbered in a truncated Palestine. The newly appointed High Commissioner, Sir Herbert
Samuel, a prominent Jewish leader in Britain, did his best to
reduce the resulting tensions.

In October 1922 the Lloyd George Coalition government of
Britain resigned and was replaced by the Conservative government of Bonar Law. Churchill disappeared from the scene.
Lord Curzon became the dominant figure in the Foreign
Office. The Northcliffe press began an anti-Zionist campaign.
Curzon, no pro-Zionist, was for the time being preoccupied
with affairs other than Palestinian. The French had occupied
the German Ruhr; the Bolshevik government of Russia had renounced its claims for expansion into the Middle East. Both Persia and Turkey required attention. Egypt was seething with
resentment over the continued British occupation after the
protectorate had nominally been lifted. Sir Herbert Samuel
was left more or less on his own to deal with the impossible
Palestinian mandate. He did so ably and fairly, but just because
he was fair, he alienated both Zionists and Arabs before he retired in 1925.

In Persia, Curzon obtained an agreement from the weak Qajar
Shah which, if consummated, would have placed that oil-rich

* A brilliant picture of the Hashemite kingdoms has been painted by
James Morris in his charmingly written book *The Hashemite Kings*.

country completely under British domination. Even though the Majlis (the recently created Persian Parliament) repudiated the agreement, the episode left lasting resentment and hostility toward Britain.

In Turkey, Allied plans for the dismemberment of the Ottoman Empire had to be reconsidered when, in 1923, as the result of defeat and humiliation, the Sultanate was overthrown by revolution and a republic established. Under the leadership of Mustapha Kemal Pasha, who later took the name of Atatürk, a modern state was rapidly created. The Turkish capital was moved from its vulnerable site at Istanbul (Constantinople) to Ankara in the interior. Smyrna became Izmir. The Turkish alphabet was Latinized. Women were emancipated. The fez was abolished. In a remarkably short time the Turkish people were freed from the centuries-old oppression of the corrupt Sultanate and from the bonds of Moslem orthodoxy. Civil law began to repace the edicts of mullahs. Under Kemal's firm authoritarian leadership, the ground work was laid for the beginnings of democracy.

The example set by the Turkish revolution fired the nationalist ambitions of the Arab world.

In 1923 war broke out between Turkey and Greece when the Turks refused to surrender to the Greeks that part of Macedonia which had been allotted to them under the peace settlements. The Greeks were defeated and atrocious massacres of minority populations took place. Eventually, peace was restored by an exchange of minorities enforced by the League of Nations. This forced resettlement set a dangerous precedent, as we shall see presently.

Fortunately for Britain and its High Commissioner in Palestine, the Arab-Jewish problem remained relatively quiescent during these troubled years. There was no recurrence of violance, such as Jaffa riots of 1921 which had taken place over the Mopsi incident. When Sir Herbert Samuel retired in 1925, he left with the respect of both Jews and Arabs, although each side thought that he had favored the other. The Zionists disliked the restrictions upon immigration which Samuel had imposed, even though there was little pressure for immigration. The Arabs were dissatisfied with Samuel's handling of the question of land-purchase, although actually this was not so much a question of regulation as of the evasion of regulations by absentee Arab landowners.

In 1925 Samuel was succeeded by Field Marshal Lord Plumer, one of Britain's ablest military commanders, who had little knowledge or experience in the Middle East and who was unfamiliar with the idiosyncrasies of both Jews and Arabs. Plumer, however, did understand that he had been assigned the task of carrying out an inoperable mandate—a task in which, like his predecessor, he saw that the only hope of success rested upon an impartial effort to reconcile the almost irreconcilable, frustrated ambitions of the Zionists with the fear-inspired obstructionism of the Arabs. He tackled the job with a soldier's loyalty and rigid discipline. Distrusted at first by the Jews because he was not Jewish and feared by the Arabs because of his inaccessibility and austere appearance, Plumer rapidly acquired the respectful admiration of both. When asked what his policy was going to be, he is said to have replied: "I have no policy. I am here to carry out the instructions of His Majesty's Government." The fact that these instructions were to carry out an impossible task did not apparently trouble him. He was used to such assignments. Also he was utterly fearless. Before long, his erect figure and his bristling mustache became familiar to the Palestinians as he walked about the streets of Jerusalem, not knowing whether he was among Jews or Arabs or whether he was being cheered or reviled.

During the three years of Plumer's firm, impartial and authoritarian rule, Palestine remained calm. This was partly because both Jews and Arabs recognized that "no nonsense" would be tolerated, but also because these three years marked the low tide of Zionism and, consequently, of Arab resistance to it.

Throughout the early years of the mandate, Jewish immigration had been partially offset by re-emigration. Between 1920 and 1924, 13 percent of the immigrants had left the country. In the next four years the number of those who left rose to 33 percent of those who entered. This decline of Zionist enthusiasm was largely due to events in Poland.

Liberated Poland contained some 3 million Jews, almost 30

percent of the Polish population. At first, with the liquidation of the Russian Pale of Settlement, conditions of life for the Jews greatly improved. With greater liberty, the Polish Jews rapidly became the dominant element in the middle class which was concentrated in Warsaw, where almost 30 percent of the population was Jewish. In Pinsk almost 90 percent of the people were Jews.

In 1925 Poland went through a period of inflation and near economic collapse similar to that which had occurred a little earlier in Germany. The young Polish government was not anti-Semitic although it had not outlawed anti-Semitism as had the Soviet regime,* but now, due to the economic depression, three factors tended to produce a new anti-Semitism. As might be expected under a regime of landowning aristocrats, taxation fell most heavily upon the largely Jewish middle class. Jewish protests against the tax exemption accorded to the wealthy landowning gentry aroused aristocratic anti-Semitism. Secondly, Polish members of the middle class resented the predominance of Jews and this led to restriction of Jewish participation in the professions and universities. The Jews not only resisted the restrictions but some of them went so far as to demand the creation of a Jewish state within Poland. (This heretical form of Zionism bore a resemblance to the Black Power movement which was to develop among American Negroes some forty years later.)

One might have thought that these conditions in Poland, which contained more Jews at the time than any other European country, would have stimulated a substantial emigration to Palestine. That such was only temporarily the case was due partly to the short-lived phenomenon of heretical Zionism mentioned above and partly to the fact that Palestine was

---

* The Bolshevik regime in Russia not only made anti-Semitism illegal but abolished the ghettos and encouraged Jews to become factory workers and farmers. The American Joint Distribution Committee, together with Julius Rosenwald and John D. Rockefeller, Jr., supplied the funds for an organization, called *Agro-Joint*, which aided a large number of Russian Jews to settle on land provided by the Soviet government. Most of these settlements were in the Crimea. The story of *Agro-Joint* has been interestingly told by James N. Rosenberg, a close associate of Felix Warburg, in his memoir, *Unfinished Business*.

suffering at the time from a state of economic depression and unemployment. Nevertheless, in 1925 some 17,000 Polish Jews did emigrate to Palestine. In the following year immigration rose to over 34,000 largely due to the temporary lifting of the Soviet government's ban on emigration. This was an all-time high, but because of the depressed economic state of Palestine and the discouraged mood of the Zionists, the influx aroused little Arab protest. Perhaps, in greater measure, the quiescence of the Arabs was due to the enforcement of law and order by the imposing figure of the High Commissioner.

During his incumbency, Lord Plumer substantially reduced the British military garrison in Palestine—an action which would soon have to be reversed by his successor. Plumer's other major action was the appointment of a commission under Norman Bentwich, instructed to devise legislation that would give better protection to tenants against eviction. This reform was directed less against the small Jewish settlers than against absentee Arab landlords who evicted tenant farmers in order to make profitable sales.

Plumer retired in 1928 for reasons of ill health and old age. He was to be remembered with gratitude by both Arabs and Jews.

The year 1928 marked the end of a decade during which the British had shown considerable skill in managing the unmanagable conditions which they had created in Palestine. The successors of Samuel and Plumer did not possess the attributes of impartiality, self-confidence and cool-headedness required to maintain peace.

The year 1928 also marked the end of a period about which one might say that neither the Jews nor the Arabs made any substantial contribution toward creating the tragic conflict that lay ahead. Up to this time, the differences between the Arabs and the Zionists had been primarily economic and political with only occasional overtones of religious prejudice. From here on, the conflict was to become more and more of a religious confrontation in which emotions would supersede reason and cause irrational outbursts of violence, more often than not sparked by fanatical leadership.

9

Prelude to Tragedy— 1929–1930

Until 1929, Arab leadership in Palestine had been deceptively quiescent. The British attributed this to the moderate influence upon the Arab "notables" of Haj Amin el Husseini, the Mufti of Jerusalem. They were now to discover that the Mufti had merely bided his time, concealing his vicious, fanatical fury beneath an appearance of polite and calm reasonableness.

The first outburst of violence since the Jaffa riots of 1921 occurred in August 1929 and began, as religious conflicts usually do, over an incident so trivial as to seem in retrospect almost ludicrous. It arose over the placement at the western wall of the ancient Hebrew Temple in Jerusalem (the "Wailing Wall") of a little screen, innocently put there by a rabbi in order to separate the men from the women during the traditional Yom Kippur service. The British District Superintendent, not understanding the purpose of the screen and fearing that the Moslem Council might object to it, ordered its removal. When the rabbi refused to do so until after the service had been completed, police were ordered to take it away and some of the outraged Jewish women attacked the police officers with parasols. A few Arabs apparently participated in the relatively minor disturbance that ensued.

At this point, Haj Amin el Husseini for the first time disclosed his true colors, inciting the Moslems with rumors that the Jews intended to take over the holy sites and to destroy all the mosques. As the result of this incitement, groups of Arabs attacked a number of Jewish settlements, murdering men, women and children in the most atrociously barbaric manner. Some of the Jewish settlements defended themselves as best they could. The police, many of them Moslems, were unable or unwilling to restore order. For three days, while British troops were on the way from Egypt to reinforce the garrison which Lord Plumer had reduced, there was chaos. The worst incidents occurred at Hebron and Safed, but throughout Palestine Arab mobs rushed through the streets with knives and clubs, attacking any Jew they encountered. The British authorities refused to issue arms to the Jews and even ordered the small number of Jewish policemen to refrain from action. Before order could be restored, 133 Jews were killed and 339 wounded, while the Arabs suffered 116 killed and 232 wounded. All the Jewish casualties were due to Arab action. All the Arab losses were due to police action, except for 6 Arabs that were killed in a Jewish counterattack between Jaffa and Tel Aviv.

Sir John Chancellor, the new High Commissioner, was in London when the disorders occurred. On his return, he first issued a proclamation denouncing the Arab attacks upon "the defenseless members of the Jewish population." This statement assumed Arab guilt before any evidence had been taken. The Mufti immediately protested. Chancellor then issued a second proclamation announcing the appointment of an investigatory commission. This looked like—as, indeed, it was—a public apology to the Arabs for the High Commissioner's earlier spontaneous outburst of indignation.

The investigating commission, headed by Sir Walter Shaw, the former Chief Justice in the Straits Settlements, began its work in September and conducted hearings. It refused to credit the charges of incitement leveled against Haj Amin and the Moslem leaders by the Zionists and officially found that the Arab attacks had been "unpremeditated." The British authorities were unwilling to believe that their faith in the Mufti's moderation had been misplaced. (They were soon to have ample proof of Haj Amin's crafty, ruthless and bloodthirsty nature.)

The Jews were understandably outraged by the Shaw Commission's verdict. Chaim Weizmann had hurried to London from a vacation in Switzerland as soon as he heard the news of the riots. In the British capital he found a radically changed picture.

The Baldwin government had fallen in midsummer. Ramsay MacDonald, who had for six months in 1924 headed the first Labour Party government in British history, had again become Prime Minister. The friendly Leopold Amery was gone from the Colonial Office, replaced by the well-known socialist Sidney Webb, whom MacDonald had elevated to the peerage as Lord Passfield. All the old leaders of the Liberal and Conservative Parties who had sponsored the Balfour Declaration had disappeared from the scene.

The British Labour Party was essentially a trade union party with an intellectual socialist elite dominating its representation in Parliament. Webb and his wife Beatrice were perhaps the most prominent and influential members of this elite. One might have expected that British socialists would feel a natural sympathy for the largely socialist Zionist settlers in Palestine— a sympathy more natural, indeed, than that of the aristocratic Conservatives and the Liberals who had sponsored the Balfour Declaration. Such, however, was not the case in the early days of Britain's first Labour government.

The Shaw Commission's report contained more than an exoneration of Arab leadership from the charge of willful incitement. This alone was enough to disappoint and dishearten the Jews. The Commission went further to express its views concerning the broader questions of British policy in Palestine. It recommended a survey of land available for settlement and a limitation of future immigration, in language which seemed strongly to favor a greater protection of the Arab interests. A second commission was appointed to study the findings of the first (a favorite practice of British governments) and to devise means for carrying out the policy recommended. To head this second commission, the British government appointed Sir John Hope Simpson, who had recently arranged for the exchange and resettlement of Greek and Turkish minorities after the Greco-Turkish War. Weizmann vainly sought an appointment to see Hope Simpson before his departure for Palestine.

Recognizing the need for a greater involvement of the world's leading Jews in Palestinian affairs, Weizmann had proposed to the 16th Zionist Congress at Zurich an enlargement of the governing body of the Jewish Palestine community, the Jewish Agency, to 224, with half of the members to be Zionists and half "non-Zionists." (This dubious term, meant to exclude anti-Zionists, was defined as denoting "a person associated with the Agency otherwise than in the capacity of a member and representative of the Zionist Organization." The distinction was spurious, but Weizmann's move, adopted after heated debate, accomplished its chief purpose, namely, a broader enlistment of world Jewry's support.) The acceptance of Weizmann's proposal was a victory for the moderates over the extremist Zionists, but what the Arabs saw in the 16th Congress was not the final moderate decision but the statement of the extremist position by Vladmir Jabotinsky, the former commander of the Jewish Legion which had fought for Britain against the Turks. Jabotinsky demanded a repudiation of the 1922 White Paper, asserting that all of Palestine, including Transjordan, should be open to Jewish settlement and that the British should desist from any further attempts to appease the Arabs. It was Jabotinsky's speech and the provocative behavior of his followers in Jerusalem that probably caused the Mufti to think that the time had come to let loose the terror of a Holy War.

All this was taken into consideration by the Shaw and the Hope Simpson Commissions, except that they failed to realize the essential fact—that the Mufti had now given the Arabs a cause beyond mere obstructionism and that this cause was a Jehad, a Holy War against the Infidel, be he British or Jewish.

Lord Passfield weighed the recommendations of the two commissions and produced a White Paper accepting all the recommendations as to land, immigration and the alleged failure of the Jews to give employment to Arabs. It summed up its generally anti-Zionist conclusions by stating that, in the view of the British government, the Balfour Declaration's clauses regarding the safeguarding of the rights of non-Jewish communities in Palestine were not secondary to the establishment of a Jewish National Home and that the latter was "not the primary object for which the mandate has been framed."

Publication of the White Paper in October 1930 aroused such a storm within Britain as to force the Labour government to retreat. The document was criticized by all the surviving members of the Liberal-Conservative coalition that had issued the Balfour Declaration. Jews throughout the world were outraged. Weizmann resigned from the presidency of the Zionist Organization; Lord Melchett resigned from the chairmanship of the Council; and Felix Warburg, one of the "non-Zionist" members, resigned as chairman of the Agency's administrative committee.

Sensing the strength of the opposition, Lord Passfield decided not to fight for his White Paper. A conference with representatives of the Jewish Agency and the debate in Parliament ended with Weizmann winning over MacDonald and receiving from him a letter that completely repudiated the White Paper.

Both sides had now received a renewed recognition of their rights as hazily defined in the Balfour Declaration. The Zionists had been given a reaffirmation of British support for their aspirations, although with certain limitations. The Arabs had been given the assurance that the extremist demands of Jabotinsky and his "Revisionists" for massive colonization "on both sides of the Jordan" would receive no British support.

For a brief period there was now peace in Palestine, partly because, while the rest of the world was sinking into the depths of a great economic depression, Palestine enjoyed a sudden period of prosperity in which increased immigration was accompanied by a substantial inflow of foreign private capital that stimulated development and increased employment. The wounds of 1929 had not been healed but, for the time being, they were papered over by prosperity.

In Iraq, too, things were not going too badly for the British. King Feisal was gradually uniting the country, overcoming the hostility of the Turkish, Kurdish and Assyrian minorities and easing the tension between the Sunni and Shiah Moslems. A revised Iraqi-British treaty was in the making which would soon supplant the mandate and permit Iraq to become an independent state.*

* Iraq was admitted to the League of Nations as an independent

Unlike the British in Iraq, the French had no idea of giving up their mandate over Syria and Lebanon. Their repressive policy and their attempt to place Maronite Christians over the Moslem majority resulted in a series of insurrections that had to be put down by armed force.

---

country in 1932. Unfortunately, Feisal's premature death a year later was destined to interrupt the nation's progress.

PART TWO

10

The West with Adolf Hitler in It

For a little more than a year after Hitler's accession to power in Germany, the West regarded him as a strange and somewhat frightening figure who would probably soon pass from the world stage. Although his hatred of Jews was probably his strongest single motivating force, this was not at first evident. The first outbursts of his anti-Semitism were taken as campaign oratory, but the law passed in April 1933, limiting Jewish participation in a large part of Germany's professional, official and cultural life caused enough of an unfavorable reaction in other countries to bring about a temporary lull in overt anti-Semitic action. German Jews were, in fact, given assurances that no further limitations would be imposed upon them. However, in September 1935, at a party rally in Nuremberg, Hitler convened the Reichstag in a Nuremberg hall and proposed the notorious three Nuremberg Laws which the Reichstag obediently adopted: (1) that the swastika on a red flag become the national ensign; (2) that German citizenship should be confined to "Aryans" while "non-Aryans" were to be reduced to subject status; and (3) that sexual relationships, marital or other, between Jews and Germans should be forbidden.

The Western world, with a state that adopted such laws within it, had at that moment become a different world altogether, and nowhere was this more profoundly realized than in

Palestine. The change affected not only the Jews throughout the Western world and in the Middle East but the Arabs in Palestine as well. Anti-Semitism mixed well with the Mufti's Moslem fanaticism, even though anti-Semitism on the part of Semites might be a strange paradox.

The figures of Jewish immigration into Palestine in the years from 1931 to 1935 clearly show the effect of Hitler's ever more overt and ever more brutal anti-Semitism. In 1931, 4,075 Jews had entered Palestine. In 1932 the figure more than doubled to 9,553. In 1933, after Hitler came to power, immigration jumped to 30,327, then to 42,359 in 1934 and 61,854 in 1935. The need for a refuge in Palestine was becoming more and more urgent for European Jews, and for Jews everywhere, the National Home was becoming more and more a symbol of self-respect and of hope in a period of shameful degradation.

The vastly increased inflow was handled with the utmost skill by the *Yishuv* (Jewish community). Newcomers were quickly settled and unemployment was kept under strict control by the Jewish Agency.

The Arab leadership viewed these developments with alarm and resentment. The Arabs might have been more sympathetic if they had felt that the influx was caused by what was happening in Germany, but one of the things that disturbed them was that only about one-eighth of the new immigrants came from Germany, while almost half (43 percent) came from Poland. (It is not clear to what extent, if any, emigration from Poland was stimulated or favored by the earlier settlers, the majority of whom had come from Slavic countries.) From the Arab point of view, the nexus between German persecution and a preponderantly Polish immigration was not clear. Moreover, the Arab leadership felt, and said, that the Europeans—not the Arabs— were responsible for what was happening to the Jews in Poland and Germany. They asked why the Europeans did not take care of the refugees, pointing out that during the period when Britain had forced Arab Palestine to admit 145,000 Jews, less than 3,000 had been admitted to Britain.

Events outside of Palestine also exerted a strong influence upon the attitude of the Palestinian Arabs. Iraq had become independent and self-governing. Transjordan had achieved quasi-independent status. Even in Syria, the French had permitted the creation of a nominally self-governing Syrian Republic (though without actually relaxing their control). The Moslem Turks had not only achieved complete independence but had won a war against Greece and forced the evacuation of the Greek minority from their domain. The Palestinian Arabs felt that they were the only Arabs who were denied any form of self-government. Actually, this was to some extent their own fault. In 1922, when Churchill, as Colonial Secretary, had tried to establish a legislative council, the Arabs had boycotted the proposal, while the Jews (who were then still a small minority and might more reasonably have feared being outvoted) had agreed to Churchill's proposal. These positions were now reversed. The Arab leadership now demanded the creation of an Arab-controlled parliament, while Jewish enthusiasm for an Arab-Jewish legislative council had cooled.

Major General Sir Arthur Wauchope, whom MacDonald had appointed as High Commissioner in 1931, hoping that he would be a second Plumer, proposed to install a mixed legislative council. This did not suit the Arabs because it gave the Jews a voice. In 1933 the Arabs, inspired by the Mufti, launched a boycott against the British. Riots occurred in Jaffa, Nablus, Haifa and Jerusalem. The Mufti demanded a ban on land sales and immigration and what amounted to an abandonment of the mandate and a repudiation of the Balfour Declaration.

Wauchope nevertheless produced and proposed to the British government a plan for what was called an "Elizabethan-style Parliament" with more nominal than real power, sticking stubbornly to the long-held British idea that both sides could be made "to sink their differences." This proposal was withdrawn after a debate in the British Parliament.

At this time neither His Majesty's Government nor the League of Nations commanded great respect in the Middle East. Mussolini had begun his war against Ethiopia in defiance of the League and the economic sanctions which it halfheartedly imposed. Moreover, the Italo-Ethiopian War was disrupting trade in the eastern Mediterranean and this caused a slump in the Palestinian economy.

In April 1936 the Arabs declared a general strike and, again, there were riots and atrocities, directed more against the British than against the Jews. Roads and railroads were wrecked. A band of Arabs led by a Lebanese, Fawzi el Kawakji, apparently operating independently of the Mufti's control, at first destroyed and looted Jewish property and then turned against the British. Wauchope hesitated to suppress these disorders by force. Before the disturbances ended, there were 1,300 casualties of whom over 300 were killed.

In September 1936 the British garrison was reinforced, and the Arab rulers of Iraq, Jordan, Yemen and Sa'udi Arabia asked the Mufti to call off the strike, probably at the urging of the British government, which promised to send another commission to investigate the causes of the trouble.

In November 1936 the Commission arrived in Palestine. Its chairman was Lord Peel, grandson of Sir Robert Peel, the erstwhile Prime Minister. With him were five other members: Sir Horace Rumbold, who had been ambassador in Berlin from 1928 until August 1933; Professor Reginald Coupland, an Oxford teacher, who turned out to be the dominant intellect on the Commission; Sir Lucas Hammond, an experienced Indian civil servant; and two lawyers, Sir Harold Lucas and Sir William Morris Carter.

The appointment of the Peel Commission at first appeared to the Jews as another British move to appease the Arabs, rather like the appointment of the earlier Shaw and Hope Simpson Commissions. Nevertheless, they decided to cooperate by stating their case. The Arabs, on the other hand, boycotted the Commission during the first two months of its hearings.

Weizmann appeared on November 25 and made an eloquent statement of the Jewish case in the course of three hours of testimony. "There are," he said, "in this part of the world [Eastern Europe] six million people doomed to be pent up in places where they are not wanted and for whom the world is divided into places where they cannot live and places into which they cannot enter." The Commission was deeply impressed by the restraint with which he put forward the Jewish case.

Two months later, Haj Amin finally decided to appear before

the Commission. He, too, was eloquent. His demand was that the British government reverse its policy, stop Jewish immigration and land purchase and permit self-government by the Arabs in Palestine. He was more vehement against the British than against the Jews and, at one point, aroused the ire of at least one member of the Commission by saying that he would rather be under Turkish than British rule.

Professor Coupland recognized that it was hopeless to reconcile the Arab and Jewish positions. In a talk with Weizmann he sounded out the latter's feelings toward a partition of Palestine into separate Arab and Jewish states. Weizmann concealed his joy over the suggestion and said he must have time to think about it. Subsequently, in a private conversation with Coupland, he expressed acceptance in principle of the proposal. He did so with so much enthusiasm that Coupland, who had come prepared to convert Weizmann to the idea of partition, came away completely convinced that no other solution was possible. For Weizmann, this was perhaps his greatest moment; the idea of a Jewish state seemed about to be realized. Some time later, Weizmann met with President Eddé of Lebanon, who greeted him as the future president of a Jewish state and discussed with him how he hoped to develop friendly and mutually beneficial relations between the new Jewish state and its northern neighbor.

The report of the Peel Commission was published in July 1937. After stating why the Commission could see no way to reconcile the Jewish demand for continued and increased immigration with the Arab demand that all immigration and land purchase cease, the Commission put forward a proposal for partition drafted by Coupland. This plan called for a tiny Jewish state with the rest of Palestine to be united to Transjordan, except for a few scattered areas, including Bethlehem and Jerusalem, which were to remain under the mandate. In the north the border of the Jewish state was to be similar in outline to that of the Israel created in 1947 but without including Acre, Nazareth, Tiberias and Safed. The state was not to include but to have access to Haifa. Jaffa was conceded to Jordan. South of Tel Aviv the only Jewish territory was to consist of about 100 square miles in a strip south of Jaffa. Gaza, Hebron and the whole Negev were to belong to Jordan.

Because the Jewish state would embrace the most fertile area of Palestine, the Peel Commission proposed that it pay a yearly subsidy to Jordan. And because the Jewish state would contain very nearly as many Arabs as Jews, the Commission proposed that as many as possible of these Arabs be resettled in Arab lands, if necessary by compulsion. (This recommendation no doubt derived from the precedent set by the resettlement of the Greek minority in Turkey.)

The Peel Report was opposed by Wauchope and the Palestine administration. Perhaps for this reason it was given only lukewarm support by the government speakers when it came before Parliament. The strongest attack upon it was made by Lord Samuel, who declared the whole plan unworkable and dangerous, proposing instead that all the Arab states be joined in a single federation in which Jews would be permitted to settle and to participate in community government. The speech cost Lord Samuel much of the affection and esteem that he had earlier won as High Commissioner. Largely because of the cogent criticism directed against the plan of partition, the government dropped its advocacy and the Peel Report was laid aside.

Even before this, the Arab leadership had denounced the plan and the Arabs had once more taken to violence.

The reaction of the Jews toward the Peel Plan was ambiguous. Weizmann continued to support the idea of partition, but the details of the proposal did not seem attractive. At the 20th Zionist Congress in August, Weizmann succeeded, against considerable opposition, in obtaining a conditional approval, subject to the whole matter being once more brought up for discussion when and if a final plan for partition should be proposed by Parliament. In spite of all its obvious faults, the Peel proposal appealed to the Jews simply because, in this time of great distress and indignity, it provided for a Jewish nation, no matter how small.

At this conference Judah Magnes, supported by Felix Warburg, made another appeal for the creation of a binational state. Magnes felt that, since both sides rejected the proposed plan of partition, they might now be willing to cooperate. (It was far too late for that.) He argued, with considerable prescience, that partition would inevitably lead to an Arab-Jewish war. He lost his case, but made a proposal which was to be adopted—again too late—in 1938. This was to mobilize world Jewish leadership behind the Zionist cause as the Arabs in Palestine had mobilized the Arab leadership in other Arab states.

On September 8, 1937, four hundred Arab leaders met near Damascus in a conference attended by the top leadership in all the Arab states except Yemen. The Arab answer to the Peel proposal was unequivocal. It said to Britain that the time had come when Britain would have to choose between Arabs and Jews. Unless Britain renounced the mandate and the Balfour Declaration, the Arab states would "feel at liberty to join other European powers whose policies are inimical to Britain." Egypt, Iraq and Syria sent protests against partition to the League of Nations.

In October the Arabs again resorted to violence. Lewis Andrews, the District Commissioner for Galilee, was murdered. Wauchope resigned and was replaced by Sir Harold MacMichael.

Until now the Jews in Palestine had pursued a deliberate policy of self-restraint (*Havlagah*), but now their semi-secret and semi-illegal defense force, the Haganah, moved from strictly defensive action to occasional reprisals against Arab violence. Illegal immigration began in violation of the administration's restrictions, and landings began to be protected by the Haganah with arms often smuggled into the country. "Law and order" would soon be a thing of the past.

11

"Appeasement" in the West
1935–1939

What happened in Palestine in the last two years before the outbreak of World War II can be understood (if at all) only in the context of the Western policy of "appeasing" the fascist dictators in Italy, Germany and Spain.

This policy began when the League of Nations, dominated by Britain and France, failed to halt Mussolini's war of conquest against Ethiopia in 1934. (Actually, "appeasement" may be said to have begun in 1931, when Japan was permitted to seize Manchuria. In March 1935 Hitler suddenly announced that, in defiance of the Versailles Treaty, Germany had secretly created an air force and that a new German army was about to be raised by conscription. The League condemned this action, but three months later the British government signed a naval treaty with Germany tacitly sanctioning German land rearmament provided that Hitler would refrain from challenging British naval supremacy at sea. By the notorious Hoare-Laval Agreement, Britain and France agreed to permit Mussolini to partition Ethiopia. (France thought it could win Mussolini as an ally against Hitler. British sentiment against the agreement was so strong that the Baldwin government was nearly overthrown.) Churchill and Duff Cooper demanded rapid British rearmament. They were denounced as scaremongers.

American reaction to the rising threat of war in Europe was merely to seek more complete isolation. The Neutrality Acts of 1935 and 1936 sought to accomplish this purpose.*

On March 7, 1936, Hitler's new Wehrmacht marched into the Rhineland, without previous notice and in direct violation of both the Versailles and Locarno Treaties. French opinion favored strong counteraction. The Baldwin government deprecated Hitler's unilateral action but "After all, the Rhineland is a part of Germany; why shouldn't the Germans be allowed to occupy it?" Britain accepted the *fait accompli*. France might well have acted alone. Her army was still vastly superior to the Wehrmacht and no one knew this better than the German generals who warned Hitler against the adventure. (It is now definitely known that, if France had acted, Hitler would have been forced to make an ignominious retreat.) But powerful French interests feared the Soviet Union more than they feared Germany. The Depression had stimulated the workers' demand for social reform and had frightened conservatives and business interests into forming such reactionary organizations as the Cagoulards and the Croix de Feu. These gained considerable support among the officers in the French army; both organizations were infected with anti-Semitism reminiscent of the Dreyfus Case. Nevertheless, failure to stop Hitler's invasion of the Rhineland caused the overthrow of the French government and Leon Blum's Popular Front came to power amid sit-down strikes and disorder.

Frightened by these developments in France, King Leopold of Belgium abrogated the Franco-Belgian alliance—a fateful decision which was later to contribute to the collapse of the Allied defenses.

In the same year, Mussolini completed the conquest of Ethiopia and Victor Emmanuel assumed the title of Emperor. Francisco Franco launched a rebellion against the government of Spain with the concealed support of Hitler and Mussolini. The Moscow Purge Trials took place, and Hitler proclaimed a worldwide crusade against communism.

---

* For a fuller account of U.S. foreign policy in the years of appeasement, see J. P. Warburg, *The United States in a Changing World* (Putnam, New York, 1954), pp. 297-317.

The year 1937 marked the unrecognized beginning of World War II.

A military revolt in Shensi Province presented the Japanese with a pretext for intervention "to pacify China." Japanese troops overran China's northern provinces, captured Peking, blockaded China's coast, seized Shanghai and moved inland up the Yangtze Valley.

In Europe the British government signed a "gentleman's agreement" with Mussolini. By this time Italian "volunteers" were fighting side by side with Franco's rebels at the gates of Madrid and Hitler was testing his latest weapons by sending "a few technical groups" to Franco's assistance. Russia was providing planes and pilots to the hard-pressed Spanish government.

Britain and France entered into a farcical "neutrality agreement" with other nations, *including Germany, Italy and the Soviet Union who were openly participating in the Spanish Civil War*. British and French warships patrolled the Spanish coast to "enforce non-intervention," the effect of which was to shut off outside aid to the Spanish government. The United States Congress passed a resolution amending the Neutrality Act by providing that its restrictions and prohibitions should apply not only to belligerents but to countries engaged in civil war if, in the President's judgment, this should be in the national interest. By so declaring, President Roosevelt in effect caused the United States to aid the Franco rebellion and, in so doing, to further the designs of Hitler and Mussolini. The President presumably took this action because the American people were still deeply committed to isolationism and more afraid of communism than of fascism; because of pressure from the Roman Catholic hierarchy; and because the legitimate government of Spain had become identified in the public mind with communism by fascist propaganda. (Actually, the government against which the rebellion was launched did not contain a single communist or even left-wing socialist.*)

In France, where Leon Blum attempted to institute "a French New Deal," conservatives and business leaders were

* See U.S. Ambassador Claude Bowers, *My Mission to Spain* (Simon & Schuster, New York, 1954), pp. 190–194.

muttering, "Better Hitler than Blum." When the reforms failed of enactment, Blum was forced to resign; his place was taken by Camille Chautemps, in whom the British appeasers were to find a willing collaborator.

When Neville Chamberlain succeeded Stanley Baldwin as Prime Minister, the British appeasement policy was clearly formulated; it consisted of leisurely rearmament and an endeavor "to remove the causes of war" by making every possible concession to the aggressive dictators. It was a policy based upon the delusion that the dictators could be appeased by concessions and upon the realization that the tardy British preparations for defense would not take effect for two years.

In October 1937 President Roosevelt finally recognized the mounting danger and attempted to make the American people aware of it by his famous "quarantine the aggressor" speech. The speech fell flat because it was utterly inconsistent with the President's recent conduct of foreign affairs.

Early in 1938 Hitler summoned the Austrian Chancellor Schuschnigg to Berchtesgaden and demanded that Austria cease suppressing the Nazi Party. Chamberlain told the House of Commons that he intended to seek another "gentleman's agreement" with Mussolini in the hope that he would "give some evidence of sincerity by withdrawing a substantial number of volunteers from Spain." This produced the first showdown over the appeasement policy. Foreign Secretary Anthony Eden resigned; his stand was widely applauded in the United States, but the White House remained silent.

On March 11, Hitler proclaimed the annexation of Austria and Nazi troops marched unopposed into Vienna. Britain and France addressed sharp notes of protest to a defiant and triumphant Fuehrer. The French ambassador called at the Foreign Office to declare that France would honor its alliance with Czechoslovakia in the event that Hitler should attack that country and demanded to know what Britain would do. Chamberlain did not know what Britain would do; he felt sure that "Herr Hitler" would now be reasonable and that Mussolini would see that Germany must not be allowed to acquire domination over Europe. French public opinion was outraged, but not Chautemps, who agreed with Chamberlain and was shortly forced to resign. A second Blum administration lasted only a few weeks and was replaced, after another financial crisis, by a cabinet headed by Edouard Daladier.

Neither the British nor the French government was convinced that war was inevitable. Britain relied upon the power of a naval blockade and France upon the presumed impregnability of the Maginot Line of fortifications. Both hoped that Hitler would follow the line laid down in his book *Mein Kampf* and attack Russia. As for the attitude of the Soviet government, Maxim Litvinov, the Soviet Foreign Minister, made this unequivocally clear in a proposal for joint action sent to London, Paris and Washington.*

The Soviet proposal for collective action to halt fascist aggression received no reply from Britain, France or the United States. In part this was due to Western fear of communism; in part it was due to the erroneous belief that Stalin had "killed off all his best generals" in the purge of 1937.

No sooner had Hitler annexed Austria than the campaign for the "liberation" of the Sudeten Germans in Czechoslovakia went into high gear. . . .

It is not necessary to review here the details of the betrayal of Czechoslovakia. The shameful "Peace of Munich" in October 1938 involved more than the betrayal of Czechoslovakia. It destroyed at one stroke the whole system of French continental alliances and alienated the Soviet Union, giving Hitler the one thing he needed most—the assurance that he would not have to fight a two-front war.

Within Germany, Munich killed the last serious opposition to Hitler's policy of aggressive expansionism. Once more, as in the occupation of the Rhineland, the German generals had opposed risking major war over the Sudeten issue. Once more Hitler had said: "Wait. There will be no war." And once more Hitler had been proved right. The German people had been as frightened of war in 1938 as the people of France and Britain. Had Hitler's intuition proved wrong, there might have been serious disturbances among the German workers and disaffection in the High Command. After Munich, Hitler stood before

---

* See Warburg, *The United States in a Changing World,* p. 306.

the German people as the genius who had led them from triumph to triumph without getting them into a war. Henceforward, they would follow him blindly.

President Roosevelt had connived at the Peace of Munich by cabling Hitler and President Beneš of Czechoslovakia on September 26, urging a peaceful solution. To Hitler's uncompromising and rude reply, he had added another plea urging the avoidance of armed conflict. In addition, he had cabled to Mussolini asking this avowed ally of the Nazi leader to mediate the dispute. Undersecretary of State Sumner Welles officially hailed the Munich Pact, characterizing Roosevelt's intervention as "an historical service to humanity." The President himself asked to be "excused from an opinion." And well he might. He, who a year earlier had advocated quarantining the aggressors, now found himself in the unhappy position of having helped to bring about an abject and disgraceful surrender to aggression.

In fairness to Neville Chamberlain and his fellow appeasers in Britain, it must be said that none of them aimed at an eventual accommodation with a Nazi-controlled Europe. They were playing for time; they were not, like Joseph Kennedy, the American ambassador to the Court of St. James, or Charles Lindbergh, predicting an ultimate Nazi victory and recommending an accommodation with "the wave of the future." (The same cannot be said of the leading French appeasers. Men like Chautemps, Flandin, Bonnet and Laval were aiming at collaboration, if not an outright alliance with Hitler and Mussolini.*)

Without taking into consideration the shameful and—as it appears in retrospect—almost incredibly stupid somnambulistic behavior of the West in the face of overt fascist aggression, it is impossible to understand the actions of the British government with respect to Palestine during the last two years before World War II. Even with this background in mind, the story of these two years, as outlined in the next chapter, seems almost unbelievable. It is necessary to remind oneself of the proven qualities of courage and fairness so characteristic of the

---

* See Charles Micaud, *The French Right and Nazi Germany* (Durham, N.C.: Duke University Press, 1943).

British people before and after the years of appeasement in order to realize that British behavior during these five years was an aberration. It is also necessary for Americans to remember that they have little of which to be proud during that period.

12

Appeasement and Betrayal in Palestine

The new High Commissioner, Sir Harold MacMichael, determined to suppress the Arab rebellion. There was a strong suspicion that the Arab Higher Committee and Haj Amin had been concerned in the murder of Lewis Andrews. MacMichael disbanded the Committee, arrested five of its members and banned all Arab national associations. Haj Amin escaped arrest by fleeing in disguise with his cousin Jamal Husseini.

The rebellion mounted in ferocity. It was directed primarily against the British and only incidentally against the Jews. Most of the casualties were Arab, many of them caused by a quarrel between the Mufti's followers and the followers of a rival Nashashibi clique. While the Jewish casualties were light, much Jewish property was destroyed; fruit trees were cut down and crops damaged. It was said that the Jews planted ten new trees for every one destroyed. Inevitably, the Jewish population undertook measures of defense and these were now no longer purely defensive. A Jew named Isaac Sadeh organized some of the Haganah men into armed patrols which tracked down the Arab marauders. These little striking forces were known as the *Fosh* groups. Their activities were known to the British, who made no effort to suppress them.

In 1938 a young English intelligence officer named Orde Wingate arrived in Palestine from Africa. In a short time he became a passionate supporter of the Zionists and a close friend of the Weizmanns. Wingate, who was later to distinguish himself in Burma, conceived the idea of organizing a small number of Jews for what today would be called counterinsurgency. He showed them how a relatively short period of training would enable them to deal with Arab forces that greatly outnumbered them. The secret, he found, was to operate at night instead of following the British custom of moving only by day against the Arab rebels. Wingate's "Special Night Squads" continued to operate throughout 1938 and during the first part of 1939. They were composed of something like 200 men from *Fosh* plus a few British non-coms and privates. More important than what these Night Squads accomplished in the field was their psychological effect upon the whole *Yishuv*. The Jewish policy of *Havlagah* had prevented the development of a martial spirit. Many Jews had never thought of bearing arms and lacked confidence in their ability to become good soldiers. Wingate proved to them that, properly trained, they could become better soldiers than the Arabs and, in so doing, laid the foundations for what was soon to become the extraordinary spirit of the Jewish army.

Largely due to pressure from American Jewish leaders and especially Judah Magnes, President Roosevelt finally was moved to take action with regard to the growing refugee problem. There were said to be 600,000 Jews in Germany and Austria (there were probably considerably more) who wished to escape from Nazi persecution; and there were millions more in Eastern Europe. Roosevelt issued a call for an international conference in June of 1938 and sent Myron C. Taylor as his personal representative.*) Taylor was accompanied by James G. Macdonald, the League of Nations High Commissioner for German Refugees. The leading British delegates were Lord Winterton, known as an Arab apologist, and Victor Cazalet, a strong Zionist sympathizer.

The conference met at Evian, with the understanding, insisted upon by Britain, that Palestine would not be discussed. Its purpose was to find asylum elsewhere for the victims of

* Myron C. Taylor was a former president of the U.S. Steel Corporation and later became Roosevelt's first ambassador to the Vatican.

Nazi persecution. It was attended by representatives of 31 nations and a number of Jewish groups from Central Europe whom, surprisingly, Hitler permitted to attend. The United States, once the haven for the oppressed, was now hampered by the immigration laws enacted in 1924. The most Roosevelt could do was to allocate the entire German quota (30,000 a year) to Jewish refugees from Germany. (Another 10,000 was later added.) Britain feared that if she opened her doors to refugees the pressure on Palestine would be increased. The only nation at the conference that took any generous action was the tiny Dominican Republic, which offered to take in 100,000 German or Austrian refugees provided that help would be forthcoming from other nations to defray the cost of their resettlement. The British produced a plan for resettlement in Northern Rhodesia which was vetoed by that colony's 11,000 white inhabitants. Another plan for resettlement in tropical British Guiana was unacceptable to the Jewish delegates. The United States could have absorbed any number of refugees, but Roosevelt was unwilling to antagonize an isolationist Congress by asking for a modification of the immigration laws.* Canada refused to take in any refugees. In the end, the entire British Commonwealth provided refuge for slightly less than the pitifully small number admitted to the United States during the years 1938–1940, which amounted to approximately 100,-000.

The Zionists did not attend the Evian Conference and were little concerned by its tragic and disgraceful outcome. They

---

* In the following year the United States refused admission to over 900 refugees who had sailed from Hamburg for Cuba, erroneously thinking that the permits they had bought would permit them to stay in Cuba pending their admission to the United States. The ship cruised off the Florida coast while an agent of the Joint Distribution Committee vainly sought to persuade the Cuban government to permit the refugees to land. The American government remained adamant. While the vessel was on its way back to Hamburg, the JDC managed to arrange for the admission of the refugees to Holland, Belgium, France and Britain.

A similar negative attitude was taken by the American government when Senator Robert Wagner of New York and Congresswoman Edith Nourse of Massachusetts introduced a bill to admit 10,000 refugee children. In spite of the pleas of Christian as well as Jewish groups, and a personal appeal from Mrs. Roosevelt, the President refused to support the proposal.

did not want those European Jews who could escape to go to other countries; they wanted them to come to Palestine. Their harsh attitude made little difference, since the Western world had all but closed its doors to the victims of Nazi persecution.

Meanwhile, the British government had appointed yet another Palestine Commission to see how the rebellion might be brought under control. This Commission, under the leadership of Sir John Woodhead (a name perhaps not entirely inappropriate), went to Palestine and made its report in November 1938. The Woodhead Commission recommended partition but, unlike the Peel Commission, provided that the Jewish state to be created should consist solely of Tel Aviv and a total area of about 400 square miles! The report was published in the same month in which hundreds of Jews were murdered in the Berlin pogrom of the *Kristallnacht*. On November 24, less than a month after the betrayal of Czechoslovakia at Munich, Malcolm MacDonald,* the Colonial Secretary, presented the Woodhead Report to the House of Commons.

When both the Zionists and the Arabs denounced the report and grave misgivings were voiced in Commons, the British government decided to call an Arab-Jewish conference at London. Both sides sent delegations, but the Arabs refused to attend any meetings at which the Jews were present. After futile attempts by Malcolm MacDonald to bring the two sides together, the Chamberlain government decided that since reconciliation was impossible, a solution would have to be imposed by the mandatory power.

The White Paper of 1939 announced the policy which His Majesty's Government had decided to impose. It was a stark and utter betrayal of the Jews for the sake of appeasing the Arabs. Its outstanding feature was that Jewish immigration should be limited as follows: 25,000 were to be admitted at once; thereafter immigration was to be limited to 10,000 a year for five years.

While the cruel limitation of immigration in the face of the conditions existing within Hitler-dominated territory outraged not only the Zionists and other Jews but decent people throughout the world, the White Paper also stated that "it was

* Malcolm MacDonald was the son of the former Prime Minister.

no part of British policy to create a Jewish state in Palestine." It was a complete surrender to Arab demands.

Yet the Arabs did not think so. The Mufti denounced the proposed admission of 75,000 more Jews.

Thus "appeasement" reached its sorry climax. For the sake of Britain's strategic and commercial interests in the Middle East, not only the Jews in Palestine but, in a sense, the Jews throughout the world were betrayed. Forced to choose between Jews and Arabs, the Chamberlain government chose the Arabs. If there was to be war—and war seemed imminent after Hitler marched into Czechoslovakia in defiance of the "Peace of Munich"—the Jews would have no choice in their allegiance; no matter what Britain did, they could not join Hitler and the enemies of Britain. On the other hand, the Arabs had a choice; they, whose lands were essential for the protection of the Suez Canal and from whose lands came Britain's oil, might, if antagonized further, join Britain's enemies. This was true, but it did not alter the moral crime. Nor was the moral issue affected by the fact that, in this case, "appeasement" paid off in at least some strategic dividends, as we shall see in the next chapter.

Even before the White Paper was published, the British government committed an act so incredibly heartless that it alienated the opinion of much of the Western world.

As Hitler's policy toward the Jews in Germany changed from ill-treatment to persecution and concentration camps, and from persecution to mass expulsion, the pressures for the admission of refugees into Palestine inevitably mounted. The Evian Conference had shown that there was practically nowhere but Palestine for them to go. Part of this pressure was deliberately caused by the Nazis in their determination to make their domain *Judenrein* (cleansed of Jews).

Hitler's Gestapo and its agents, many of them corrupt, threatened the Jews with being sent into concentration camps unless they agreed to go to Palestine. By persuasion, threat or force they herded thousands of Jews onto the unseaworthy, vermin-infested freighters of the German Danube Shipping Company for delivery, via Rumania, the Black Sea and the Dardanelles, to Palestine. The Jews were forced to pay for their passage as well as for the forged passports and visas furnished them by the Gestapo at exorbitant prices. The secret police and their agents reaped handsome profits.

Filthy and overcrowded, "the little death ships," as Arthur Koestler called them, set out for Palestine. Some foundered. Some succeeded in setting their passengers ashore at night under the protection of the Haganah, while others were intercepted by the British. Three of these intercepted vessels were ordered by the British authorities to take their wretched passengers back to their ports of embarkation. When asked in Commons whether this meant that, in effect, these refugees had been sent back to the concentration camps, the Colonial Secretary replied that "the responsibility for this matter must rest upon those who are responsible for organizing this traffic in illegal immigration."

The reaction to this inhuman behavior was so great that the Colonial Office changed its policy—but this was not until war had broken out, as we shall see presently. It is not clear whether, as claimed by the Zionists, additional ships were turned back before the policy was changed in 1940.

In a sense, the publication of the White Paper in April 1939 came as an anticlimax.

13

World War II in the Middle East

So far as the Middle East was concerned, World War II did not begin until June 1940, when Mussolini declared war upon Britain and an already defeated France. When the Italian dictator launched his troops against the British in Somaliland and Egypt, Hitler had already conquered Poland, Denmark, Norway, Holland, Belgium and the northern part of France. In southern, unoccupied France, Marshal Pétain headed a collaborationist government at Vichy which controlled the French African Empire, the French Fleet and the French forces in Syria. In July 1940 Pétain broke off diplomatic relations with Britain after a British squadron had attacked part of the French Fleet at Mers el Kebir. Charles de Gaulle was rallying the Free French from his refuge in London. Britain herself was in imminent danger of invasion. The United States was still neutral. Britain's sole belligerent ally was Greece.

For one who anxiously followed the early campaigns in Africa and later became intimately involved in the planning of the Anglo-American invasion of Morocco and Algeria, it is difficult to bear in mind that this book is not a military history; it is concerned, not with battles and campaigns, but with the reactions of the people of the Middle East to the ebb and flow of the fortunes of war.

The appeasement of the Arabs at the expense of the Jews

and General Wavell's early successes against the Italians in Egypt and the Libyan desert, as well as the Italian defeat in East Africa and in the early naval actions in the Mediterranean, served to keep most of the Middle Eastern states in a condition of non-belligerent neutrality, waiting to see which way the war would go.

In the spring of 1941 the Greeks beat off an Italian attack launched through Albania but, by this time, the Germans had given up their plan to invade Britain and were descending into the Balkans. In a heroic but vain attempt to save Greece from Nazi conquest, Britain detached part of its forces in North Africa, thereby sacrificing much of what Wavell had gained in his advance into Tripoli. Unable to hold Greece, the British force retired to Crete, but that island soon fell to the first Nazi paratroop operation of the war. These reverses touched off the first Arab move toward affiliation with the Axis.

Inspired by the Mufti Haj Amin, the Iraqis launched a pogrom against the Jews in Baghdad and Rashid Ali staged a pro-Axis coup. Advance elements of the Luftwaffe were said to be near Baghdad and the Iraqis momentarily expected a descent of the Nazi paratroopers who had taken Crete. Churchill ordered Wavell to undertake the almost hopeless task of rescuing Iraq. A British motorized column set out from Amman across the Syrian desert, accompanied by Abdullah and his Arab Legion, and succeeded in overthrowing Rashid Ali and in re-establishing the Hashemite king. Had it not been for the fact that Hitler was preparing for his June attack upon the Soviet Union, Iraq would almost certainly have been lost. The story of the rescue of one Hashemite king by another is vividly told by James Morris in the work already cited (*The Hashemite Kings*). This was one case in which British pro-Arab policy paid dividends.

The Mufti escaped to Berlin from where he would soon be heard broadcasting Nazi propaganda to the Arab countries.

In June, July and August 1941 the Germans drove deep into Russia. As a precautionary measure, British and Russian troops occupied Iran.

In spite of their tremendous commitment in Russia, the Germans managed to reinforce the Italians in Libya with a specially trained Afrika Korps commanded by General Rommel. In May 1942 Rommel began an advance into Egypt; in June he captured Tobruk with its large garrison, much to the dismay of Churchill, who was then in Washington conferring with Roosevelt. As a result of this conference, a large consignment of American Sherman tanks was rushed to Egypt; General Wavell was relieved of his command and transferred to India, his place in Egypt being taken by General Claude Auchinleck.

(By this time, the United States had, of course, been in the war for six months but its forces were heavily engaged in the war against Japan. The tide had begun to turn against Japan with the decisive American victory in the naval battle of Midway on June 5.)

By the end of June, Rommel stood at the gates of Alexandria and Cairo. Even when their own country was being invaded, the Egyptians maintained a non-belligerent neutrality. King Faruq carried on something of a flirtation with the Axis, but strong measures by the British put an end to this intrigue. On July 1, Auchinlek stopped and defeated Rommel at the first battle of El Alamein.

A hard-pressed Stalin was insistently demanding that the Allies open up a second front in Europe. American troops were gathering in Britain. Should they and the re-equipped British armies be launched across the Channel or used in some other diversionary offensive? The writer was in London while this question was resolved after much debate in favor of launching an invasion of North Africa in November. The decision involved much careful planning and an intensive study of which French and native elements in Morocco and Algeria might be expected to resist an Anglo-French landing and which, if any, might be expected to render assistance. The French forces were under Vichy command but secret intelligence revealed that some of the higher officers might wish to aid the war against the Germans by offering only token resistance. The Arabs and Berbers, while hostile to the French, were not necessarily to be counted upon as friendly to Western invaders, although one powerful Berber chieftain appeared likely to offer assistance. On the whole, it seemed likely that Americans would be accorded a more friendly reception than the British and,

accordingly, the operation was put under American command
and given as much American coloration as possible. When the
invasion fleet arrived off Casablanca and Oran on November 8,
loud-speakers and radio transmitters delivered a carefully prepared proclamation by President Roosevelt.

The outcome is well known. Due to the arrangement made
by General Eisenhower with Admiral Darlan, French resistance was minimal, although the political consequences might
have been disastrous if Darlan had not been assassinated shortly
after he was given command of the French forces in North
Africa. The Arabs and Berbers caused no trouble as the Allied
forces occupied Morocco and Algeria. The trouble came when
the Allies encountered strong resistance from German forces
landed in Tunisia. However, by this time, the tide had turned,
not only in the Middle East but in the entire war against the
Axis powers. Ten days before the Anglo-American landings,
General Montgomery, now in command of the British Desert
Army, had decisively defeated Rommel at the second battle of
El Alamein and had forced him to retreat out of Egypt. A day
later, on October 29, the Russians began their great counteroffensive at Stalingrad. Before the end of the year, Montgomery reached Wavell's old high-water mark at El Agheila,
driving the Afrika Korps westward toward Tunisia. When
Roosevelt and Churchill met at Casablanca in January 1943, in
order to decide upon future operations in the Mediterranean
Theater, Churchill could declare that while this was not "the
beginning of the end," it was "the end of the beginning."

On February 2, 1943, the Russians announced that the battle
of Stalingrad had been won and that the entire Sixth German
Army had surrendered.

On May 7, the Allied armies captured Tunis and Bizerte; five
days later, the last Axis forces in Africa surrendered at Cap
Bon.

So far as the Middle East was concerned, the war was over.
During the subsequent campaigns in which the Allies conquered Sicily, Italy and, finally, France, the North African
bases remained important, but the scene of battle was now in
Europe.

Apart from the campaigns in Africa, there had been only

two other minor scenes of conflict in the Middle East. One, the attempted Nazi coup in Iraq, has already been mentioned. The other episode took place early in the war when an Allied force composed of British, Free French and Haganah units had defeated the Vichy French forces in control of Syria and Lebanon. The Syrians and Lebanese had welcomed their liberators but had been justifiably suspicious of the intentions of the Free French who were left in supposedly temporary occupation. It was not until 1945 that Churchill forced De Gaulle to order their withdrawal. (It was in this campaign that Moshe Dayan, later to become famous as an Israeli commander, lost an eye when a bullet struck the telescope through which he was examining the Vichy positions.)

In Palestine the outbreak of the war in 1939 at first caused a serious economic depression. The consequent distress, shared by Jews and Arabs alike, and a common uncertainty about the future had for a short time driven the two peoples toward a certain degree of economic cooperation. This, however, had no effect upon the political leadership on either side. The Arabs, in spite of the appeasment offered by the White Paper, remained hostile to the British. For the Jews, the outbreak of the war presented a fearful dilemma.

No Jew in possession of his senses could even remotely consider joining Britain's enemies; yet how could the Jews join the British who had betrayed them?

David Ben-Gurion, who had become chairman of the Jewish Agency, provided the answer:

"We shall fight with Great Britain in this war," he said, "as if there were no White Paper; and we shall fight the White Paper as if there were no war." Throughout the war, neither purpose was ever laid aside. The Jews became, to the extent that they were permitted to do so, stout fighting allies of the British in the war against Hitler; and they maintained throughout the war that the White Paper restrictions on land purchases and, above all, on immigration were not only cruel and unjust but without legal validity, since they violated the League of Nations mandate. Holding the White Paper to be illegal, the Zionists took the position that whatever they might do to evade the restrictions could not be considered illegal. And, throughout the war, the British government and the British administration in Palestine continued to stand with incredible callousness upon the letter of the White Paper.

Although thousands of Jews enlisted in the British armed forces, what the Zionists wanted was permission to create a Jewish army, so that they might fight the hated Nazis under their own flag. This they were not permitted to do until the last months of the war, and then only to the extent of forming a single division. At the beginning of the war, the chief reason for the denial was undoubtedly Britain's inability to equip and supply another fighting force in the Middle East.

As a matter of fact, Churchill, shortly after he became Prime Minister, promised Weizmann that a Jewish Army would be created, but not even Churchill at the height of his power could overcome the objections of the British Middle East Command. Sir Archibald Wavell, commander of the British forces in the Middle East, had been in Palestine in 1938–1939 and had noted with approval the disciplined and effective work of the Haganah and the special night patrols organized by Orde Wingate. But Wavell had his hands full with chasing the Italians out of Egypt and across the Libyan desert, then having to give up most of his gains in order to go to the rescue of Greece and then, after that effort failed, having to fight a losing war in Crete.*

The problem of equipment and supply was real but could not be fully disclosed for obvious reasons. The Jews interpreted the protracted stalling of the British government as the policy of an anti-Jewish Palestine administration carrying out the anti-Jewish White Paper. This interpretation was not without foundation in fact, although Churchill was certainly not motivated by any such attitude.

Whatever the balance of the political and military factors involved, British refusal to permit the Jews to fight as Jews against the Nazis had a disastrous effect upon Anglo-Jewish relations.

The question of whether or not to create a Jewish Army was

* Christopher Sykes, in *Crossroads to Israel*, pp. 205–215, gives a detailed and lucid account of the protracted negotiations concerning the formation of a Jewish Army. They lasted from 1940 until 1944.

complicated by the ambivalent attitude taken by the British toward the Haganah. The Palestine administration consistently maintained that the Haganah was illegal, yet at times, when it suited the administration, Haganah's actions were tacitly permitted.

The British Military Command, or rather the branch which handled clandestine operations—the Special Operations Executive (SOE)—occasionally made use of Haganah men in some of its secret work. Several teams of Haganah men were trained by SOE and sent on extremely dangerous missions; some of them were wiped out in the course of their work. One such group was lost in an attempt to blow up an oil refinery in Tripoli; another was sent to Iraq in an attempt to abduct or assassinate the Mufti. Haganah scouts were used by the Anglo-French force that invaded Syria in order to oust the Vichy French. On a few occasions, SOE was said to have employed even members of the Irgun Zvai Leumi,* which was considered an outlaw organization by both the Palestine administration and the Jewish Agency.

Haganah and the Palestine administration came into their sharpest conflict over the High Commissioner's determination to enforce the cruel White Paper restrictions on migration and the Zionist refusal to abide by these restrictions.

In 1940 the Palestine administration altered the policy under which "illegal" Jewish immigrants had been sent back to Germany early in 1939. It was still determined not to let the immigrants land unless they had proper papers and came within the White Paper restrictions, but instead of shipping them back to Germany, the British authorities now decided to intern "illegal" arrivals in Cyprus or Mauritius for the duration of the war. Sir Harold MacMichael broadcast an explanation of this new policy in these terms:

> His Majesty's Government are not lacking in sympathy for refugees from territory under German control. But

* When the Revisionist followers of Jabotinsky split away from the Zionist leadership in 1937, they formed their own military underground, the Irgun Zvai Leumi, known for short as ETZEL. Irgun terrorist activities were directed against the British but not in such a way as to interfere with the British war effort.

they are responsible for the administration of Palestine and are bound to see to it that the laws of the country are not openly flouted.

Moreover, they can only regard a revival of illegal Jewish immigration at the present juncture as likely to affect the local situation most adversely *and to prove a serious menace to British interests in the Middle East* [emphasis added].

The effect upon "the local situation" of this announcement was to give the Jews every reason to consider that the British administration was utterly without heart and concerned solely with the appeasement of the Arabs for the sake of "British interests in the Middle East." From here on, even the most moderate Zionists would not hesitate to assist in flouting the restrictions, while the less moderate would resort increasingly to terror tactics and murder.

The first application of the new immigration policy led to a horrible disaster. The British intercepted and brought into Haifa two old hulks, the *Pacific* and the *Milos*, with more than 1,700 refugees aboard. These people were transferred to a French liner, the *Patria*, for transshipment to Mauritius. Then a third hulk, the *Atlantic* was intercepted and brought into Haifa and the British decided to add its human cargo to that of the *Patria*. But before this transfer was completed, an alarm was sounded on the *Patria* and her passengers were ordered for safety to jump overboard. A few minutes later, there was an explosion on the ship which caused it to keel over and sink. Two hundred and forty refugees were drowned or killed by the explosion and a number of policemen lost their lives.

The Zionist leadership announced that the sinking was caused by an attempted mass suicide of the refugees in protest at being shipped away from Palestine. This story was widely believed, and as late as 1949 it was repeated in a widely read book,* although by this time the facts were known. These were that the Jewish Agency had sent a few Haganah men aboard the *Patria* to disable her engines and thus to prevent her from sailing, with the object of keeping the refugees in Pales-

* Arthur Koestler, *Promise and Fulfillment.*

tine and increasing the pressure upon Sir Harold MacMichael to alter his new policy.

The mass suicide story was deliberately invented by the Jewish Agency to cover up its action in attempting to disable the vessel's engines. The truth must have been known to a considerable number of the survivors who were permitted to remain in Palestine. From this point on, it is extremely difficult to separate fact from fiction in the tragic story of the Zionist struggle against the White Paper, because both sides—the British as well as the Jews—made increasing use of planted rumors and cover stories.

It is impossible to ascertain how many of the continuing flow of refugee-loaded hulks foundered. The passengers of those that were intercepted continued to be deported to Mauritius, an island which Zionist propaganda quite inaccurately described as another Devil's Island.

During 1941 an overloaded vessel, the *Salvador*, arrived at the Bosporus where the Turkish authorities refused the refugees permission to land because they had no valid passports or visas. Ordered to proceed, the vessel sank in a storm in which some 230 out of the 350 refugees were drowned. Fifty-nine survivers reached the Turkish shore and were sent back to Bulgaria, from where the *Salvador* had sailed; the remainder somehow reached Palestine.

In December 1941 another horribly overloaded vessel, the *Struma*, carrying 769 Jewish refugees, reached the Bosporus, and its passengers, too, were refused permission to land. For two months the Jewish Agency argued with the British authorities, desperately seeking to obtain permission for the refugees to land in Palestine, while the wretched people remained confined to their filthy prison-ship lying within sight of the Turkish shore. Finally, the British agreed to issue visas to the children between the ages of eleven and seventeen that were aboard the ship, but before the necessary arrangements were made, the Turkish authorities ordered the *Struma* to be towed out into the Black Sea where she sank after an explosion of unknown origin. There was only one survivor.

The Jewish Agency declared that this had been another case of mass protest by mass suicide, blaming the British for the disaster. Whatever happened aboard the *Struma*, whether or not she was sunk by the passengers, the British administration certainly was to blame. Instead of arguing for two months with the Jewish Agency, it could quite easily have had the ship sent to Haifa and, from there, sent the refugees to Mauritius. If the Jewish Agency had been more strongly moved by humanitarian rather than by political considerations, it, too, might have suggested letting the ship come to Haifa while it argued the case for permitting the refugees to land in Palestine.

It is important to realize that the *Struma* disaster occurred at the time when Rommel's Afrika Korps stood at the gateway to Cairo and Alexandria, and when there was great fear in Palestine that Egypt might have to be evacuated. This gave new urgency to the Agency's demand for a Jewish Army. If the British were to give up the Nile Delta, they might also withdraw from Palestine. If the Jews were to be abandoned to the Nazis, they wanted at the very least to go down fighting under their own flag. Churchill was in Washington and Weizmann put the case to him there with his usual eloquence. The Prime Minister had always favored the creation of a Jewish Army but, as stated earlier, had been unable to overcome the objections of the British Middle East Command. Even though he now obtained the support of President Roosevelt* and General Marshall, he was still unable to win over the British Chiefs of Staff. Auchinlek was, with good reason, as anxious as Wavell had been earlier not to have his stream of equipment and supplies diluted.

It was not only the question of supplies and equipment that made both the British military command and the Palestine administration reluctant to create a Jewish Army. There was also the fear that relations between the administration and the Jews had become so bad, due largely to the immigration disasters, that a Jewish Army might not necessarily fight for the objectives that commended themselves to the British, especially if it

* At the urging of Undersecretary of State Sumner Welles and Secretary of the Treasury Morgenthau, Roosevelt telephoned Field Marshal Sir John Dill, the British representative on the Combined (U.S.-British) Chiefs of Staff, urging the creation of a Jewish Army and the appointment of Orde Wingate as its commander.

came to the question of defending or evacuating Palestine. Another factor militating against the desire of the Jews to fight under their own flag was the fact that so many of them enlisted as individuals in the British armed forces. Ironically, this enabled some of the opponents of a Jewish Army in Britain to say: "Why a Jewish Army? There are thousands of them enlisting in our forces."

As Weizmann continued his patient negotiations, Ben-Gurion began to emerge as a far less patient and less moderate leader of the Zionists. The two men had little in common except for a shared objective. Weizmann was an aristocratic, highly intellectual diplomat who had pursued a sometimes devious course of patient gradualism—a course which, had it not been for the advent of Hitler, would almost certainly have led to the creation of a Jewish state, perhaps within the British Commonwealth. Ben-Gurion was much more a man of the people, a socialist labor leader and a fiery orator. He was also very much younger than the aging Weizmann, whose spirit had been crushed but not broken by the death of his son while serving in the Royal Air Force.

In 1942, as the first news of Hitler's policy of extermination sifted through to the West, great anxiety and restlessness was aroused among Jews everywhere. In May some six hundred American Jewish leaders, many of them non-Zionist, met with a large delegation of Zionists at the Biltmore Hotel in New York. Both Weizmann and Ben-Gurion were present. The latter ardently advocated the abandonment of gradualism and a demand for the immediate abrogation of the White Paper, asking that the Arabs be clearly told that there was going to be a Jewish state in Palestine and that the Jews would control their own immigration. The manner in which Ben-Gurion succeeded in winning the overwhelming support of the conference over Weizmann's opposition was interesting.

In the January issue of *Foreign Affairs*, the influential quarterly published by the Council on Foreign Relations in New York, Weizmann had written an article entitled "Palestine's Role in the Solution of the Jewish Problem." The article traced the history of the Jewish settlements in Palestine, emphasizing the benefits which these settlements brought to both Jews and

Arabs and which a Jewish state could bring to the whole area. The article endeavored to show how, by the proper agricultural development of land and the growth of industry and urban development, there could *eventually* be room for 400,000 additional Jewish families, and ended by a rather quiet statement that "the Arabs must be clearly told that the Jews will be encouraged to settle in Palestine, and will control their own immigration; that here Jews who so desire will be able to achieve their freedom and self-government by establishing a state of their own and ceasing to be a minority dependent on the will and pleasure of other nations."

Ben-Gurion used these words of Weizmann's as the basis for a resolution which, in effect, made the statement of an ultimate objective into a demand for immediate fulfillment. The resolution was adopted by an astounding majority but was sharply criticized by the conservative American Jewish Committee.

Ben-Gurion then went to Palestine to arouse the Yishuv and to obtain the sanction of the Central Executive of the Jewish Agency. Weizmann's leadership suffered from the fact that he did not go to Palestine and that, consequently, the majority of the Palestinian Jews assumed his approval.

At the crucial meeting of the Central Executive of the Jewish Agency in November 1942, Ben-Gurion won approval of the Biltmore resolution but only after overcoming stiff opposition. The German-speaking Jews declared that nothing of this sort should be done until after Hitler's defeat. A number of the smaller political parties objected. The most formidable fight was put up by Judah Magnes and his *Ihud* (equality) group of binationalists. Had the binationalists been able to adduce any evidence whatever of Arab support for a binational state, they might have succeeded in defeating the Biltmore resolution. But there was no such Arab support. From here on, Ben-Gurion became the dominant Zionist leader. Weizmann remained the greatly revered and greatly loved father figure.

The idea of the Biltmore program had been to force Great Britain into an immediate abrogation of the White Paper and the immigration restrictions which it imposed. No such result was achieved. The effect of the adoption of the program was, as Weizmann had foreseen, to put an end for the time being to his negotiations for a Jewish Army. Its further effect was to harden the cleavage between the Jewish Agency and the British administration. Denied the privilege of fighting the war "as if there were no White Paper," there was now nothing for the Jews to do except to "fight the White Paper as if there were no war."

Unfortunately but inevitably, given the unwillingness or the inability of the Palestine administration to see any connection between the mass murders being perpetrated in Nazi-controlled Europe and the feelings of the Jews in Palestine, the hardening Jewish attitude toward Britain resulted in a rapid growth of terrorism. This was not the fault of the Jewish Agency, which had endeavored to restrain all such activities. Until now, even the Irgun had avoided using its terror tactics against the British in such a way as to hamper their war effort; but that time was now past. Worse yet, a separate small group of terrorists organized by a ruthless fanatic, Abraham Stern, began to murder not only British officials but any Jews who did not agree that there was now no difference between the British and the German Nazis. No one was more horrified by these activities of the Irgun and the Stern Gang than the Jewish Agency, but unfortunately the Agency did not publicly denounce the terrorists for fear of splitting the Yishuv. This gave the Palestine administration reason to believe that the Zionist leadership was inspiring the terrorists. As we shall see presently, it would take a particularly atrocious terrorist crime to bring about some degree of cooperation on the part of the Agency-directed Haganah and the British administration in suppressing terrorism.

As Hitler proceeded with the extermination of six million Jews while Britain kept the doors of Palestine locked against all but a few thousand immigrants, the temper of the Yishuv rose and acts of terrorism against the British increased, with the Agency still unwilling to disclose its very real abhorrence of such activities.

The Agency probably knew and Weizmann in London certainly knew all through 1943 and 1944 that Churchill was sponsoring and trying to win support for an abrogation of the White Paper of 1939 and a return to a plan for partition similar to the Peel proposal but slightly less favorable to the Jews. During the same period, however, Foreign Secretary Eden let it be known that Britain would like to see the Arab countries develop a certain degree of national unity, and it was probably to promote this idea that Lord Moyne, a former Colonial Secretary, was sent to Cairo as British Minister of State to replace the Australian Richard Casey, whose term had expired. This was in January 1944. In October 1944 a number of Arab leaders met at Alexandria under the chairmanship of the Egyptian Prime Minister, Nahas Pasha. They issued a statement urging the British to cooperate with the Arabs by enforcing the White Paper and threatened to withhold their cooperation if the White Paper were abandoned.

As seen from Palestine, this was a typical act of British duplicity consistent with Britain's past history of playing both sides and, as usual, ending up by appeasing the Arabs and betraying the Jews. As a matter of fact, it seems extremely doubtful whether either Churchill or Lord Moyne had anything to do with the statement issued by the Arab group. Churchill was consistently and sincerely working toward an abandonment of the White Paper, and it is difficult to conceive of his appointing Lord Moyne to the Cairo post if he had had the slightest doubt of his loyalty. The worst that could be said of Lord Moyne was that he was imbued with the typical British diplomat's habit of trying to "be fair to both sides." This, in view of the Zionists' experience with such "fairness," was enough to damn Moyne as a pro-Arab anti-Semite.

On November 4, 1944, Churchill had a long talk with Weizmann and explained what he had in mind with respect to partition. Weizmann's report of the lunch at Chequers (contained in the Weizmann Archives) shows that Weizmann was greatly encouraged and pleased, even though Churchill made it clear that no steps would be taken until the conclusion of the war. When Weizmann said that he was about to go to Palestine, the Prime Minister suggested that he stop off at Cairo to see Lord Moyne.

Two days later, on November 6, Lord Moyne and the driver of his car were assassinated by two young Jews, presumably members of the Stern Gang. Both of them were arrested, tried before a court-martial and hanged. Arthur Koestler's version, already mentioned, suggests that one of these young men, Ben Hakim, had witnessed the sinking of the *Patria* and believed that this tragedy had come about through the mass suicide of its desperate passengers. If that was the case, the young assassins were clearly the victims of the false cover story put out by the Jewish Agency at the time of the *Patria* disaster. But there may have been another reason.

At the trial of Adolf Eichmann, years later, a strange story came to light, revealing a different possible motive for the murder. By the middle of 1944 the Jews in Germany, Austria and Eastern Europe under Nazi control had just about been exterminated, but there were still 800,000 to 1,000,000 Jews alive in Hungary. Possibly to prepare the way for a separate peace with the West, Eichmann, acting upon Himmler's or perhaps Hitler's orders, offered Yoel Brand, an agent of the American Joint Distribution Committee in Hungary, an exchange of "one million Hungarian Jews for certain strategic goods, notably ten thousand new, winterized trucks to be used exclusively in the campaign against the Soviet Union." Brand, on his way to see Mosche Shertok of the Jewish Agency, was arrested by British Intelligence and taken to Cairo, where he disclosed the offer to Lord Moyne. According to Brand, Moyne is reported to have said: "What can I do with a million Jews? Where can I put them?"

If this story was known in Palestine, Moyne's reported remark may have been the cause of his murder.*

Whatever its motivation, the Jewish Agency and the entire Yishuv were shocked and horrified by the murder. The Agency at last openly stated its condemnation and ordered the Haganah to cooperate with the British authorities in tracking down the members of the terrorist Stern Gang. Stern himself

---

* See Moshe Pearlman: *The Trial of Adolf Eichmann*, pp. 363–366 for Brand's testimony. Ira Hirschmann in *The Embers Still Burn* suggested that British Intelligence kept Brand in seclusion for four or five months in order to keep the "Jews for goods" scheme from being seriously considered. During this period the Pope and Roosevelt are said to have lost interest, if, indeed, Roosevelt had ever given the plan serious consideration. Eden, informed by Weizmann of the proposal, is said to have considered it "impractical." See also Gerold Frank, *The Deed*.

was already dead, but almost three hundred terrorists were rounded up, most of them Sternists along with a few members of the Irgun. Menachem Begin, the leader of Irgun, protested violently to the Agency without altering its determination to suppress terror.

For the remaining months of the war, a truce prevailed between the Zionists and the Palestine administration, due in part to the changed policy of the Agency. But perhaps in even larger measure it stemmed from the fact that Sir Harold Mac-Michael's term as High Commissioner expired in the autumn of 1944. His place was taken by Lord Gort, the distinguished soldier who had commanded the Malta garrison during its darkest moments of siege. It seemed that the British government had at long last found "another Plumer."

The new High Commissioner introduced a better atmosphere. He issued an order permitting the return to Palestine of the refugees that had been deported to Mauritius, but, like all his predecessors, Gort found himself charged with the task of carrying out an impossible policy, a policy which, among other things, insisted upon considering the Haganah "illegal" even when it was cooperating with the British administration. Unfortunately for what might have been the future, Gort was stricken with cancer and died after about a year in office.

During the last months of the war, Weizmann spent much time in Palestine, making frequent speeches to the Yishuv, urging moderation. He was adored by the people, many if not most of whom admired his preaching of the ancient Jewish doctrine of *Havlagah* (self-restraint), but his influence upon the impatient leaders of the Agency, and especially upon Shertok and Ben-Gurion, was slight.

Once the war against Hitler was over and won, the war against the White Paper redoubled in intensity.

The murder of Lord Moyne severely hampered Churchill's efforts to win support for the partition plan that had been worked out by Colonial Secretary Oliver Stanley. Churchill found it necessary to announce in Parliment that if the Zionist leadership were to condone such acts of terrorism, the British "would have to reconsider their attitude." Nor was the furtherance of Churchill's partition plan aided by the fact that the

Jewish Agency sent a memorandum protesting against partition.

In spite of Weizmann's appeals for moderation, Ben-Gurion and Shertok made public this protest in December 1944 and obtained confirmation of their action by the Va'ad Leumi (the National Council for the Jews in Palestine). Ben-Gurion was now in the saddle and would not consider any retreat from the Biltmore program.

The British Labour Party held its annual conference in the same month (December 1944) and adopted a resolution put forward by its leader, Clement Attlee, committing the Labour Party to a Palestine policy which went even further than the Biltmore program of the Zionists. The resolution proposed to permit Jews to become a majority in Palestine by increasing immigration and "encouraging the Arabs to move out as they move in." The Arabs were to be "compensated handsomely for their land" and their "resettlement elsewhere" was to be "carefully organized and generously financed." Noting that the Arabs had "many wide territories of their own," the resolution declared that they "must not claim to exclude the Jews from this small area in Palestine, less than the size of Wales." Indeed, the resolution proposed examining the question whether the "present Palestinian boundaries" might not be extended "by agreement with Egypt, Syria and Transjordan."

This action on the part of the Labour Party gave added impetus to the Zionists' determination to carry out the Biltmore program, although the Zionist leadership hastened to dissociate itself from the proposal to effect a transfer of the Arab population.

Whatever had been the chances for Weizmann and Churchill's gradualist program they were now all but eliminated.

Few people—not even the most optimistic leaders of the Labour Party—entertained the thought in December 1944 that, within eight months, the British electorate would reject their great and victorious war leader and bring the Labour Party to power.

14

Anglo–American Relations in World War II

From the outbreak of the war in 1939 until the fall of France in May 1940, American public opinion had remained preponderantly isolationist. From May 1940 until the Japanese attack upon Pearl Harbor in December 1941, American opinion had been sharply divided between isolationists and a growing number of Americans who felt that the United States should come to the aid of Britain, then standing alone, except for Greece, against the Axis powers. Between these two groups, Roosevelt moved cautiously, preparing the country for a war which he thought inevitable and, at the same time, assuring the American people that their sons would not be sent overseas.

Immediately after the fall of France, arms and supplies were sent to Britain, which then stood in danger of immediate invasion. In September 1940 Roosevelt, with the concurrence of his Republican rival Wendell Willkie, put through the "destroyers-for-bases" deal to help the hard-pressed Royal Navy defend the vital sea-lanes against the German submarine campaign. In March 1941, under the slogan of "defending America by aiding the nations resisting Axis aggression," the Lend-Lease Act was passed as the culminating effort in what was known as short-of-war aid.*

* For a detailed account of this period by an avowed interventionist, see J. P. Warburg, *Our War and Our Peace* (Farrar & Rinehart, New York, 1941).

Hitler's attack upon the Soviet Union in June 1941, while of vital assistance to the Allied cause, for a short time fortified the isolationists in the United States. Not only was communism extremely unpopular, but Soviet unpopularity had been increased by the now-ended alliance with Nazi Germany and by the Soviet attack upon Finland. The interventionists now found themselves suddenly and unhappily allied to the American Communist Party. And so the debate went on, until Pearl Harbor put an end to it.

Even before Pearl Harbor, in August 1941 Roosevelt had met with Churchill at sea and signed the Atlantic Charter defining Anglo-American war aims, although the United States was not yet at war.* Had the principles laid down in the Atlantic Charter been adhered to, instead of being jettisoned at Yalta in 1945, the postwar world might have assumed a happier shape.

Roosevelt's direction of the American war effort was almost solely aimed at achieving victory as quickly as possible and at the lowest possible cost of American lives. Military expediency, as largely determined by the American Chiefs of Staff and, in some cases, by the commanders in the field,† took precedence over political considerations.

Churchill's aim, once Britain's own survival was assured, was essentially political. Churchill did not, to use his own words, "become the King's first minister in order to preside over the liquidation of His Majesty's Empire." The British war leader gave less latitude than Roosevelt to his field commanders.

These differences became more pronounced toward the end of the war when doubts arose as to the intentions of Josef Stalin. Roosevelt inclined to interpret the Soviet leader's aggressive attitude in Eastern Europe as primarily motivated by the desire to assure Soviet security and, until the last days of his life, held to the aim of preserving the wartime coalition during

* Winston Churchill's monumental *History of the Second World War* gives the fullest and best account of the "Grand Alliance." Robert E. Sherwood's *Roosevelt and Hopkins* gives the most intimate account of Roosevelt's views and actions during the same period.

† The decision whether or not to push on to Berlin was, for example, left to General Eisenhower. Admiral Nimitz and General MacArthur decided between them what Japanese strongpoints were to be captured or bypassed and left to "wither on the vine."

the period that was to come after victory. Churchill, on the other hand, was more distrustful of Stalin, more fearful of his encroachment into Europe, and more conscious that Soviet ambitions might well constitute a threat to Britain's imperial interests; this applied particularly to traditional Russian ambitions in Southeast Europe and the Middle East.

When the three great war leaders met at Tehran in 1943 and again at Yalta early in 1945, Roosevelt's primary concern was not only to preserve the Soviet alliance against Germany but to obtain Soviet aid against Japan after Germany's surrender. To accomplish these ends, Roosevelt was willing to jettison the pledges in the Atlantic Charter (later subscribed to by the other members of the anti-Axis coalition) against territorial annexations or "territorial changes that did not conform to the wishes of the peoples concerned." In spite of Churchill's misgivings, the Soviet Union was conceded (at Yalta) the right to annex the Polish Ukraine and the northern part of German East Prussia, while Poland was to be granted in compensation certain "accessions of German territory in the West."*

Because Roosevelt put military expediency and the maintenance of the Soviet alliance first, he avoided so far as possible any discussion of the shape of the postwar world, except for his insistence that, after victory, the world's peace should be preserved by a world organization dominated by the United States, Britain, the Soviet Union, China and France. (China was made one of the Big Five at Roosevelt's insistence while Churchill insisted upon the inclusion of France.) Beyond this rather vague blueprint of the future, Roosevelt either ducked or straddled political issues. This was notably the case with respect to the Middle East.

Until 1938, American interest in the Middle East had been chiefly cultural and commercial. Broadly speaking, the area was recognized to be a sphere of British influence in which, as in China, the United States merely insisted upon equal commercial rights; this applied especially to the right to obtain oil concessions in the area. The United States government did not, as did the British government, itself enter into oil exploration

---

* For the fatal consequences of this decision, see J. P. Warburg, *Germany—Bridge or Battleground* (Harcourt Brace, New York, 1947).

and production, but it insisted that private American enterprises should have equal rights with foreign governmental or private enterprises. Until 1938, about two-thirds of the oil produced in the Middle East came from Iran. In that year, however, huge oil reserves were discovered in Sa'udi Arabia in concessions obtained by American oil companies. This was to have an important bearing upon future American policy.

Besides cultural, missionary and commercial interests, the only important political involvement of the United States in the Middle East prior to World War II had been the development of a somewhat curious relationship with Iran, where Britain and Russia had long maneuvered for control. On two occasions, from 1911 to 1912 and again from 1922 to 1927, United States citizens, nominated by the Department of State at the request of the Persian government, became to all intents and purposes the controllers of Persian finance. Both Morgan Shuster (1911–1912) and Arthur C. Millspaugh (1922–1927) were held to be employees of the Persian government. Both endeavored to reorganize taxation and tax collection with a view to balancing the government's budget. The Shah had turned to the United States for this unusual form of financial assistance because it was remote from the scene and presumably neutral in the Anglo-Russian contest for hegemony. Shuster's plan ran afoul of both foreign interests; he and his staff were forced to resign as the result of Russian armed intervention. Millspaugh was more successful and prevented the Soviet Union from reacquiring the Caspian fisheries concession.

During World War II the United States again became an important factor in Iran through the creation, at Britain's request, of the United States Persian Gulf Command. This time Britain was interested not in opposing Russia as in the past, but in opening up a supply line to the Soviet Union via Iran, over which Lend-Lease supplies from the United States might flow more easily than via the difficult and dangerous northern route across the Atlantic.*

* The operations of the Persian Gulf Command left bitter resentment in Iran against the United States because its operations brought the Russians back into northern Iran. (They were supposed to withdraw at the end of the war, but stayed until 1946, when a United Nations Security Council resolution forced their withdrawal.)

Apart from the campaigns in North Africa, the operations of the Persian Gulf Command constituted the sole American military intervention in the Middle East during World War II. The United States, fully preoccupied with two wars, one in Europe and the other in the Far East, considered the eastern Mediterranean and the Middle East a British responsibility; and, indeed, throughout the Arab lands, Britain possessed the only bases and military alliances that existed for the defense of the area.

As for Palestine, Roosevelt had no desire to become involved in that nest of trouble, although here he was subjected to increasing pressures. Not only American Jews but a large part of the non-Jewish American population became so outraged by the Nazi persecutions that many previous anti-Zionists became Zionists or Zionist sympathizers. The creation of a Jewish state in Palestine was no longer an idea in which one might or might not believe; it had become a desperate necessity. In the summer of 1942 the State Department received the first news of Hitler's incredible plan for the total extermination of all Jews within his reach. For six months the Department first questioned and then deliberately suppressed the reports, on the theory that any attempt to intervene on behalf of the Jews or to rescue those that could be rescued would "interfere with the war effort." *

In November 1942, 68 Senators and 200 Representatives signed a resolution denouncing the British White Paper. Appeals from Jewish leaders failed to move Roosevelt to action until the spring of 1943, by which time it was too late, even if the action taken had been more forceful than that undertaken after Treasury Secretary Morgenthau had opened the President's eyes to what had been going on in the State Department. After a meeting with the British at Ottawa, it was decided to call another conference to discuss what might be done about those of Hitler's victims who were still alive. The conference, held at Bermuda in April 1943, accomplished nothing. At Evian, in 1938, it had still been possible to take effective action if the United States, Britain and the Commonwealth had been

---

* The full ugly story was revealed in 1967 by Arthur Morse in a carefully researched book, *While Six Million Died* (Random House, New York).

willing to open their doors to the refugees. In 1943 such action was held to entail the risk that among the refugees there might be enemy agents. Another excuse for inaction was the alleged shortage of available shipping. (There were plenty of empty supply ships returning from Europe to the United States.)

The simple truth was that the State Department was not interested in the fate of Europe's Jews. The State Department was oil- and Arab-oriented. Some of its officials were all but openly anti-Semitic; all but a few were indifferent, looking for excuses for inaction. It is hard to say whether the President was ill informed or too preoccupied with military affairs to be greatly concerned. Certainly, there was not a trace of anti-Semitism in his make-up. Probably, his concern for maintaining the British alliance at a time when preparations were under way for the cross-Channel invasion of France overrode all other considerations. Perhaps he realized with regret that it was now too late to do what should have been done much earlier.

Apart from the question of any attempt at a rescue operation, the President was undoubtedly reluctant to express whatever disagreement he may have felt concerning Britain's policy in Palestine. In these circumstances Roosevelt did not declare, as he might have, that he intended to take no part in solving the Arab-Jewish problem. Instead, he curried favor with both Arabs and Jews, thereby incurring alternately the distrust of both, as well as the British. He several times assured the Zionists that the United States shared their aim of establishing "a Jewish Commonwealth" in Palestine, while at the same time he promised King Ibn Sa'ud that the United States would do nothing to injure the Arab cause. (The latter assurance was conveyed to Ibn Sa'ud by letter on May 26, 1943 and again in 1945, in a personal shipboard interview with Ibn Sa'ud on Roosevelt's return from Yalta, shortly before his death.*

The net result of this two-sided policy was negative insofar as solving the Arab-Jewish problem was concerned, but it had one very definite consequence: it gave the British the right to

---

* See Bartley C. Crum, *Behind the Silken Curtain.* Also, for the State Department messages to the rulers of Egypt, Sa'udi Arabia and Yemen of March 13, 1943, see Cordell Hull, *Memoirs* (Macmillan, New York, 1948), Vol II, p. 1535.

assume that the United States would take a hand in finding a solution.

This was the position which Harry S Truman, a far less devious man than Roosevelt, inherited on April 12, 1945.

In mid-July 1945 Clement Attlee became Prime Minister of Britain and his legacy included not only the steadily more intractable problem of Palestine but the obligation to fulfill the promise which he and the Labour Party had given to the Jews eight months earlier. Unfortunately for all concerned, Attlee assigned this task to Ernest Bevin as Foreign Minister—a man wholly unqualified by experience and temperament.

In passing any judgment upon the British government's lamentable handling of the Palestine mandate from the end of the war until British withdrawal two years later, several factors should be borne in mind.

First, while the United Kingdom emerged from the war victorious and still in possession of its empire, Britain itself was so exhausted and weakened that its apparent position of power had become largely illusory. The sudden cutting off of American Lend-Lease aid left Britain in dire need of a large American loan—a need which was aggravated by unusually harsh climatic conditions and the necessity for reconverting British production to peacetime requirements. This alone tended to make British policy subject to American pressures.

Second, the attitude of the Truman administration during 1945 and 1946 was not marked by any understanding or consideration of Britain's plight. Under the pressure of American business, the government hastily abolished wartime rationing and controls at a time when the whole world needed food, fuel, tools and every other kind of necessity that could be obtained only in the one country—the United States—which had emerged from the war with greater economic strength than it had ever had before. In order to buy in the United States, Britain and the other would-be purchasers needed dollars, and dollars could be earned only by selling goods in the United States market or by borrowing from the United States. In effect, this meant that, before Europe could begin to earn dollars, it would have to borrow in order to restore its productive capacity. It took the Truman administration the better part of two years to comprehend and eventually to act upon this situation. Sympathetic understanding of British needs was not helped by the fact that many Americans looked with suspicion upon a socialist Labour Party government.*

Third, Stalin's aggressive behavior in Eastern Europe caused both British and American policy to become increasingly anti-Soviet. In the United States particularly, there was emerging a policy which, while actually directed against old-fashioned Russian expansionism, rapidly became an ideological crusade against communism—a crusade soon to become a worldwide Jehad against "the international communist conspiracy."†

And finally, fourth, the defeat of the European powers by Japan and the anti-colonial revolution in the Far East was having its effect upon Britain's empire in Asia and was beginning to show repercussions in the Arab world of the Middle East.

These were all factors affecting the behavior of the Attlee government which did not excuse but partially explained its behavior in Palestine.

In the Arab world, the Attlee government continued the efforts made by Churchill and Eden to bring about a certain amount of Arab unity. These efforts had produced meetings of the Arab leadership in 1943 and 1944 from which little resulted except a reaffirmation of the Arab demand that Jewish immigration into Palestine be halted. Curiously enough, these meetings were not attended by any representative of the Arabs in Palestine who were most directly concerned. This was due to constant squabbling among local factions contending for Arab leadership, chiefly between a local Palestine Party and a group inspired by Tewfik Saleh el Husseini, a cousin of the exiled Mufti whose leadership in the whole Arab world Tewfik hoped to restore. Finally, in March 1945, the Arab League was

---

* See Chapter 3, "Postwar Myopia," pp. 29–35, in J. P. Warburg, *The United States in the Postwar World* (Atheneum, New York, 1966). The American ideological attitude led many Americans to consider at this time that socialism was only a step toward communism.

† Churchill, although no longer in power, is considered by most authorities to have keynoted the Cold War in his speech at Fulton, Missouri, in March 1946. But Churchill took a less ideological view of the Soviet menace than Truman and his advisors; Churchill saw Stalin as a lineal descendant of Peter the Great rather than as the spider in the center of a web of worldwide communist conspiracy.

established with Egypt and Transjordan vying for leadership. The Mufti, who had been in prison in France since the Nazi surrender, "escaped" and showed up in Cairo in 1946.*

Because of the formation of the Arab League under British auspices and the liberation of Syria and Lebanon, Britain's stock rose in the Arab world and raised expectations as to Palestine which Britain would find itself totally unable to fulfill without repudiating entirely the Labour Party's promises to the Jews. Correspondingly, Britain's standing among the Zionists sank to a new low.

Truman acted in accordance with the ambivalent policy that he had inherited from Roosevelt. At Potsdam in July 1945 he informed both the outgoing Churchill and the incoming Attlee that he hoped for the admission of as many Jews as possible into Palestine. Asked whether the United States would help actively in bringing this about, Truman answered in the negative. Upon his return to the United States he repeated this attitude, which amounted to telling the British what to do without assuming any responsibility for devising or carrying out a plan of action.

On August 1, 1945, a World Zionist conference met at London, at which Weizmann expressed optimistic hopes of collaboration with a British Labour government, while Ben-Gurion took a less optimistic view, urging active and passive resistance to the White Paper. Rabbi Abba Hillel Silver, head of the Zionist Organization of America, supported Ben-Gurion by stating that it could be that "the height of statesmanship might be to be unstatesmanlike"—a strong hint that virtue might lie in extremist action.

In June 1945 Truman had asked Earl G. Harrison, dean of the Law School of Pennsylvania University, to make a survey of the number of "non-repatriable" Jews in Europe. In the second half of August, Harrison reported his findings: that there were about 100,000 Jews in camps for displaced persons who had no other place to go than Palestine. Truman submitted this

---

* Whether he actually escaped or was let out by the French is not clear. It was suspected that the French government of Charles de Gaulle had released him to cause trouble for the British in retaliation for their liberation of Syria and Lebanon in 1945–1946.

report to Attlee and received an icy response, pointing out what the Arab reaction would be to an abrogation of the White Paper and reminding Truman of Roosevelt's assurances to Ibn Sa'ud. The British reply was in part conditioned by intelligence that the Haganah, with the approval of the Jewish Agency, was about to enter upon an alliance with Irgun. Perhaps in greater measure, Attlee was deeply concerned over what effect Truman's recommendation might have upon the Arabs in relation to the question of resisting Soviet penetration into the Middle East. (The Russians were acting with ominous aggressiveness in Iran.) As for Bevin, he seems to have flown into the first of his many "black rages" against the United States.

In the United States opinion was divided. The State Department urged the President to consider the Arab point of view and its effect upon the defense against Soviet intrusion. The Democratic Party leadership urged Truman to make a move which would "capture the Jewish vote" from Thomas E. Dewey, his Republican opponent in the forthcoming presidential election. Partly because of sincere sympathy for the 100,-000 unrepatriable Jews and partly for domestic political reasons, Truman decided to give public support to the Harrison Report. At the same time, in order to be true to Roosevelt's two-faced legacy, he authorized the publication of his predecessor's letter to Ibn Sa'ud.

October was the last month of Lord Gort's incumbency as High Commissioner and relative peace prevailed in Palestine, reinforced by the transfer there of the British 6th Airborne Division, a distinguished unit now assigned to an impossible task. While overt incidents were few during a period when there still seemed to be some hope that the Labour government would find a way to fulfill its promises, preparations for its failure to do so were going on. Above all, there was increased arms smuggling and increased activity by the Committee for Illegal Immigration.

The Jewish operators of a well-organized clandestine "underground railway" for the transfer of Central European Jews to Palestine received aid from a number of sources, among them workers for UNNRA, demobilized Jewish veterans

and—most important of all—from the hitherto solely charitable American Joint Distribution Committee ("Joint"), which
now decided to assist in the organization and financing of illegal immigration. This change of the Joint's old-established policy reflected the rapid "Zionization" not only of the American
Jewish community but of a large part of Gentile opinion.

On the night of October 31 the Agency acted to nudge the
British government into fulfillment of its promises. Haganah
shock troops (*Palmach*) wrecked railway lines in fifty different locations and sank three small British naval vessels. Sternists
attacked the Haifa oil refinery, and the Irgun attacked the railway station at Lydda. The attacks were carried out skillfully
and with only slight and unintentional loss of life. The effect
was to infuriate Bevin but also to move him to action.

In view of Truman's intervention and British dependence
upon American assistance, the action took the form of appointing an Anglo-American Committee of Inquiry, consisting of
six British and six American members, with instructions to "examine political, social and economic conditions in Palestine as
they bear upon the problem of Jewish immigration" and to
"examine the position of the Jews in those countries of Europe
where they have been the victims of Nazi and fascist
persecution." This was announced on November 13.

The American members of the Committee were Professor
Frank Aydelotte, Frank W. Buxton, Bartley C. Crum, Judge
Joseph C. Hutchinson, James G. MacDonald, and Ambassador
William Phillips. The British members were W. F. Crick, R.
H. S. Crossman M.P., Sir Frederick Leggett, R. E. Manningham-
Buller M.P., Lord Morrison, former M.P., and Sir John Single-
ton, High Court Judge.

Foreign Secretary Bevin met with the Committee and assured its members that if they adopted a unanimous report, he
would abide by it.

In announcing the appointment of the Anglo-American
Committee and in the press conference that he held after the
announcement on November 13, Bevin made the first of many
subsequent statements that were to earn him the reputation of
being an anti-Semite. When asked about the prospects for increasing the development potential of Palestine, Bevin said that

80 percent of the so-called potential was nothing but propaganda. This was an obvious reference to a then widely read book, *Palestine: Land of Promise* by Walter Clay Lowdermilk, an American soil conservationist and a member of the American Christian Palestine Committee. The main thesis of the book was a carefully researched plan for river development which Lowdermilk called a "T.V.A. (Tennessee Valley Authority) on the Jordan." Far from being 80 percent propaganda, Lowdermilk's plan was destined to form the basis for several later proposals sponsored by the American government which, if adopted, would have benefited the entire region. The significance of Bevin's remark was that it betrayed his hostility toward a development that would make possible a vastly greater population of Palestine.

Bevin's second ill-chosen remark on this occasion was made to reporters in summarizing his statement to the House of Commons and deserves to be directly quoted. "I am very anxious," he said, "that Jews shall not in Europe overemphasize their racial position. The keynote of the statement I made in the House is that what I want is the suppression of racial warfare and therefore, if the Jews, with all their sufferings, want to get too much at the head of the queue, you have the danger of another anti-Semitic reaction through it all." Whatever Britain's Foreign Secretary may have meant by this statement, his choice of language earned him a reputation that he was never thereafter to lose. In the Yishuv, Bevin's name became a hate-word.

For the time being, the situation in Palestine remained relatively peaceful under the new High Commissioner, Sir Alan Cunningham. There was still a chance for the British government to indicate its intention of fulfilling Attlee's pledges. Zionist hopes centered upon the Anglo-American Committee, which began its work in December 1945. Despite the efforts of the Agency to avoid provocative incidents, just before the end of the year Irgun committed a major outrage in which nine British soldiers were murdered. Ben-Gurion and Shertok disavowed the action but told the High Commissioner that they were powerless to prevent it.

Meanwhile, the United States Congress passed the anti-White

Paper resolutions which it had withheld at Stimson's request in 1944. The State Department pointed out the danger of telling the British what to do without being willing to take a hand in settling a problem that was theirs to solve. On December 22, Truman attempted to make a move which, if undertaken in the previous decade, could have led to a peaceful solution, namely, to open the gates of the United States to the refugees. Due to the need for legislation to implement his executive order, it would be two years before there would be any substantial result. This period might have been shortened if the groups of citizens clamoring for greater immigration into Palestine had diverted at least a part of their effort toward unlocking the doors of the United States.

The Anglo-American Committee held extensive hearings in the United States, in Britain, in Palestine, in Cairo and in the European refugee camps. The result was what might have been expected: the Arabs were adamant against partition or any further Jewish immigration; the Jews were adamant against the White Paper although they showed a degree of willingness to retreat from the full demands of the Biltmore program; the refugees wanted to go to Palestine and nowhere else. The Committee delivered its unanimous report in April 1946; it was not published until the last day of that month in order to give the British and American governments an opportunity to examine its findings.

The report rejected partition as impracticable and likewise rejected making Palestine into either a Jewish or an Arab state. Its recommendation was for a binational state—an idea which, however sound years earlier, had now become hopelessly impractical. The report further recommended the immediate admission to Palestine of the 100,000 Jews in the European assembly centers and the facilitation of further immigration "under suitable conditions," as well as the removal of the White Paper restrictions on Jewish land purchases. As a concession to the Arabs, the Committee proposed that it be made illegal to exclude Arab labor in enterprises financed by the Jewish National Fund.

The British Ministers were outraged by the report, not so much because of its recommendation of the outdated idea of binationalism as by the one-sided concessions to Zionism and by what seemed to them a total disregard of British interests. At the same time, because the American loan was still in the process of negotiation, they were frustrated in their desire to reject utterly a report made by an Anglo-American Committee. To make matters worse, five days before the report was to be published, two incidents occurred in Palestine which aroused violent emotions. On April 25 the Sternists in Tel Aviv attacked a British car park and killed seven of the eight British soldiers on guard; this seemed to have been their sole purpose. On the following night of April 26 British troops committed a counteratrocity, wreaking their anger on the innocent Jewish inhabitants of a nearby village by breaking up four houses and brutally beating up a number of villagers. In London shame and anger added to the already tense climate of opinion.

Bevin flatly refused to see any of the British members of the Committee. Richard Crossman, whose two books* on the Committee's mission are still well worth reading, did manage to see Attlee. The interview was extremely unpleasant, with the Prime Minister telling Crossman that he and his British fellow members of the Committee had "let us down."

The climax of British anger came when, upon the Report's simultaneous publication in America, President Truman issued a statement lending his approval to the admission of the 100,000 refugees and the other concessions to Zionism while stating that the longer-range recommendations required careful study. Bevin vented his rage in a sharply worded protest to Washington. The Prime Minister, speaking to the House of Commons, vigorously criticized Truman's approval of the Committee's concessions to the Zionists and wanted to know whether his intervention meant that the United States would be willing to share in the cost of the mass immigration and in the military commitments that it entailed. Then Attlee added a statement the effect of which Crossman correctly described as "catastrophic." (Crossman himself had considered Truman's intervention "lamentable.") Attlee stated to the House that there could be no question of admitting 100,000 refugees unless and until

* R. H. S. Crossman, *Palestine Mission* and *A Nation Reborn*.

the "illegal armies" in Palestine, *Arab and Jewish,* surrendered their arms and disbanded. This was a condition not only impossible for the Zionists to accept but wholly impractical; it would take greater military force to disband and suppress the Haganah than to supervise the immigration and, with Haganah's help, to suppress an Arab revolt. This was pointed out to the British government by friendly critics, but the government stubbornly stuck to its position.

No one seemed to realize that in concentrating its demand upon the admission of the 100,000 refugees, the Zionist leadership had, out of humanitarian concern, almost abandoned the essential demands of the Biltmore program; i.e., that there should be a Jewish state and that the Jewish state should control future immigration after the 100,000. If Bevin, who had promised to abide by a unanimous committee report, had kept his promise, the Zionists would have been in an extremely difficult position. They had so sharply focused attention upon the admission of the 100,000 refugees that, with this demand granted, they would have found it difficult to obtain a hearing for anything more. In all probability, the Biltmore program would have been unattainable; a Jewish state might never have come into existence.

The very moderate reaction of the Zionist leadership to the Anglo-American Committee report, amounting almost to a tacit renunciation of its own program, stood in sharp contrast to the Arab reaction. In the first week of November 1945, just before the Committee's appointment was announced, there had been an Arab uprising in Tripoli during which 100 Jews had been murdered in a pogrom similar to the earlier Mufti-inspired incident in Iraq. When the Committee Report was published five months later, Ibn Sa'ud had sent a strong protest to Washington, and the Arab League had threatened to suspend all trade with the West if the Report were adopted. Arab intransigence no doubt strongly influenced the British government's uncompromising rejection of the Report.

In answer to Attlee's sarcastic query as to what the United States proposed to do to help carry out the Committee's recommendations, if they should be adopted, Truman offered to finance the cost of transferring the 100,000 refugees to Palestine and appointed a cabinet committee to confer with the British government. However, by the time this group arrived in London in July, the situation had changed.

At the annual Labour Party Conference in June, a large group of delegates, led by the Party Chairman, Professor Harold Laski, sharply criticized the Foreign Secretary and deplored "sacrificing the Jews who escaped from the tortures of Hitlerism to the Arab leaders." In defending himself, an enraged Bevin made a number of wild assertions as to the cost of admitting the refugees and leveled an accusation against the United States which was never to be forgotten or forgiven: the reason for the American pressure to admit the 100,000 to Palestine, Bevin said, was "that they don't want them in New York." In view of Truman's recent efforts to obtain the power to admit a greater number of refugees to the United States, and considering Britain's consistent refusal to open its own doors, this outburst was inexcusable. It was not surprising that, when Bevin later came to the United States, longshoremen refused to handle his baggage and crowds booed him on the streets.

With the British government's rejection of the Anglo-American Committee's Report, leadership toward some sort of peaceful Palestinian settlement passed, in effect, into the anything but eager hands of President Truman. Yet it was almost impossible to see how Truman could take any effective action so long as the British government remained in control of the Palestine administration. This soon became evident.

It did not take long for Ben-Gurion and Shertok to realize how narrowly they had escaped from sacrificing their major aim of establishing a Jewish state. On the 16th of June, with the seeming approval of the Jewish Agency, terrorists in conjunction with elements of Haganah destroyed the Allenby railroad bridge and eight other bridges. On June 29 the Palestine administration ordered the arrest not only of Palmach and the terrorists but of the Agency leadership, including Shertok. Ben-Gurion escaped arrest only because he was in Paris at the time. Weizmann's protest in London was backed by British and American Zionist leadership. There were reports, some no doubt exaggerated, of atrocities committed by British troops against innocent Jewish settlers. In mid-July the Irgun, apparently acting on its own, blew up one wing of the King David Hotel in Jerusalem, the fourth floor of which had been used as British Army Headquarters. British, Arabs and Jews were among the 91 persons killed and 45 wounded.

The revulsion caused by this outrageous crime might have led to a cooling off of tempers on both sides had it not been for the reaction of Lieutenant-General Sir Evelyn Barker, commander of the British garrison. In an order to his troops ordaining strict non-fraternization with Jews, he referred to his plan as a means of "punishing the Jews in a way the race dislikes—by striking at their pockets." This evidence of overt anti-Semitism on the part of the British garrison's commander partly overshadowed the revulsion inspired by the Irgun's atrocity. Both the Jews and the British in Palestine had now descended to a new low of primitive hatred and barbarism. All this happened at a time when the American and British governments were making a real effort to reconcile their differences.

In July 1946 an American mission under Ambassador Henry Grady arrived in London to consult with the British government. Fortunately, Bevin was ill and Herbert Morrison conducted the negotiations. These resulted in a Grady-Morrison Plan which amounted to a somewhat revised version of the plans for partition recommended by the Peel Commission and later considered by Oliver Stanley at Churchill's request. There was, however, one important modification: the Grady-Morrison Plan provided that, within one year of its adoption, the 100,000 refugees should be admitted to Palestine. In accepting this proposal, the British government gave up its objection to the one feature of the Anglo-American Committee Report to which it had most strenuously objected. However, by this time the Zionist leaders in the United States had also recognized that they had given up too much for the sake of the 100,000 refugees and refused to consider the new proposal. But for this, Mr. Truman would have accepted the Grady-Morrison Plan. As it was, he rejected it.

Meanwhile, the Jewish Agency leaders,* shocked by the

---

* The arrested members of the Agency Executive were still held. Those at large joined Ben-Gurion, who had escaped arrest and had remained in Paris.

King David outrage perpetrated by Irgun, met at Paris in August under the chairmanship of Ben-Gurion and drew up a plan
that showed a willingness to retreat from the extreme demands
of the Biltmore program. They proposed a plan of partition in
which no claim was made to Jerusalem as part of the proposed
Jewish state. The plan was flown to Washington for submission to President Truman and presented to the British government by Weizmann and two members of the Agency Executive.

The British government, which was planning a British-Jew-
ish-Arab conference for September, refused to put the new
Zionist plan on the agenda for fear of hopelessly alienating the
Arabs. When the time came for the conference, the usual thing
happened. The Arabs would not sit down with the Jews and
the British conferred with the Arabs alone. All they got for
their pains was an Arab demand for an independent Palestinian
state in which the Jews were to hold one-third of the seats in
the legislature, Jewish land purchase would remain restricted
and all further Jewish immigration would be prohibited.

One thing could be said for the Arabs: their position was
clear and never changed. Had it not been for the religious fanaticism inspired by the Mufti, the Arab case was not without
moral support: they had had no part in creating "the Jewish
problem"; they could see no reason why it should be solved at
their expense.

Prodded by Laski and Crossman, Bevin gave evidence of
some degree of softening in his harsh attitude. He proposed to
Weizmann that Palestine should be governed for from three to
ten years as a trusteeship pending an advance toward self-
government. To lend credence to Bevin's apparent change of
heart, Attlee appointed Arthur Creech-Jones, a strong Zionist
sympathizer, as Colonial Secretary. Bevin later claimed that he
had been making excellent progress with Weizmann when, according to him, Truman once more upset all his plans.

Whether or not Bevin was actually making any progress,
which seems highly doubtful, it was true that Truman did intervene in a manner considered unfortunate by many of his
advisors.

Once more, an election was imminent in the United States

and, once more, Truman's Democratic Party advisors urged
him to outbid the Republicans for "the Jewish vote." In spite
of Attlee's pleas to the contrary, Truman issued a statement
endorsing the Agency's partition plan and renewing the demand for the admission of the 100,000 refugees. As might be
expected, Bevin blamed the Americans for the breakdown of
his negotiations.

Conciliatory moves by Creech-Jones caused a brief period
of relative peace in Palestine during the remainder of the year.
The imprisoned Agency leaders were liberated and 2,700 Jews
interned in Cyprus were admitted to Palestine. The Agency, in
turn, ended the Haganah alliance with the terrorists and urged
the whole of the Yishuv to join in action against the criminals.

On December 22, 1946, the Zionist Congress assembled for
the first time since the war. The meeting was held at Basel.
Here, for the last time, Dr. Weizmann rose to the full heights
of his moderate statesmanship, condemning the murder of
Lord Moyne, the Irgun and Sternist crimes and the encourage-
ment given to violence by Rabbi Silver and other rabid American Zionist leaders. He was given an ovation, but the time for
moderation had passed. During the winter of 1946–1947 terrorism increased and the British army resorted to the revolting
tactics of corporal punishment and counter-terror. In February
1947 the long tragedy drew to a close with a thoroughly bewil-
dered Bevin confessing his failure and announcing that the
British mandate would be surrendered to the United Nations.

15

A Nation is Born out of Chaos

British behavior during the last months of the mandate is almost impossible to understand and utterly impossible to excuse. Yet certain developments outside of Palestine deserve attention because they had a bearing upon the British government's conduct.

In 1946 there was a crisis in Iran over the Soviet Union's refusal to withdraw its troops from that country's northern provinces in accordance with the wartime agreement reached with Britain. Not only that, but it was apparent that the Russians aimed at a quasi-annexation of Azerbayjan. The matter was taken to the Security Council of the United Nations. After difficult negotiations, the Soviet Union finally agreed to withdraw its troops. (It was during this period that Churchill delivered his famous speech at Fulton, Missouri, calling for united Anglo-American determination to halt Stalin's aggressive expansionism.) It must not be forgotten that the final years of the Palestine mandate coincided with the beginnings of the Cold War and that these were years when any disturbance in any part of the world aroused suspicion of communist activity. Bevin seems for a time to have suspected that Zionism had become part of a communist conspiracy.

Although it was not apparent in 1946, Britain's empire was in the course of breaking up. India was demanding independence

and the problem Britain faced there was in some respects mis-
leadingly similar to the problem of Palestine. In both countries
only the presence of British troops prevented open war—in
India between Hindus and Moslems, in Palestine between Arabs
and Jews. There was however, this great difference: in India,
Britain was free to act without previous commitments to
either side; in Palestine, Britain was bound by conflicting promises to both sides. This meant that Britain could and eventually
did withdraw her troops from India, leaving Hindus and Moslems to fight out a solution by partition, whereas in Palestine
Britain was obligated by the League of Nations mandate to remain so long as the mandate was not surrendered. The false
analogy between the two problems undoubtedly contributed
to the British government's confusion and to its sense of being
trapped in a position from which it would have liked to withdraw.

On the other hand, a withdrawal from Palestine would, as
the British government saw it, endanger Britain's whole position in the Middle East. Egypt was no longer a secure base.
The Egyptians were not receptive to any prolongation of the
British presence after more than sixty years of occupation,
originally proposed in 1882 as temporary. And Cairo was demanding an end of the condominium in the Sudan. Egypt
could not be evacuated without danger, unless Palestine replaced it as a base for British power. The British had not
learned the lesson that no base is secure in a country that is
determined to become independent.

Finally, Britain's defense position in the Middle East rested
upon treaties with Egypt, Iraq and Transjordan, her colony at
Aden and the protectorates along the Persian Gulf. Her three
major allies were rivals for Arab leadership, united only in
their hostility toward the creation of a Jewish state in Palestine.

To these factors must be added the unexpected decline of
Britain's own military and economic power, the full realization
of which came as a shock to the United States early in 1947,
when the British government asked the United States to take
over its responsibilities in Greece and Turkey.*

* The manner in which this resulted in the declaration of the Truman

It is evident from the foregoing that the last months of the Palestine mandate coincided with a complicated and extremely difficult period in which neither the British nor the American government had very much time to devote to the Palestinian problems. They were both preoccupied with preparing their defenses in the nascent Cold War with the Soviet Union. Bearing this in mind, one is inclined to be a little less critical of Britain's Foreign Secretary, although it is impossible to condone the cruelty and irrationality of his behavior during the dying days of the mandate. As we shall see, the Attlee government was not helped during this period by the uncertain vacillations of American policy.

In May 1947 a special session of the United Nations, convened at the request of Britain, appointed a United Nations Special Committee on Palestine, UNSCOP, consisting of representatives of Australia, Canada, Czechoslovakia, Guatemala, India, Iran, Holland, Peru, Sweden, Uruguay and Yugoslavia. (In order to prevent the Soviet Union from being on the committee, all members of the United Nations Security Council were excluded.) Emile el Ghuri, the fiery spokesman for the Mufti, declared: "It is the determined and unequivocal will of the Arabs to refuse to consider any solution which even implies the loss of their sovereignty over any part of their country, or the diminution of such sovereignty in any form whatever." *

When the UNSCOP arrived in Palestine in June, the country was wracked by constant atrocities committed by Jews against the British, by the British against the Jews, and by the Arabs against both and against each other. (There were three Arab factions contending for leadership, among which the Mufti-led Al Futuwah was the strongest.) But the main con-

---

Doctrine, the consequences of that declaration and the subsequent evolution of the Marshall Plan have been described by the writer in *Put Yourself in Marshall's Place* (Simon & Schuster, New York, 1948), *Last Call for Common Sense* (Harcourt Brace, New York, 1949), and, more recently, in *The United States in the Postwar World* (Atheneum, New York, 1966).

* Cited by J. C. Hurewitz in *The Struggle for Palestine*. This work and *A Clash of Destinies* by Jon and David Kimche throw more light on this period than any other works known to the author, except Sykes, *Crossroads to Israel*, liberally used throughout as a source.

flict was Anglo-Jewish, marked by murders, arrests and kid-
napings. The most dreadful affair was that of the liner *Exodus
1947*, so named by Haganah sympathizers who had bought the
vessel from an American shipping company under whose flag it
had sailed as the *President Garfield*.

The ship was brought into Haifa by British naval vessels that
had intercepted it. Some 4,500 Jewish refugees were aboard—
by far the largest group to arrive on a single ship. By this time,
the Agency had developed great skill in making propaganda
use of all such arrivals. In this case it was claimed that the passengers unanimously refused to debark anywhere except in
Palestine. (This was probably true of the majority. If there
were any passengers not quite so determined, Haganah men
aboard the vessel took care to keep them under cover.)

Enraged over the continuing atrocities and wanting to
"teach the Jews a lesson," Bevin ordered the *Exodus* passengers
to be taken back to the French port near Marseilles from which
the ship had sailed. For this purpose, they were placed aboard
three British vessels and the French government was asked to
permit them to land. De Gaulle, still smarting over Churchill's
forcing him to liberate Syria and Lebanon, agreed but only on
the condition that no passenger was to be forced to debark. As
the ships lay at anchor, the passengers were bombarded with
propaganda by Haganah agents in small boats equipped with
loudspeakers, urging them to refuse to go ashore. The British
consul came aboard to try to reason with the passengers but was
able to see only Haganah men. And then Bevin committed the
supreme and cruel folly of ordering the people to be taken
back to Hamburg. The three ships sailed with the passengers
under British guard!

This tragic episode provided Zionist propagandists with their
greatest opportunity. (It also provided inspiration for a number of sensationalist writers who added imaginary horrors to a
horror that required no embellishment.) The whole thing happened while the United Nations Committee was in Palestine
and inevitably affected the Committee's judgment of British
policy.

On the 1st of September UNSCOP produced its proposals.
Since the plan was greatly modified, the details need not con-

cern us. In essence, the UNSCOP plan was a proposal for partition only slightly less favorable to the Jewish state than the
plan devised by the Jewish Agency. It deprived the Jews of
Acre in the north but allotted Jaffa to them as well as the
Negev as far as Beersheba. However, the UNSCOP report was
not unanimous and the concession of the Negev was later
erased. Nevertheless, the report was enthusiastically welcomed
by the Yishuv and accepted in principle by the Agency, subject to its being adopted by the United Nations Assembly.
When the Assembly met, the matter was put into the hands of
a special committee.

Colonial Secretary Creech-Jones declared that the plan was
not acceptable to the British government, that Britain would
not impose it by force and that "in the absence of a settlement,
it had to plan for an early withdrawal of British forces and of
the British administration of Palestine." For a short time, it
seemed incredible that the British would actually withdraw; it
was true that they had withdrawn from India but not in the
total absence of a settlement. But on October 8 the British High
Commissioner in Jerusalem confirmed that Britain would, indeed, withdraw at an early date.

Late in November the United Nations General Assembly
adopted the UNSCOP partition plan, considerably modified in
the vain hope of appeasing the Arabs by subtracting about 500
square miles from the proposed Jewish state. Even this was accepted by the Jews.

There was never any question of the Arabs accepting the
UNSCOP proposal. Abdullah of Transjordan was the most ra-
tional among the Arab leaders and possessed, in the British-
trained Arab Legion commanded by Sir John Glubb, the only
efficient military force. Abdullah proposed to Bevin that if the
partition should go into effect, his forces should occupy that
part of Palestine west of the Jordan that was to be allotted to
the Arabs. Bevin told him that this seemed the sensible thing to
do. In a secret meeting with Jewish emissaries, Abdullah said
that he would not attack Jewish territory unless his forces
were attacked. Had this plan been generally known, much of
the later bloodshed might have been avoided; it was kept secret
for intra-Arab political reasons. The Mufti was known to as-

pire to leadership of an Arab Palestine; the Egyptians did not
want Arab leadership to fall into Hashemite hands; and Iraq,
the most violently anti-Jewish of the Arab states, was still resentful of Abdullah's cooperation with the British in suppressing the Mufti-inspired revolt of Rashid Ali.

At this time, anti-Jewish pogroms took place in Aleppo, Damascus and, worst of all, in Baghdad where a large Jewish community had lived ever since the Babylonian captivity. Within
Palestine, Arab terrorism mounted while the British garrison
looked on. Sir John Glubb described the situation during the
last months of the mandate in a single sentence: "With the ma-
chinery of the Palestine government still in position, with officials still going to their offices every morning, with the police
still in the streets and a considerable army still in its barracks,
raging battles were going on in the country almost unhin-
dered." *

Dov Joseph, one of the Zionist leaders, described the final
months in this way: "Our final fight for freedom after two
thousand years of exile came at a moment when a war-weary
nation, unwilling to go on paying the price of empire and unwilling to give it up, was capable only of a massive, wavering
indecision." †

On December 11, 1947, the British announced that the mandate would be terminated on May 15, 1948. (As it turned out,
they packed up and left one day earlier.) One may search in
vain for a reliable account of the war that raged, undeclared,
between the Arabs and the Jews from December 1947 until
Israel declared its independence on May 15, after which the
real war began. Broadly speaking, the Arabs took the initiative
while the Jews remained for the most part on the defensive.
This was in part due to the fact that Haganah lacked offensive
weapons or even an adequate supply of small arms. (This lack
was remedied in the nick of time by the successful accomplishment of an extraordinary mission entrusted by Ben-Gurion to
an agent named Ehud Avriel, who purchased large quantities of
arms in Czechoslovakia, pretending that he was an agent for a
South American country, and arranged for them to be smug-

---

* Cited in Sykes, *Crossroads to Israel,* p. 335.
† *Ibid.*

gled into Palestine.* The money required for this purpose was
said to have been furnished by American Zionists.)

We must now take note of the remarkable vacillations of
United States policy during the first months of 1948. The best
sources of information concerning this almost incomprehensi-
ble period are the *Memoirs* of Harry S Truman and Dr. Abba
Eban's chapter in *Chaim Weizmann: A Biography by Several
Hands.* The story is well summarized by Christopher Sykes.†
Very briefly, these were the gyrations through which Ameri-
can policy passed between January and May 1948.

In March the tide of battle in the undeclared war turned in
favor of the Jews, largely due to the first shiploads of smuggled
weapons. But this was also the period in which plans were
under way for a European Recovery Program, although Secretary of State Marshall did not make his famous announcement
until June. If such a program was to be undertaken, it was
thought that its success would depend, among other things,
upon the continuation of large shipments of oil from the Middle East to Europe. Furthermore, at this time the West was in a
state of shock over the Czechoslovakian coup and a major consideration of the Pentagon and State Department planners was
how to stop further Soviet encroachment upon what was beginning to be called "the Free World." (This term included
the far-from-free Arab countries!) In addition, the pro-Arab
pressure of the oil companies was mounting. All these factors
operated to cool off the American government's enthusiasm for
the UNSCOP partition plan. This became evident from several
utterances of Secretary Marshall and from the statement of
Senator Warren Austin, U.S. Ambassador to the United Nations, to the effect that the Security Council's task was to preserve peace and not to enforce partition.

In response to Zionist protests, Marshall, Austin and Truman
himself denied that there was an American retreat from the
UNSCOP proposal, and on March 14 the Security Council
passed a United States resolution that the Council "will do ev-

* The coup d'état by which communists took over the government of
Czechoslovakia occurred in mid-February 1948. It seems likely that the
Czech authorities knew, or at least suspected, where the arms were going.
† *Crossroads to Israel*, pp. 344–349 and 357–360.

erything it can to give effect to the recommendation of the
General Assembly." This seemed as if the retreat had been
called off. However, only five days later, on March 19, in another complete reversal of policy, Austin announced that his
government would like action on partition suspended and
asked that the General Assembly be called into session to discuss a temporary United Nations "trusteeship" over Palestine,
"without prejudice to the character of the eventual political
settlement."

Nothing was said by Truman to explain this incomprehen-
sible reversal. It was not until the publication of the President's
memoirs in 1955 that the matter was cleared up, although some
parts of the answer were given in 1950 through the publication
of Jonathan Daniels' biography of Mr. Truman. What had happened was this:

Dr. Weizmann was in New York and had witnessed the earlier symptoms of the American cooling off toward the
UNSCOP plan with alarm. He had tried without success to see
the President, whom he had met once in November 1947. As
Truman tells it, he had become thoroughly fed up with the un-
remitting pressures of the Zionists, and he had decided to shut
his door against them. This was why he did not reply to Weizmann, whom he actually liked and admired. And now a curious
thing happened to affect the course of history.

Eddie Jacobson, a non-Zionist Kansas City Jew, had been
Truman's partner in an unsuccessful haberdashery business
shortly after both men had returned from World War I. Jacobson did not know Weizmann but greatly admired him.
When he learned of the old gentleman's distress at not being
able to see the President, Jacobson went to Washington and
saw Truman on the plea of personal business. When the real
purpose of his visit was disclosed, Truman was not pleased. He
told Jacobson that his seeing Weizmann "would only result in
more wrong interpretations." But Jacobson was not to be put
off. (The story of the interview is charmingly told in Eban's
biography of Weizmann.) Knowing Truman's hero-worship
of Andrew Jackson, Jacobson likened his own admiration
for Weizmann to Truman's feeling for "Old Hickory" and
pointed out that Weizmann was an old and very sick man.

"He has traveled thousands of miles to see you, and now you put off seeing him. That isn't like you." After a long pause, Truman gave a typical answer to his old friend: "All right, you bald-headed son of a bitch, you win." Jacobson went to New York to tell Weizmann that he was expected at the White House on March 18. The meeting was secret and, as later described by Truman in his *Memoirs,* resulted in a complete and cordial understanding.

The next day was the day of the great American reversal at Lake Success, described above. When Truman learned what had happened, he was furious and greatly agitated. "How could this have happened?" he asked an assistant. "I assured Chaim Weizmann that we were for partition and would stick to it. He must think I am a plain liar." But Weizmann thought nothing of the sort. He had no doubt that Truman would keep faith with him. He alone among all the Zionists remained calm.

Weizmann's confidence was not misplaced. The action of the American delegation at Lake Success, undertaken without reference to the President, finally caused Truman's anger at the pro-Arab State Department to boil over. He was sick and tired of being a prisoner in the White House. The openly pro-Arab and less openly anti-Semitic top official, hitherto in charge of Middle Eastern affairs in the State Department, was replaced by Major General J. H. Hildring, an outspoken supporter of the partition plan. (Secretary of State Marshall was at this time in Moscow, attending the ill-fated four-power conference on Germany.*)

Inevitably, it took some time for the ponderous American ship of state to come about once more at Lake Success. The accomplishment of this task was replete with details which need not concern us here. While a series of confusing maneuvers went on, Truman remained silent. British policy, if such it may be called, was equally confused and confusing. Both the British and American governments appeared to fear at this time that a Zionist victory in Palestine might benefit the Soviet Union which was then beginning to put pressure upon the Western enclaves in Berlin. Even Truman was reluctant to let

* See J. P. Warburg, *Germany—Key to Peace* (Harvard University Press, Cambridge, Mass., 1954), pp. 40–45.

nature take its course in Palestine too fast. By this time (mid-April) the Jews had established a clear military superiority.

Originally, the fighting had been chiefly over control of the roads connecting the various settlements. The Arabs were better armed but operated under divided leadership. In the north the Syrian invading forces, which called themselves the Arab Liberation Army, were commanded by the Lebanese, Fawzi el Kawakji, of whom mention has been made previously; this army was acting under the authority of the Arab League. In the Jerusalem area the Arab forces were commanded by Abd el Kader el-Husseini,* whose orders came from the Mufti. Until he was killed leading an assault, Abd el Kader showed himself an effective commander and achieved a certain amount of success. Kawakji, on the other hand, was a boastful brigand whose forces were poorly led and suffered heavy defeats between Jaffa and Tel Aviv. The Jordanian Arab Legion, commanded by Glubb Pasha, was by far the best-trained and best-equipped Arab force, but it was hampered by having to obey the confused orders of the British, whereas Kawakji and Abd el Kader did not hesitate to violate the laws of the administration.

By the middle of April, the Jews had taken full control of the coastal area and controlled most of the roads, except that leading from Tel Aviv to Jerusalem. Jerusalem itself was under siege.

In March and April a huge flight of the civilian Arab population was under way. From Jaffa alone, 40,000 Arabs fled although the city authorities urged them to remain. The Jewish victories created a panic throughout the country; the "notables" were the first to leave and were then followed by the leaderless masses. We shall revert to this mass exodus presently.

Abdullah, the only Arab leader who seriously wished to avoid a full-scale war, had occupied Palestine east of the Jordan up to the outskirts of Jerusalem, according to his agreement with Bevin. But in April the British government became more nervous than ever about its strained relations with Egypt and, to appease the Mufti, ordered the Arab Legion to retire across the Jordan. Abdullah held another secret meeting with Golda

---

* Son of Musa Kazim el-Husseini, the first Arab major of Jerusalem and a cousin of Haj Amin.

Myerson and proposed a plan whereby the Jewish communities would be given autonomy within an Arab state pending a final settlement. Mrs. Myerson said that it was too late for that kind of a solution. Her parting with Abdullah was friendly.

While the debate at the United Nations went around in ever more confusing circles, Dr. Weizmann wrote President Truman a letter on April 9 stating that "the choice for our people, Mr. President, is between statehood and extermination." By this time, British policy had taken another one of those inexplicable turns and Creech-Jones was talking about a revision of the UNSCOP plan of partition in such a way as to give all but a tiny enclave to the Arabs. Yet, at the same time, the British insisted upon the withdrawal of the Arab Legion. At Lake Success the whole affair was now in a whirlpool of confusion.

On the night of April 23, which happened to be the night of the Jewish Passover, Weizmann received a message asking him to go immediately to the apartment of Judge Samuel Rosenman, an intimate advisor of Roosevelt and now a close friend of Truman. From Rosenman, Weizmann received a message from the President which he never revealed and which became known only ten years after his death. The message was that Truman had told Rosenman, "I have Weizmann on my conscience." Truman had reviewed the whole muddle of March 19 and to a certain extent blamed himself. He declared that his aim was now to get American policy back to where it belonged, in support of the Assembly resolution of November 1947. If this could be done and if a Jewish state were proclaimed, the President said that he would accord it immediate recognition.

The question was now one of timing. Secretary Marshall sent a message to the Jewish Agency warning against undue haste. Shertok flew to New York to consult Weizmann. Weizmann's answer was flat: "Proclaim the state, no matter what ensues!" Ben-Gurion needed no urging. On May 13 Weizmann wrote the President that the state of Israel would be proclaimed on the next day. When the letter arrived at the White House, it was realized that Weizmann occupied no official position. However, Eliahu Epstein, an Agency official, was in Washington. He was brought to the White House in a taxi to hand the President an official notification.

At four o'clock on the afternoon of May 14, Ben-Gurion convened the Va'ad Leumi in the Tel Aviv Museum of Modern Art and announced the establishment of a Jewish state to be known as Israel.

Earlier on the same day, Sir Alan Cunningham and the British garrison and administration had left Palestine by the port of Haifa.

True to his promise, Truman accorded Israel *de facto* recognition as soon as the news of Ben-Gurion's declaration had been received in Washington. "The old doctor will believe me now," he said.

16

The First Arab-Israeli War and Its Consequences 1948-1949

The day before the Jewish proclamation of independence, the Arab League Council met at Damascus and announced that "a state of war" existed between its members and "the Jewish rebels." On the following day, May 14, Assam Pasha, Secretary-General of the League, said at a press conference in Cairo:

"This will be a war of extermination and a momentous massacre."

In short order, Egypt, Iraq, Jordan, Lebanon and Syria declared war on Israel and sent their regular armies into action.

On May 15 the Provisional Government of Israel was organized with Ben-Gurion as Prime Minister. On the following day, Dr. Chaim Weizmann was unanimously elected President.

At Lake Success, during the confused debate which followed President Truman's announcement of recognition, Soviet Ambassador Gromyko declared that the Soviet Union would likewise extend recognition. (It did so on May 17.)

Simultaneously with their declaration of war, the Arab states imposed an economic blockade upon Israel, denying it the use of the Suez Canal. (The blockade remained in force after the armistice.)

During the first four weeks of the war, the Israelis asserted their complete supremacy, pushing back the Arab armies and partially lifting the siege of Jerusalem, although the Arabs remained in possession of the "Old City." On May 24 the United Nations Security Council called for a cease-fire; Israel yielded to the Council's demand but the Arabs rejected it. By this time the Syrians had been driven out of Israeli territory and the Iraqi army had been soundly defeated at the crossing of the Jordan near Beisan. The only serious setback was suffered by those Israeli forces which had driven through to Jerusalem but were forced with great bitterness to surrender the Jewish quarter in the Old City, a section within the walled city that had been inhabited by Jews since Roman times and contained a part of the ancient walls of the Temple.

On May 20 a special committee of the five big powers in the United Nations appointed a mediator, Count Folke Bernadotte, head of the Swedish Red Cross. On June 11 Bernadotte was able to arrange a four-week truce and to appoint a United Nations Truce Supervision Organization (UNETSO) to observe the truce and report violations. Neither this truce, which was broken on July 6, nor the truce which followed on July 18 brought peace. Israel was willing to halt the fighting and so were the Transjordanian, Iraqi, Sa'udi Arabian and Lebanese leaders, but the Syrians and Egyptians insisted upon an immediate resumption of the war. Between the 6th and the 18th of July, Israeli forces established themselves in almost the whole of what was to become the northern part of Israel. The towns of Lydda, Ramleh and Nazareth were captured and communications between Tel Aviv and Jerusalem were restored.

Now Israel was in no mood for compromise. Bernadotte's efforts to be fair to both sides earned him criticism from both. Sporadic fighting continued in spite of the truce of July 18. On September 17 Bernadotte was assassinated by Jewish terrorists. Although the assassins, presumably members of the Stern Gang, acted entirely on their own initiative, the murder added one more stain to the long list of incidents in which the Irgun and the Sternists had besmirched a Jewish record which, on the whole, had been as honorable as could be expected in the circumstances. (Lawlessness and savagery inevitably breed their counterparts even among the most highly civilized peoples.

What the Nazis had done reopened an age of primitive barbarism, as witness not only the terrorism practiced by Jews and Arabs in Palestine, but also the counter-atrocities committed by British troops.) Dr. Ralph Bunche, an American, was appointed as Bernadotte's successor—a man who proved himself admirably suited to the difficult task.

On September 20 a "government of Palestine" was set up by proclamation of the Mufti. Happily, on this occasion Haj Amin was disavowed by the Arabs. Five thousand Arab notables met on October 1, 1948, and acclaimed King Abdullah. (Haj Amin had hurt the originally just Arab cause as much if not more than Irgun and the Sternists had injured the cause of Zionism.)

Continued aggression by the Egyptian army in the south gave the Israelis a welcome excuse to continue the war. An attack launched on October 14 resulted in the capture of Beersheba. On the following day, Dr. Bunche managed to reimpose the truce but on October 28 fighting again broke out, this time in the north. This resulted in the final defeat of Kawakji's Syrians and the Israeli capture of the small part of Galilee that had remained in Arab hands.

The last campaign of the war began on December 22 after a confused period of skirmishing between the Israeli and Egyptian forces and resulted in Israel's gaining control of the Negev, including an Arab police post at the head of the Gulf of Aqaba. A strange feature of this last campaign was a British attempt to intervene on Egypt's behalf in accordance with the Anglo-Egyptian Treaty of 1936, which the Egyptians were seeking to annul! (The empire dream was slow in dissolving.)

In January 1949 Dr. Bunche established himself on the island of Rhodes and began with patience and skill the arduous task of getting the Arabs and Israelis to sign armistice agreements. Israel and Egypt signed on February 24, Lebanon on March 23, Jordan on April 3, and Syria on July 20. The long Syrian delay was caused by internal upheavals in the country.

In his last report, signed the day before his assassination, Count Bernadotte had recognized that the postwar frontiers should "not be rigidly controlled by the territorial arrangements envisaged in the resolution of November 29" (the U.N.

partition resolution). The armistice agreements signed in 1949
did not settle any frontiers, but as they provided for no further
use of force and the recognition of each party's right to "security from fear of attack," they implied that any territorial
changes from the armistice lines would have to come about by
mutual agreement. Since there were no peace treaties, there
were no such agreements.

The 1947 United Nations plan of partition had awarded Israel about 5,500 square miles of territory. Victory left the Israelis in possession of slightly over 8,000 square miles. The
gains were in Galilee and Acre to the north, in the central area
west of Jerusalem and in the Negev southwest of Gaza (see
map). The contention of Israel after the war was that the Jews
had accepted the partition terms while the Arabs had rejected
them; that, therefore, the United Nations boundaries were no
longer valid and Israel had a right to retain the additional conquered territory. The failure of the United Nations to make
any attempt to enforce the 1947 partition terms and the statement of Count Bernadotte above quoted made this contention
almost unassailable.

The question of boundaries was not, however, the chief
question at issue. The Arab aim had been to destroy Israel altogether, and it was the utter failure to do so that rankled, rather
than the fact that Israel's victory had expanded its boundaries.

A much more burning question was that of the Arab refugees from Palestine. At the beginning of the undeclared war, it
was estimated that there had been 650,000 Arabs living in the
territory allotted to the Jewish state. Of these, all but about
175,000 had fled before the advance of the Jewish forces. Arabs
and Jews accused each other of having caused this mass flight
by calculated measures. There was a relatively small element of
truth in these charges either way, but the known facts belie
both basic contentions.

There is no evidence of an agreed Jewish policy to evict the
settled Arab population; on the contrary, there is considerable
evidence, such as that already cited with respect to Jaffa, that
up to the July armistice the Jews tried to prevent the flight. It
is known that when the Jewish mayor of Jaffa appealed to the
Arab leadership to halt the flight, the Arab Committee not only

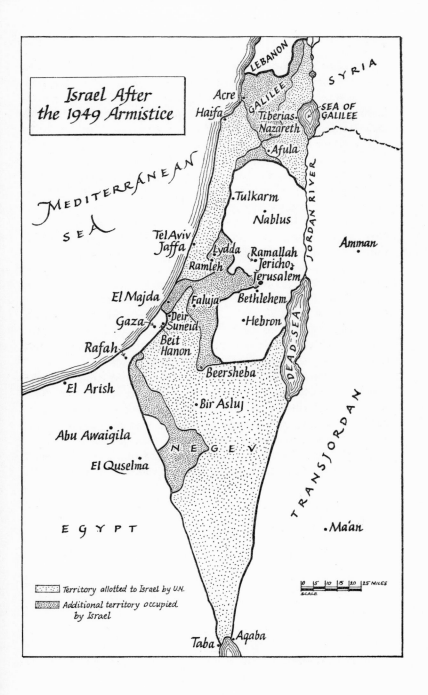

Israel After
the 1949 Armistice

LEBANON
SYRIA
Acre
Haifa
GALILEE
Tiberias
Nazareth
SEA OF
GALILEE
Afula

MEDITERRANEAN
SEA

Tulkarm
Nablus

Tel Aviv
Jaffa
Lydda
Ramleh
Ramallah
Jericho
Jerusalem
Amman

JORDAN RIVER

El Majda
Faluja
Bethlehem
Gaza
Deir
Suneid
Hebron
DEAD SEA
Rafah
Beit
Hanon
Beersheba
El Arish

Bir Asluj

Abu Awaigila
NEGEV
TRANSJORDAN

El Quselma

EGYPT
Ma'an

0 5 10 15 20 25 MILES
SCALE

Territory allotted to Israel by U.N.

Additional territory occupied
by Israel

Taba
Aqaba

refused but afterwards declared that it had ordered the flight from the city. A year later the Arab leaders declared that they had "proudly asked for the removal of the Arabs to the neighboring Arab countries." * The Jews did not invent although they later made extensive use of the myth created by the Arabs to the effect that the mass exodus was a planned Arab maneuver to clear the ground for the invading Arab armies. Until mid-1948 the mass exodus seems to have been mostly a fear-inspired movement of ignorant people who had been badly led and then deserted by their panic-stricken leaders.

In June and July 1948 the situation changed. Realizing that they were no longer bound by the UNSCOP provisions, which the Arabs had rejected, the Israelis adopted a more ruthless policy of encouraging if not actually forcing the Arab population to leave the villages they captured. Even then, when the Arabs refused to be stampeded by Jewish propaganda and stood firm, no harm was done to them. When Nazareth fell to the Jews, the mayor refused to be intimidated and kept his people together, with the result that Nazareth remained the largest and most prosperous Arab community within Israel.

To say, however, that the claims and counterclaims as to the cause of the exodus were exaggerated or untrue is not to deny that more than half a million mostly innocent Arabs were rendered homeless, and this tragic result was to plague Arab-Jewish relations in the years to come.

For the time being, we must now turn our attention away from Palestine and toward other developments in the Middle East.

* Rony E. Gabbay, *A Political Study of the Arab-Jewish Conflict.*

PART THREE

17

The Truman Years—
Cold War in the Middle East

During the years when Israel was being born out of the chaos
of the British mandate, the great wartime coalition disintegrated and Europe became divided into two hostile camps separated by what Sir Winston Churchill called the Iron Curtain.
A year after Churchill's sounding the trumpet of the incipient
Cold War between the Soviet Union and the West, Truman
declared his global anti-communist crusade; the last effort to
solve the problem of Germany failed and Germany became the
major battleground of the Cold War. With the final failure of
the Potsdam agreement, the Marshall Plan, originally offered to
all of Europe, inevitably became a program to strengthen only
Western Europe, including the western part of a divided Germany, against communist encroachment or penetration. The
communist coup in Czechoslovakia, early in 1948, caused Britain, France, Holland, Belgium and Luxembourg to form a defense alliance (the Brussels Treaty). The United States, Britain
and France merged their zones of occupation in Germany into
a new West German state. The Soviet Union created a communist satellite state in East Germany and attempted by blockade to force the Western powers to evacuate the three western
sectors of Berlin.

In the same year American intervention helped to bring
about the defeat of the powerful Communist Party in the Ital-

ian elections; the French Communists were excluded from participation in the unstable French government; and Yugoslavia defected from the Soviet orbit. The latter development deprived the Greek Communist rebels of their sanctuary and enabled the Rightist Greek government to suppress the rebellion.

In 1949 the West European defenses were further bolstered when the United States and Canada signed the North Atlantic Treaty with Britain, France, Holland, Belgium, Luxembourg, Norway, Denmark, Iceland and Portugal. The signatories pledged themselves to consider an attack upon any one of them as an attack upon all. For the first time in its history, the United States entered upon a commitment of this sort.

Before the ink was dry on the treaty, the commitment was stretched at French insistence from a simple declaration of solidarity into an American undertaking to defend Western Europe at its frontiers. Since the Iron Curtain ran through the heart of Germany, this commitment clearly foreshadowed the inclusion of a rearmed West Germany in the North Atlantic Treaty Organization, although Secretary of State Acheson assured the Senate that such would not be the case.*

While the Cold War in its early stages was concentrated in Europe, contemporary developments in Asia had an equal if not a greater impact upon the Middle East. These developments were:

1. The freeing of India, Burma and Ceylon from British rule and the subsequent division of the Indian subcontinent into two nations—India and Pakistan.

2. The unsuccessful attempt of the United States to prevent the defeat of the Chinese Nationalist regime and the subsequent flight of the Nationalists to Formosa.

3. The success of the American occupation policy in Japan.

4. The vacillation of the United States in first supporting the

---

* The writer's persistent criticism of American postwar policy in Europe (except for the Marshall Plan, which he supported) has been stated in five books: *Germany—Bridge or Battleground* (1947); *Put Yourself in Marshall's Place* (1948); *Last Call for Common Sense* (1949); *Germany—Key to Peace* (1954); and *The United States in the Postwar World* (1966). A sixth study, *Agenda for Action Toward Peace Through Disengagement* (1957), linked a possible disengagement in Germany to an arms embargo and a mutual hands-off agreement in the Middle East.

Dutch in their attempt to keep the Dutch East Indies as a colonial possession and in then supporting the Indonesian struggle
for independence.

5. The aid given by the United States to France in its attempt to re-establish colonial rule over Indo-China.

6. The division of South Korea at the 38th parallel; the
North Korean attack upon the South; the U.N.-sanctioned
American intervention; the conversion by the United States of
a successful police action into a war of conquest, provoking
Chinese intervention and resulting in defeat; and the stalemate at
the 38th parallel.*

The broad impact of these Asian developments upon the
Middle East was to make the Middle Eastern nations aware of
European weakness, of American vacillation and American obsession with communism and, above all, of the growing power
of revolutionary, anti-colonial nationalism.

With this European and Asian context in mind, we may now
consider the course of events in the Middle East during this
period.

Turkey

In spite of Churchill's strenuous efforts to win Turkey as an
ally, Turkey had maintained her neutrality throughout most of
the war. In 1945 Turkey was permitted to declare war on Germany in order to qualify as a founding member of the United
Nations. (Turkish neutrality had tended to favor the Axis;
large amounts of chrome were shipped to Germany in spite of
Allied protests. Pro-Axis sentiment was largely due to the fact
that Russia, Turkey's traditional enemy, was allied with the
United States and Britain.)

Since Britain had with Turkey no such contractual alliance
relationship as it had with other Middle Eastern states, the
United States was able, at the conclusion of the war, to deal
directly with Ankara. And when Britain handed over its responsibility in both Turkey and Greece to the United States in

* For a brief discussion of American postwar policy in the Far East,
see J. P. Warburg, *Western Intruders* (Atheneum, New York, 1967).

1947, the United States obtained a free hand in helping the
Turks to modernize, train and equip their large but antiquated
army. This task was so ably performed by an American military
mission that Turkey was able successfully to resist Stalin's demands for the cession of Turkish territory in the region of
Kars, as well as Stalin's insistence upon a revision of the Montreux Convention in such a way as to give the Soviet Union
joint control with Turkey over the Bosporus and Dardanelles.*

Once Turkey's army was modernized, it became, until West
Germany was armed, the strongest ground force in Europe,
except for the Soviet Army. In order to link this powerful
force with NATO (the newly formed North Atlantic Treaty
Organization), Turkey was offered an associate membership in
1950, but this did not suit the Turks, who wanted full membership if they were to guard NATO's southern flank. However, Britain and the United States were thinking of Turkey not
only in that capacity but as the cornerstone of a vaguely conceived defense of the Middle East against the Soviet Union.

Middle East defense rested upon relatively small British
forces in the area and upon bilateral British treaties with
Egypt, Iraq, Jordan and Iran. British rights and bases under
these treaties were non-transferable, even if Britain had wished
to transfer them to the United States. This vastly complicated
the whole problem, especially as Britain lacked the necessary
military and economic strength to forge an effective alliance.
More important, apart from Turkey and Iran, none of the
Middle East countries, except possibly Iraq, was aware of any
Soviet menace. The Arab states were far more concerned with
ridding themselves of the familiar and deeply resented imperialism of the West than with protecting themselves from any
Soviet threat that might be lurking behind the Caucasus. Moreover, the Arab states were deeply disunited, and the dissension
among them was exacerbated when defeat at the hands of Israel
left them blaming each other for their humiliation.

Ever since its liberation from French rule, Syria had been the

* Stalin had several times raised this question during the war. Truman
had proposed at Potsdam the internationalization of all the major
international waterways, but nothing had come of the suggestion. The
Montreux Convention gives Turkey the right to close the straits in time
of war.

focal point of intra-Arab dissension. Historically, Syria had always been a bone of contention between the rulers of the Nile Valley and the successive rulers of Mesopotamia. After World War II, Syria became the object of rivalry between Egypt and the Hashemite kingdoms of Iraq and Jordan. The Hashemite dream, backed by Britain, was a union of the Fertile Crescent which, if consummated, would have dominated Arab western Asia. This ran counter to Egyptian aspirations toward leadership of the Arab world.

Syria itself was unstable, flirting first with one side and then with the other. The first of a long series of revolutions against a so-called republican government dominated by the wealthy landowners was followed by a succession of army coups d'état, in spite of which a social-revolutionary movement gained increasing political power. Limited measures of land reform antedated the similar reforms of the Egyptian revolution, and vague ideas of pan-Arabism took shape in Syria before they developed in Egypt. The extremely complicated postwar history of Syrian political development has recently been described in two British studies undertaken under the auspices of the Royal Institute of International Affairs (Chatham House).*

The traditional rivalry between Egypt and the rulers of Mesopotamia received a new dimension in the postwar period by reason of the fact that the Hashemite kingdoms of Jordan and Iraq were client states of Britain, while Egypt was traditionally and increasingly anti-British.

In the early part of World War II, the Wafd Nationalists in Egypt, led by Nahas Pasha, had been loyal to Britain as against the Axis Powers, while the Palace had indulged in pro-Nazi intrigues. In 1942 British troops surrounded the Palace and forced King Faruq to appoint a Wafd government under Nahas Pasha which, in spite of vast corruption, remained intermittently in power throughout the war. However, once the tide of war had turned in 1943, Wafd Nationalism became increasingly hostile to Britain, and by 1950 the Wafdists were

---

* Patrick Seale, *The Struggle for Syria*, and Malcolm Kerr, *The Arab Cold War*. The latter work is particularly valuable for anyone seeking to understand the convolutions of Egyptian-Syrian relationships during the 1961–1967 period.

demanding the abrogation of the 1936 Treaty and the termina-
tion of the Anglo-Egyptian condominium in the Sudan. Egypt
was no longer a secure base for British power in the Middle
East, yet no other base for defense of the Suez Canal was available. Iraq was too far away and Jordan was not sufficiently
strong.

Under American pressure to multilateralize Middle East defense, the British government invited Australia, New Zealand,
the Union of South Africa, France and Turkey to join in an
Allied Middle East Command in the hope of persuading Egypt
to allow itself to become an international rather than a British
base. The Wafd government brusquely declined this overture
and proceeded unilaterally to abrogate the 1936 Treaty—an action denounced as contrary to international law by Acheson,
the American Secretary of State.

As anti-British disorders grew in frequency and violence,
King Faruq dismissed the ministry, dissolved the legislature,
postponed new elections and entrusted government under martial law to a Palace clique authorized to govern by decree. Such
a government could obviously remain in power only with the
consent of the army.

On July 23, 1952, a group of young army officers—except
for Major-General Mohammad Nagib, none was above the age
of forty or held a rank higher than that of lieutenant-colonel—
seized power in a sudden coup. The junta was originally ani-
mated by little more than a desire to correct corruption and
inefficiency in the armed forces. However, once General
Nagib became Chief of Staff, it became a relatively easy matter
to compel Faruq to abdicate and to force the resignation of his
political advisors. The old-guard army leaders were likewise
compelled to resign and the junta found itself in control of the
government. Having undertaken its action with the intention of
remaining non-political, the junta soon discovered that corruption could be cured only by far-reaching reform. Attract-
ing to its service a number of Western-trained fiscal and agricultural experts, the junta embarked upon tax reform and a
radical redistribution of land ownership. In contrast to the ideo-
logically inspired Syrian revolutionaries, the men of the junta
were essentially pragmatists in their efforts at reform.

So far as foreign policy was concerned, Nagib and his followers were no more interested than their Wafd predecessors in any plan for Middle East defense in which Egypt would be used as a base by foreign powers. In Egypt and elsewhere in the Middle East, Britain and the United States were slow to realize that the desire for national independence was infinitely stronger than fear of Soviet invasion. As a matter of fact, the socialist organization of the Soviet Union and Soviet hostility to Western imperialism caused many Arab revolutionaries to regard the Soviet Union as a possible friend rather than as a potential enemy. This tendency was particularly marked in Syria, where communism quickly gained a foothold. In Egypt, on the other hand, there developed an attitude of non-alignment in the Cold War—a posture soon to be defined as "positive neutrality"—quite similar to that adopted by India under Jawarharlal Nehru.

The failure of the Hashemite kingdoms to win Syria to their side against Egypt, the hostility between the Hashemites and Egypt and Egypt's hostility to Britain thus left the would-be planners of a Middle East defense with little to build upon in the Arab world, except Britain's two client kingdoms.

Iran

There remained, as possible allies in the Cold War, Turkey, which has already been discussed, and the other Moslem but non-Arab northern state of Iran.

The ancient Persian throne had been seized from the weak Qajar dynasty in 1925 by Reza Pahlevi, a strong man who had risen from the ranks of the army, assumed the title of Shahinshah and changed the name of his country to Iran. This strong ruler had energetically set about modernizing his country and had accomplished much, but because of his pro-German leanings during World War II, he had been deposed in 1941 in favor of his young Swiss-educated son, Muhammad Reza Pahlevi.

In view of Iran's long experience with aggressive Russian imperialism, it might have been expected that Iran, like Turkey, would willingly become a Cold War ally against the Soviet Union. But here, as elsewhere, the British had overplayed their hand.

Unlike Britain's difficulties with Egypt, which were strictly political and military, her trouble with Iran stemmed from commercial as well as political considerations. The Anglo-Iranian Oil Company (originally the Anglo-Persian Oil Company) was owned by the British government and had secured immensely profitable concessions for the exploitation of Iran's oil resources. Since 1908, when oil was first discovered in Persia, Iran had developed into the chief supplier of petroleum products not only to Britain but, through Britain, to most of Western Europe. The AIOC had built a huge refinery at Abadan, from where a great fleet of AIOC tankers carried Iranian oil to the world markets. Under the terms of the concession, Iran shared only to a minor extent in the profits gained from the sale of oil and not at all in the profits of the refinery or the tanker fleet.*

The terms of the concession had come increasingly under attack by the Nationalist Front, which opposed the authoritarian rule of the Shah. In 1950 the pro-Western Prime Minister 'Ali Razmara had proposed to Britain a modest increase in the Iranian share of the profits, pointing out that the Arabian-American (ARAMCO) consortium was paying Sa'udi Arabia 50 percent of its profit after paying United States income taxes. The AIOC had turned down Razmara's request on legalistic and commercial grounds without considering the political implications. In March 1951 Razmara was assassinated by a religious fanatic. A month later Mohammad Mossadeq, leader of the National Front, became Prime Minister and the Shah left the country. Mossadeq proceeded promptly to nationalize the whole Iranian oil industry, including the refinery at Abadan.

The immediate consequences of nationalization were neither as beneficial to Iran nor as disastrous for Britain as might have been expected. Iran lacked the trained personnel to operate the properties, particularly the refinery. Large-scale unemployment resulted. So far as Britain was concerned, reserves stored

---

* Iran's share of AIOC's profits was variously estimated at from 15 to 30 percent, depending upon who made the calculations.

at Abadan were sufficient to supply her needs for over a year
and production at Bahrein was easily and rapidly increased.
However, the political effect upon Anglo-Iranian relations was
disastrous, for the time being destroying the hope that Iran
might, like Turkey, become a strong link in Middle East defense.

Israel-Arab Relations

Once the armistice agreements were signed, the United Nations appointed a Conciliation Commission composed of
French, Turkish and American members. Its task was to promote the negotiation of peace treaties, but instead of following
Dr. Bunche's successful procedure in bringing each of the
Arab states into a bilateral meeting with Israel, the Commission
made the mistake of attempting to deal with the disunited Arab
states as an entity. The result was utter failure.

In spite of the negative votes cast by the Arab states, Israel's
application for membership in the United Nations was approved. The Commission then set up a Technical Committee to
study the question of what was to be done about the Arab
refugees from Palestine, whose numbers were estimated as being about 700,000. A year later a United Nations agency,
UNRWA, was set up to provide refugee relief.

The Palestinian refugees were not the only people displaced
as a result of the conflict. There were also Jewish refugees
from some of the Arab countries—47,000 Jews, long settled in
Yemen, were airlifted to Israel. During 1950–1951 approximately 100,000 more were brought in from Iraq, where the
government had confiscated their property; others came from
North Africa. The resettlement in Israel of these Jewish refugees diminished Israel's capacity to re-absorb the Palestinian
Arabs. Israel claimed that the property confiscated from Jews
in the Arab states constituted a partial offset to the property
lost by the Arabs in Palestine. There was plenty of room for
the Palestinian Arabs in sparsely settled Jordan and Iraq, but
the Arab governments insisted upon the right of the Palestinians to return to their homes, as, indeed, many of them wished

to do. The issue became a festering sore, with the Arabs refusing to talk peace unless the refugees were permitted to return and Israel refusing to discuss the refugee problem unless peace treaties were negotiated.

In its efforts to persuade the Arabs to drop their economic boycott of Israel, the Conciliation Commission was equally unsuccessful.

On May 25, 1950, the United States, Britain and France endeavored to aid the peace-making efforts of the United Nations by issuing a tripartite declaration in which the three Western nations undertook to guarantee all the participants in the recent war against any encroachment of the frontiers set by the armistice agreements.

In July of the same year Egypt closed the Suez Canal to Israeli shipping. After listening for over a year to Israel's protests against this action, the Security Council adopted a resolution on September 1, 1951, ordering Egypt to reopen the Canal. When Egypt flatly refused to comply with the order and the Security Council failed to take any further action, the prestige of the United Nations, which had been greatly enhanced by its intervention in Korea, sank to a new low in the Middle East.

Among the Arab leaders, Abdullah of Jordan was the only one who showed any inclination toward a reconciliation with Israel, partly perhaps because he had been able formally to annex to Jordan that part of Palestine west of the Jordan which his troops had occupied during the war. Probably for the very reason that he had shown an inclination toward a peaceful settlement, Abdullah was murdered by one of the Mufti's fanatical henchmen.

There matters stood when President Truman's term expired. Truman had come into office at the high tide of victory and with the United States at the summit of its power. He left a nation bogged down in the Korean War, torn by internal dissension and uncertain of itself and of its purposes in a world divided into two hostile camps. For the Middle East, the Cold War was meaningless, except insofar as the conflict between rival imperialisms presented opportunities for playing off one side against the other.

Truman's policy in the Middle East had been a strange mixture of conflicting aims and interests arising from disparate,
deeply rooted forces in the American society. A feeling of kin-
ship with Britain was contradicted by traditional American
anti-colonialism. Sympathy for Israel, reinforced by the large
Jewish community in the United States and by American outrage at the Nazi atrocities, was offset by pro-Arab feelings engendered by Protestant and Catholic missions courting what
was believed to be a disintegrating Moslem world. (There
were probably more Christian proselytizers than communists in
the Middle East at this time, except in Iran, where a strong
communist-influenced Tudeh Party existed, and in Syria,
where Marxism appealed to parts of the revolutionary Left.)
Above all, there was the powerful influence silently exerted by
the fabulously rich oil lobby, closely linked to the armed services. And over the whole of this mixture of forces lay the fer-
vor of anti-communism which each pressure-group used as the
rationalization for its activities. The result could hardly have
been anything other than a shapeless vacillating policy that
made more enemies than friends.

18

The Disastrous Diplomacy of John Foster Dulles— The Crises of 1956 and 1958

Between late 1951 and early 1954 almost the entire cast of major characters operating in the Middle East changed.

When Dwight D. Eisenhower became President of the United States and appointed John Foster Dulles as his Secretary of State, Attlee and Bevin had already passed from the scene; Churchill was back as Prime Minister with Anthony Eden as his Foreign Secretary.

In March 1953 Josef Stalin died and Georgi Malenkov briefly became the top man in the Soviet Union. In August of that year Mossadeq was overthrown and the Shah returned to Tehran. Before the end of the year France expelled the Sultan of Morocco.

In February 1954 Gamal Abdel Nasser replaced General Nagib as head of the Egyptian government, and in the same month an army coup ousted Syria's President Shishekly.

Early in 1953 Secretary Dulles took a trip to the Middle East in order to see for himself the existing state of confusion. The first conclusion he reached was that the United States must rid itself of the incubus of being known in the Middle East as the chief supporter of Israel. Setting out to woo the Arabs, he called upon General Nagib and, presenting him with the symbolic gift of a pistol, assured him that the previous administration's pro-Israel policy was a thing of the past.

Dulles had been a Wall Street corporation lawyer and no doubt appreciated the importance of the rapidly growing investment of American oil companies in the Middle East. But in even larger measure his pro-Arab orientation derived from his determination to complete a band of physical encirclement around the entire vast periphery of the Sino-Soviet orbit of power. Although he had sharply criticized the Truman administration's policy with respect to Europe, he adopted it lock, stock and barrel, determined to fulfill Acheson's aim of bringing a rearmed West Germany into the NATO alliance and to extend this policy into Asia and the Middle East. (One of Acheson's last acts had been to bring Greece and Turkey into NATO as full members, and this had predisposed the Turkish government to cooperate in setting up some sort of Middle East defense.)

The full story of Mossadeq's overthrow in Iran still remains to be revealed, but enough has leaked out to make it practically certain that this event was engineered by the United States Central Intelligence Agency, whose head was the brother of the Secretary of State. Whether the plan was hatched by the Dulles brothers or whether it had been set in motion under the Truman administration is not clear, nor is it known whether the secret operation was revealed to President Eisenhower. The effect of the action was to strengthen the hands of the Shah and of the conservative, pro-Western elements in Iran.

As it turned out, the chief beneficiaries of Mossadeq's overthrow were the American oil companies. After almost two years of negotiations, a deal was made (in August 1954) with the Iranian government under which Iran obtained the same 50 percent share of profits as that which ARAMCO granted to Sa'udi Arabia, but the deal was no longer between Iran and the British concessionaire; it included a substantial participation by American interests, and this aroused strong resentment in Britain.*

---

* The new consortium agreement left the newly formed British Petroleum Company with a 40 percent interest. The remaining 60 percent was divided as follows:

The Royal Dutch-Shell Company	14 percent
The French Petrol Company	6 percent
The Gulf Oil Corporation	8 percent

Anglo-American relations were further strained by the pressure exerted by Dulles upon Britain to settle its differences with the Egyptian government by relinquishing its condominium rights in the Sudan and moving up the date of its evacuation of the Suez base. (The condominium was ended in February 1953, and in July 1954 Britain agreed to evacuate Suez ahead of the schedule provided by the 1936 Anglo-Egyptian Treaty.) Beyond antagonizing the British, Dulles accomplished little by his wooing of Egypt and what little goodwill he gained was soon to be lost by his subsequent Middle East maneuvers.

When it became apparent that Egypt wanted no part of an alliance with the Western powers, Dulles turned his thoughts to the creation of a "Northern Tier Alliance," consisting of states bordering upon the Soviet Union. Turkey, the most willing of these states, undertook to form an alliance with Moslem Pakistan. The two widely separated countries signed a defense pact on April 2, 1954. A month later, the United States signed a mutual assistance treaty with Pakistan. All that was needed now was to fill in the gap between the two flanks. Iran joined willingly, under the impression that it was joining Turkey and the United States. As it turned out when Dulles was through maneuvering, Iran was to discover that it had joined not the United States but Britain. (When the British saw what Dulles was up to, they had demanded the right to join in the alliance and to bring in their Arab ally, Iraq.) Dulles, probably because of his attempt to woo Sa'udi Arabia and Egypt, decided not to sign the Baghdad Pact, although the United States did later join the military committee of what became known as the CENTO alliance. The signatories were Turkey, Iran, Iraq, Pakistan and the United Kingdom.

It is impossible to overstate the havoc wrought by this American diplomacy. In order to understand its ramifications,

Socony-Vacuum (now Socony Mobil)	8 percent
Standard Oil of California	8 percent
Standard Oil of New Jersey	8 percent
The Texas Company	8 percent

In 1955 one-eighth of the interest of the five American Oil companies was transferred to and divided among nine other American companies.

For further details of the exceedingly complicated arrangement, see Donald N. Wilber, *Iran, Past and Present*, pp. 225–226.

we shall have to shift our focus temporarily to Asia.

In 1953–1954 France was fighting a losing battle in Indo-China. The United States had extended massive economic assistance to the French effort, but in 1954 the French faced complete defeat. Dulles and Admiral Radford, Chairman of the American Joint Chiefs of Staff, together with Vice President Richard Nixon, wanted to intervene with American air power to save the French from final defeat in the battle of Dienbienphu. They were prevented from doing so by Britain's refusal to join in any such venture and by President Eisenhower's veto, backed by the advice of General Matthew Ridgway, the U.S. Army Chief of Staff. Eden's refusal to join in Dulles' plan aroused the lasting enmity of the American Secretary of State.

After the French defeat, French Premier Mendès-France signed the Geneva Accords of 1954, by which Indo-China was divided into three independent states—Laos, Cambodia and Vietnam—and Vietnam was temporarily partitioned at the 17th parallel into a communist-controlled North Vietnam and a non-communist South Vietnam, with the understanding that all-Vietnamese elections would be held in 1956. Dulles refused to sign the Geneva Accords, but the United States agreed to respect them. The remainder of the Vietnamese story need not concern us here.*

Frustrated in his desire to keep France in Indo-China as part of the encircling wall against the Sino-Soviet orbit, Dulles proceeded to organize a Southeast Asia Treaty Organization (SEATO) to fill the gap. The only two mainland Asian nations whom he could interest in this alliance were Thailand and Pakistan. Dulles saw Pakistan as the link between SEATO and the Middle East alliance which he was trying to construct. Pakistan cheerfully joined both organizations, not because it was vitally interested in the Cold War but because it wanted military and economic assistance from the United States. It wanted arms, not to resist Soviet or Chinese aggression, but to strengthen its position vis-à-vis its neighbors, India and Afghanistan. The result achieved by Dulles in rearming Pakistan was to alarm India and to force that hard-pressed country (whose neutrality Dulles denounced as "immoral") to divert funds much needed

* See Warburg, *Western Intruders,* pp. 209–220.

for economic development into countervailing armament. A
further result was to drive Afghanistan toward closer relations
with the Soviet Union.

We may now return to the effect of Dulles diplomacy upon
the Middle East.

Having antagonized the British by his attempts to woo
Egypt, Dulles now alienated Egypt by arming Iraq, Egypt's
rival for leadership in the Arab world. Iraq was under the
strong pro-Western leadership of Premier Nuri-as-Said, but
Iraq wanted to be armed, not against possible Soviet aggression,
but against Israel and to fortify its position as the would-be
leader of the Arab world.

As for Iran, the Shah, who had wanted close relations with
the United States to fortify Iran's position against both the Soviet Union and Britain, now found himself allied with Britain,
Iraq, Turkey and Pakistan without having the United States as
an ally.

Of all the CENTO signatories, only Turkey remained relatively undisturbed by the machinations of the American Secretary of State. Turkey was not particularly anti-Israel, it was
not involved in Arab politics, and it really did want to be
armed against possible Soviet aggression.

Thus, what Dulles accomplished was not to unite the Middle
East nations as allies in his anti-Soviet crusade but to split the
Arab world, alienating both Egypt and Britain and increasing
the danger to Israel. So far as Israel was concerned, Dulles
acted as if the United States had no commitment whatever to
preserve Israel's existence.

Before we consider the next chapter in Dulles diplomacy, we
must turn to the developments in the Arab Maghreb during
this period.

A long-simmering revolt of the North African Arabs against
French colonialism first broke out into the open in 1950. The
conditions which inspired the rebellion in Morocco were common to all of French North Africa.

The population of Morocco was roughly 9,000,000, of which
some 350,000 were French and other European settlers. The
European minority managed, controlled and ruthlessly exploited the Arab-Berber majority. During their forty years

of occupation of Morocco as a protectorate, the French made many physical investments and improvements, but their development schemes were undertaken exclusively for their own benefit. They built up an economy based upon discrimination in which Europeans owned the best land, most of the mines and practically all of the industries. The natives were serfs living in slums and performing manual labor at discriminatory low wages. There were only about two dozen primary schools for the entire native population. Child labor was viciously exploited. Education, like every other sort of privilege, was reserved for the French. U.S. Supreme Court Justice William O. Douglas was quoted as saying after a visit to Morocco: "The French have fastened a milking machine on Morocco for their own benefit." *

In 1950 Sultan Sidi Mohammed V proposed some mild, long-overdue reforms. He did not propose to expel the French; in fact, he proposed to guarantee them against expropriation. He demanded an educational program, a free press, freedom of assembly and a freely elected representative government. He asserted the right of Moroccan labor to form trade unions.

The French broke with the Sultan over these moderate demands, using force and terror to suppress a strike and to maintain their police-state rule. The Istiqlal nationalist party was outlawed and many of its leaders were jailed. In 1953 Marshal Juin, appointed as Resident-General to suppress the revolt, arranged a coup d'état with the help of the powerful Thami El Glaoui, the Berber pasha of Marrakesh. The Sultan was deposed and sent into exile and his unpopular cousin Moulay Mohammed Ben Arafa was installed in his place. From then on, the relations between the French and the natives went from bad to worse. In 1955 there were bloody disorders. The new Sultan agreed to "reforms" that were purely nominal and increased the spirit of revolt. New "popular assemblies" were, for example, created in which the French minority was given the right to elect half of the members. The French continued to control the bureaucracy and the police, backed by ever-increasing military forces. Probably the only reason why the French colons refrained from demanding complete French sovereignty was that this

* *Look*, October 19, 1954.

would have subjected them to French taxation.

From Morocco the spirit of revolt spread to Algeria and Tunisia. The 8,000,000 Algerians were theoretically French citizens, but of the 30 representatives Algeria sent to the National Assembly in Paris, 15 were elected by less than 1,000,000 European settlers. In local affairs one European's vote was equal to that of eight Moslems. In both Algeria and Tunisia the nationalist movements were outlawed.

The majority of the French people were unsympathetic toward their government's policy in North Africa, but the power of the colons and the business interests allied to them in their political lobby was such that no French government could see its way to break with the past.

In 1954, with Tunisia momentarily the focus of rebellion, Pierre Mendès-France, who had just brought about the French withdrawal from Indo-China, proposed to grant Tunisia autonomy within the French Union. One of the key figures in the parliamentary intrigue that brought about his subsequent fall was René Mayer, a former Premier whose constituency was in Algeria. Edgar Faure, succeeding Mendès-France, eventually managed with the help of Tunisia's remarkable leader Habib Bourguiba to put through Tunisian autonomy. By this time— April 1955—all of the Maghreb was seething with revolt.

When Faure moved to depose the unpopular Sultan of Morocco and to establish a regency, it was already too late for anything less than a grant of complete independence. This was finally conceded to Morocco and Tunisia in 1956.

When revolt had broken out in Algeria in 1954, Mendès-France had not followed the moderate policy which he had pursued in Tunisia. Drawing a sharp distinction between giving autonomy to a protectorate and permitting a nationalist movement to make headway in a part of Metropolitan France, he had sent in troops to suppress the revolt. In the following year Faure called up reservists and raised the number of troops to 180,000—and still the rebellion grew. When Guy Mollet came into office in 1956, the situation was completely out of hand. By July of that year there were over 400,000 French troops in Algeria, many of them withdrawn from NATO. "Pacification" was costing France about $1 billion a year. Such reforms as were undertaken were too little and too late.

One might have expected the anti-colonial United States to make an effort to persuade its French ally not to repeat the errors made in Indo-China. After all, the United States was indirectly paying for much of the French effort in Algeria. No such effort was made. Secretary Dulles did not wish to antagonize his French NATO ally, although he had shown no such consideration for Britain.

The Algerian Liberation Front received encouragment and help from most of the Arab states, especially from President Nasser. This had the important effect of causing France to become extremely friendly toward Israel—a friendship which was soon to be expressed in supplying Israel with arms and in open hostility toward Egypt.

Egypt sought countervailing arms from the United States, and when these were not obtainable upon acceptable terms, Nasser turned to the Soviet bloc, obtaining a large supply of modern weapons from Czechoslovakia. The deal was consummated in 1955, at a time when President Eisenhower was preparing for a meeting with the Soviet leaders at Geneva, but the news of the transaction did not come out until after the Summit meeting.

Dulles was enraged. What his Middle East diplomacy had accomplished now appeared to be this: he had constructed a Northern Tier Alliance at the expense of alienating Egypt, splitting the Arab world and thereby permitting the Soviet Union to leapfrog over the frontier defenses to obtain in Egypt its long-sought political foothold in the Middle East.

Faced with the collapse of his policy, Secretary Dulles made frantic efforts to forestall further Soviet penetration of Egypt by hastening American aid toward building the Aswan High Dam, President Nasser's pet development project. When he encountered reluctance in the Congress and discovered that Moscow was apparently in no great hurry to outbid the United States in carrying out this giant project, Dulles abruptly reversed his course, withdrawing the offer of American aid and doing so in a message which would have offended even a government less sensitive than that of President Nasser. Nasser's reply was to seize and nationalize the Suez Canal!

(Dulles was later reported to have said that his action had been a deliberate gambit to force a showdown in the Cold War. It seems more likely that he simply wanted to "teach Nasser a lesson." Whatever the motivation, the United States government was totally unprepared for the crisis which this action precipitated. According to C. L. Sulzberger's column of April 7, 1957 in *The New York Times*, "the State Department's Planning Staff did not even have a position paper covering the eventuality.")

When Britain and France reacted to the seizure of the Canal by threatening military action, Dulles was apparently surprised and shocked. President Eisenhower sent him to London to urge a peaceful solution. Throughout August and September, Dulles put forward various schemes for the participation of "the Canal Users" in its management. Egypt showed itself not unwilling to accept a proposal which would not involve a derogation of its sovereignty, but Eden was unwilling to make any such proposal. He was enraged at Nasser because he attributed the earlier dismissal of General Glubb by King Hussein of Jordan to Nasser's influence. Even before the seizure of the Canal, Eden had determined to destroy Nasser, if necessary by the use of force. A more flexible and less devious diplomat than Dulles might have restrained Eden, whose uncharacteristic rage at Nasser was in part due to illness; but Eden and Dulles disliked and distrusted each other. The full story of these negotiations and of the subsequent collusion of Britain and France with Israel has only recently been revealed by Anthony Nutting, who resigned from the Foreign Office during the Suez crisis.*

As a matter of fact, there was one possible solution to the Canal crisis. In a letter to *The New York Times* dated September 12, 1956, the writer had suggested the resurrection in modified form of a proposal that had been made by President Truman at the Potsdam Conference in 1945 to internationalize all the world's strategic waterways, including the Turkish Straits, the Rhine-Danube Waterway and the Suez, Panama and Kiel Canals. Churchill, according to Truman's *Memoirs*,† had not cared to discuss the question of Suez, explaining that "the Brit-

* Anthony Nutting, *No End of a Lesson.* See also Hugh Thomas, *Suez.*
† Volume I, p. 386.

ish had an arrangement with which they were satisfied and under which they had operated for some seventy years without complaints." To this, Molotov had prophetically replied: "You should ask Egypt." Other more pressing business intervened and nothing came of Truman's proposal.

When the writer suggested the resurrection of this project six weeks before the 1956 crisis erupted into war, two objections were raised in letters to the *Times* and in others addressed privately to the writer:

1. It was argued that there was no analogy between the "lawfully established" position of the United States as to Panama and the "illegal seizure" of Suez by Nasser. As a matter of fact, there was an analogy. The procedure by which President Theodore Roosevelt had acquired the Panama Canal Zone in 1903 was so flagrantly in violation of treaty rights and international law that, some twenty years later, the United States had paid the Republic of Colombia an indemnity of $25 million. Roosevelt himself made no bones about saying in his autobiography: "I took Panama." However, this was not the point. Even if the American position as to Panama had been impeccable, this would not have constituted a reason not to relinquish it if, thereby, the Suez crisis might be resolved.

2. The second objection was that turning over the Panama Canal to the United Nations, provided that Egypt would turn over Suez, would seriously weaken the security of the United States. In reply, it was pointed out that a single atomic bomb could wreck one of the giant locks or, worse yet, breach the Gatun Dam, turning Gatun Lake into a mudhole and putting the Canal out of business for a very long time. It was precisely for this reason, and because the Panama locks would not accommodate our new supercarriers and supertankers, that a sea-level canal was being considered. This project, if adopted, would take about ten years to complete. In the meantime, the writer contended, the Canal might well be safer if owned and operated by the United Nations; it would certainly be no less safe because its air defense would in any case have to be conducted from far out in the Caribbean or the Pacific Ocean.

Although the proposal attracted some public support, it did not appeal to the Eisenhower administration. The writer later

developed it further by suggesting that, if Nasser could be persuaded to cede or sell the Suez Canal to the United Nations, he
might also be persuaded to cede or sell a strip of land to the
United Nations running from Gaza to the entrance to the Gulf
of Aqaba, thereby creating a demilitarized neutral zone between Israel and Egypt which could serve as a base for a permanent United Nations peace-keeping force.* (Secretary-
General Dag Hammarskjold did eventually establish the
UNEF between Egypt and Israel but the Canal was left in
Egypt's hands and the United Nations did not acquire title to
the neutral zone, with the result that UNEF would be able to
remain in place only at the pleasure of the Egyptian government.)

While the Security Council was debating the Suez affair, the
world's attention was suddenly diverted to the Polish and Hungarian revolts against Soviet domination. Was a new dawn
breaking over Eastern Europe? Was the Soviet Union in serious trouble? Would it use force to suppress the rebellions?

Before these questions could be answered and at the very moment when the Soviet monolith appeared to be crumbling, the
Western Alliance fell apart.

On October 29 Israel suddenly invaded Egypt. The decision
to attack had been so carefully guarded a secret that the action came as a surprise not only to Egypt but the entire
world except the British and French high commands. Israel's
war plan aimed at the capture within ten days of the Sinai peninsula with the objectives of eliminating the bases from which
Egyptian forces had been raiding deep into Israel and of capturing Sharm el Sheikh at the entrance to the Gulf of Aqaba.
The campaign opened with a drop of paratroops at the Mitla
Pass and rapidly developed into a three-pronged armored drive
aimed at the Suez area, at Ismailia at the middle of the Canal
and at Kantara in the north. Within eight days all these objectives were achieved. The Egyptian forces were completely
routed without being able to bring into play their superior
ground and air equipment. The background and history of the
campaign were later recounted in detail by Moshe Dayan, the

* These suggestions were put forward in the February 7, 1956, issue
of *The Reporter*.

Israeli Chief of Staff.*

What caused the Israeli government's decision to incur the military and political risks involved in an invasion of Egypt? What caused Britain and France to enter the conflict a few days later with the alleged aim of separating the belligerents?

These questions cannot be answered without a brief review of the developments in the Middle East between 1949 and 1956, a period notable for the failure of the United Nations to bring about peace treaties between Israel and the Arab states, due in part to a lack of skill on the part of the Conciliation Commission and perhaps in greater measure to the unwillingness of the Arab states to reconcile themselves to the existence of Israel.

Apart from belligerent rhetoric, the Arab states pursued provocative policies which fell into three categories:

1. *Economic warfare.* On the first day of the 1948 war, the Arab League declared an economic boycott against Israel which remained in force after the 1949 armistice. Individual Arab states undertook additional measures such as boycotting Jewish-owned concerns in other countries and blacklisting non-Jewish-owned concerns that did business with Israel. For example: Sa'udi Arabia demanded that the Arabian-American Oil Company employ no Jews even in its home offices and requested the American government to exclude Jewish servicemen from the American troops stationed at the air base at Dahran.

Egypt, asserting its "belligerent rights," continued after the armistice to keep the Suez Canal closed to Israeli shipping and applied the doctrine of "visit and search" to all ships of whatever nationality bound to or from Israel. A Security Council resolution of September 1, 1951, ordering Egypt to end these practices met with Egypt's flat refusal. A second resolution demanding compliance was vetoed in March 1954 by the Soviet Union—an action denoting a radical change in Soviet policy which implied a warning that Israel would be able to place little reliance upon the United Nations. In September 1954 Egypt had seized an Israeli vessel, the *Bat Galim*, that was carrying a cargo of cement to Israel, confiscated its cargo and

---

* Moshe Dayan, *Diary of the Sinai Campaign.* See also Abba Eban, *The Voice of Israel*, pp. 255–293.

detained its crew for several months. No action was taken by the Security Council upon Israel's complaint.

2. *Water rights and river development.* Water from the Jordan River was essential to Israel's development of the Negev. In September 1953 Syria protested against Israel's commencing work on a hydroelectric project on the Jordan near B'not Yaacov. The United States sent Ambassador Eric Johnson to the Middle East to attempt to gain consent to a regional river development program similar to that suggested earlier by Walter Lowdermilk. Israel promptly agreed to the proposal. Syria and Jordan objected. At this time there were a number of Jordanian commando raids in which Israeli property was damaged or destroyed and a number of lives lost. Israel adopted a policy of quick reprisal by regular shock troops against Jordanian command posts or police stations. The Security Council took no action condemning the Jordanian raids because they were supposedly undertaken by individuals, but it condemned a reprisal assault by Israeli troops on the Arab post at Qibya and thereafter ordered suspension of the work on the hydroelectric project. On January 24, 1954, the Soviet Union vetoed a Security Council resolution that would have permitted resumption of the work.

3. *Egyptian Fedayeen raids into the Negev.* Beginning in 1954, Israeli settlements in the Negev suffered a growing number of Egyptian commando raids that destroyed crops, water pipes, trees and houses and caused serious civilian casualties. Israeli farmers were forced to go armed into the fields and to guard their houses at night. No action was taken by the Security Council upon Israel's complaints, lodged in April 1955 and again in August, against these raids.

The climax came on September 17, 1955. Egypt announced that it had purchased large quantities of arms from Czechoslovakia. It was later learned that, in exchange for its cotton crop, Egypt had acquired 230 tanks, 200 armored troop-carriers, 100 self-propelled guns, 500 pieces of artillery, almost 200 fighter planes, bombers and troop-carriers, plus a number of destroyers, motor torpedo-boats and submarines.*

The arms deal was a shock to Israel, not only because it gave

* Dayan, *Diary of the Suez Campaign*, p. 4.

Egypt an enormous superiority in armored vehicles but because the arms were obtained from the very country that, in
1948, had sold Israel the weapons with which it had successfully
fought its war of liberation.

On October 18 Israel applied to the United States for a security pact and for permission to purchase arms. Dulles, although
he was furious over the Czech deal with Egypt, took until November 1 to reply that he would "give the matter sympathetic
consideration."

In the face of continuing Fedayeen raids throughout the
next three months that caused serious Israeli casualties, the Security Council declined to take action. Edward B. Lawson, the
United States Ambassador, praised Israel's "remarkable restraint in the face of Arab suicide-squad terrorism." On May
29, 1956, Nasser announced that he himself was directing the
Fedayeen activities. By October Israeli casualties amounted to
over 500.

At some time in September 1956 Israel got wind of a French
plan for the Anglo-French seizure of the Suez Canal. The
French suggested that Israel invade Sinai and provide an excuse
for Anglo-French intervention. In spite of the Egyptian provocations and Nasser's declared intention to destroy Israel, Ben-
Gurion was reluctant to become involved in the Suez affair. At
the time, he was concerned over the reported movement of
Iraqi troops into Jordan, which seemed to imply a British-
directed attack by Jordan and Iraq upon Israel. (Incredible
as it may seem, Eden was, in fact, contemplating at one and
the same time a Jordanian move against Israel and the use of
British troops against Egypt. The Jordanian move was frustrated by the victory of the pro-Nasser forces in the Jordanian
election, since these were hostile to King Hussein and Britain.*

On October 22, 1956, Egypt, Jordan and Syria announced
the formation of a joint military command, declaring their purpose to be "a war of destruction against Israel." This appears to
have been the determining factor in Britain's agreement two
days later to participate in the French plan; and at this point
Ben-Gurion apparently agreed to launch an invasion of Sinai,

---

* Eden's confused maneuvering is described by both Nutting (*No
End of a Lesson*) and Dayan (*Diary of the Suez Campaign*).

provided that the British would knock out the Egyptian bombers that might otherwise blast Israel's cities. The British agreed
and actually did bomb the Egyptian airfields on the night of
October 31–November 1, but by this time victory was already
within Israel's grasp. (The alleged reason for the bombing was
that Egypt had not agreed to the Anglo-French ultimatum
of October 31, to which reference will be made presently.)

These, then, were the major developments between 1949 and
October 29, 1956, when Israel launched its full-scale attack
upon Egypt.

Whether Israel's action was justified in these circumstances
is a matter of opinion. It seems certain, however, that the action would never have been undertaken if the Soviet bloc had
not rearmed Egypt, if the United States and Britain had lived
up to their commitments to Israel and if the United Nations
had been both willing and able to enforce its demands that
Egypt cease its acts of belligerency against Israel. Both the reversal of the Soviet attitude toward Israel and the impotence of
the United Nations were products of the Cold War. In its obsession with communism and its preoccupation with the con-
tainment of Russia, the United States had all but forgotten its
commitments to Israel. Britain's concern had not been for Israel's security but for the overthrow of Nasser, whom Eden considered "another Hitler." France had helped Israel to rearm and
provided the collusive plan of action against Egypt less out of
concern for Israel than out of hostility to Nasser because of the
support he had given to the Algerian rebels.

It is not clear just when the Franco-Israeli collusion began.
Whatever the correct date, it is reasonably clear that there had
been something of a "hawk-dove" debate going on in Israel for
some time. Moshe Sharett (formerly Shertak) evidently believed
that a reconciliation between Israel and Egypt was possible and
appears to have had some indirect contacts with Nasser. Ben-
Gurion, Dayan, Defense Minister Lavon and his successor,
Shimon Perez, apparently believed that the Arabs understood
no language other than that of force. Very little of this internal
conflict has come to light.

The plan of action which Dayan developed with the French
provided the "hawk" faction with a unique opportunity to ob-

tain air and naval support in a major operation against Egypt, but it also involved Israel in an unclean and dishonest Anglo-French conspiracy that, apart from moral contamination, made Israel appear as the tool of Western imperialism. In this writer's *ex post facto* judgment, Israel would have been wiser and, in the long run, would have fared better had it acted alone. As it turned out, the Arab naval and air forces were so ineffective that the absence of French and British support would probably have made little difference. One may or may not feel that Nasser's provocations justified an Israeli attack. Assuming that a major action was justified, if Israel had operated alone its case would have been stronger and Nasser would have had no alibi for defeat.

Events showed that Israel, in fact, made a great effort to achieve its military objectives before there was any outside intervention and had in great measure succeeded by October 31, when Britain and France sent their ultimatum threatening to intervene "to separate the belligerents" unless both sides ceased from hostilities or came within ten miles of the Canal.

Besides being dishonest, the Anglo-French ultimatum was actually an absurdity since, if it were accepted, there would be no excuse for the intervention to which both governments were committed, with forces already launched that could not arrive at Port Said before November 6. When both Egypt and Israel tentatively accepted the cease-fire demand, the French implored Ben-Gurion to delay his final acceptance while they prodded the British to advance the date of the landings. Ben-Gurion complied, but by the time the slow-moving Anglo-French forces reached Port Said from Cyprus, Israel's war was about over, and pressures had been built up at the United Nations to a point at which Britain and France would be compelled to abandon the adventure. An infuriated Eisenhower found himself compelled to join the Soviet Union in condemning the action of America's closest allies, as well as that of Israel. Whatever defense could have been made for Israel's attack upon Egypt was now compromised by Israel's association with the wholly indefensible actions of Britain and France.

While the Security Council was able to condemn the three invaders of Egypt and to demand their withdrawal, the Soviet

Union used its veto to prevent a condemnation of its own brutal suppression of the Hungarian revolt. (Technically, the Russians had an excuse for sending their tanks into Budapest because the puppet Premier had asked for support.)

Had Dulles not driven Britain and France to distraction by first precipitating the Suez crisis and then engaging in his ambiguous diplomatic maneuvers, the point would not have been reached at which London and Paris, no longer trusting Washington, would secretly embark upon a plan for invasion. And had Britain and France not committed the incredible folly of intervening, Israel would have pulled their chestnuts out of the fire along with its own. It was highly unlikely that Nasser could have survived a defeat at the hands of Israel had he not been able to lay his defeat to Western intervention.

To say this is not to say that an utter defeat of Egypt by Israel would have brought peace to the Middle East or that the overthrow of Nasser would necessarily have been a good thing. Indeed, such an outcome might have brought about Soviet armed intervention and precipitated a third world war. Before Britain and France withdrew under Soviet-American pressure, the Soviet government had, in fact, threatened to use rockets against them and had threatened Israel with sending "volunteers" to aid Egypt. Whether or not this was bluff, it had a decided effect upon the outcome.

The dual crisis—in Hungary and Egypt—brought about a hopeless confusion of legalistic and moral judgments on the part of the United States.

From the legalistic point of view, the Security Council held that Israel, Britain and France had committed aggression in violation of the United Nations Charter. Leaving aside the fact that the Security Council did nothing to condemn the Soviet Union's brutal armed intervention in Hungary, while condemning the invaders of Egypt, it also wholly ignored those clear violations of the Charter by Egypt which, in defiance of the Council's injunctions, had provoked Israel's attack. Yet surely there was a moral distinction between the desperate act of a small nation whose very existence had been threatened and the exasperated action of two major powers whose sole complaint against Egypt had been its inconvenient but not necessarily illegal nationalization of the Suez Canal.*

It was all very well for President Eisenhower to declare that "we cannot apply one standard to our friends and another to those who oppose us," but that was precisely what the Security Council was doing with respect to the invaders of Egypt and the invader of Hungary.† And if it was true, as the President also said, that "there cannot be one law for the weak and another for the strong," then if the Council was powerless to enforce the law against Russia because of its strength, why was it just to enforce the law against a small nation too weak to resist enforcement?

Britain and France accepted the Security Council's order to withdraw. In Britain's case this was in part due to the storm of protest against the Suez adventure which arose within Britain itself and which eventually caused the resignation of Eden as Prime Minister.

Israel accepted the cease-fire but sought unsuccessfully to obtain, as a condition of the withdrawal of its forces from Sinai, the assurance of future free use of the Canal as well as a guarantee that Egypt would not be permitted to reoccupy the Gaza Strip or Sharm el Sheikh. The United States and the Soviet Union, along with a majority of the Council, took the position that Israel's withdrawal must be unconditional; otherwise, it was held, Israel would "profit from its aggression."

The height of irony was reached when the Soviet Union arose to assert that it favored the imposition of sanctions upon Israel to compel its withdrawal from Gaza and Sharm el Sheikh.

Eventually, after some months of negotiations, Israel withdrew its forces from Sinai after the Security Council had created a peace-keeping force (UNEF) to occupy both Sharm

* Two questions are involved here: (1) Egypt's right to nationalize the Canal, which seems incontrovertible if accompanied by fair compensation; and (2) Egypt's closure of the Canal. The Constantinople Convention of 1888 provided for "free and innocent passage for ships of all nations in peace and in war." The Convention was signed not by Egypt but by Turkey, and might or might not be considered binding as "law" upon a successor government.

† The Soviet Union could claim that it had been "invited" to intervene by the Hungarian government, but both the nature of the "invitation" and the independence of the Hungarian government were open to question.

el Sheikh and the Gaza Strip. Thus Israel did obtain two of its objectives: it secured free passage to its port of Eilat through the Gulf of Aqaba; and it eliminated the Egyptian base for Fedayeen harassment. It did not obtain free passage through the Canal.

For other countries the results of the fiasco were:

1. The restoration of the very conditions which had provoked the explosion, plus the blockage for about six months of the Suez Canal.

2. The strengthening of Nasser as the leader of the Arab world and of the Moscow-Cairo axis.

3. The near-destruction of British influence in the Arab world as a whole and the jeopardizing of what remained of Britain's preferential position in Iraq and in the vital Persian Gulf area.

4. The creation of a serious cleavage within the British Commonwealth (Canada had voted with the United States and the Soviet Union), and the realization on the part of the British public that Britain was no longer a world power capable of independent action.

5. The arousing of resentment on both sides of the Atlantic, with a consequent dangerous weakening of the central core of the Atlantic Alliance.

6. The strengthening of Arab resistance to France in Algeria and the diminution of the hope that a Western-oriented Maghreb federation might emerge as a counterbalance to the anti-Western Arab League centered on Cairo.

7. The strengthening of Soviet influence in the Middle East.

It should have been clear to the American government, if not to Secretary Dulles, that there was an urgent need for a drastic re-examination of United States foreign policy—and not only with respect to the Middle East.

The opportunity to revise American foreign policy was not long in coming. On November 17, 1956, a note was received from the Soviet government suggesting a mutual withdrawal of armed forces from Central Europe. While the terms of such withdrawal were in part vague and in part unacceptable, the basic suggestion of disengagement certainly seemed worth exploring. However, the State Department instantly denounced the Soviet overture as "insincere propaganda." The writer ventured to call President Eisenhower's attention to what seemed a unique opportunity to explore the possibility of combining disengagement in Germany with a mutual hands-off agreement in the Middle East. A suggested reply to Moscow, based upon the writer's letter, was addressed to the President on December 7 by the Arden House Conference and delivered to him by two Senators, one a Democrat and the other a Republican, both of whom had attended the Conference. The President found the proposal interesting but expressed the view that "Foster wouldn't like it." *

Both Secretary Acheson and Secretary Dulles had taken the position that the United States could enter upon negotiations with respect to Germany only from what Acheson called "a situation of strength." Such a situation had arisen in the autumn of 1956 because of the widespread revolt in Eastern Europe against Soviet domination, but Secretary Dulles was as unwilling to negotiate from strength as he had been unwilling to negotiate from a position of weakness. Within a short time the Soviet Union's moment of weakness passed and Chairman Khrushchev resumed the initiative with a brusque demand for Western withdrawal from Berlin.

Thus the United States lost the opportunity to extricate itself from the unfavorable position in the Middle East created by four years of blundering diplomacy. But the end of that blundering had not yet been reached.

On January 5, 1957, President Eisenhower announced a new Middle East policy which became known as the Eisenhower Doctrine. During the Middle East crisis of 1956 the United

* For the text of the proposal, see Warburg, *The United States in the Postwar World*, pp. 107–110. The writer developed further the idea of combining a relaxation of tensions in Europe with a détente in the Middle East in a book published in the following spring, entitled *Agenda for Action: Toward Peace Through Disengagement* (Academy Books, New York, 1957). A similar proposal for disengagement in Europe was put forward later in the year by Poland's Foreign Minister, Adam Rapacki; this, too, was brushed off by the State Department, as was a third effort in the same direction by George F. Kennan, former U.S. Ambassador to Moscow (the Reith Lectures of 1957, delivered over the British Broadcasting Corporation's transmitters).

States had left the untangling of the affair to the United Nations and, to all intents and purposes, Dag Hammarskjold had acted as foreign minister for all the Western powers. Lester Pearson, the Canadian Foreign Minister, had been the one to suggest the United Nations peace-keeping force which Hammerskjold had then created. The Eisenhower Doctrine now marked a reversion to the unilateral policy through which the United States had got itself into so much trouble. The President's declaration of January 5, 1957, promised military assistance and cooperation to any Middle Eastern countries "requesting aid against overt armed aggression from any nation controlled by international communism."

By no stretch of the imagination could the Eisenhower Doctrine be considered a redefinition of American policy; if anything, it constituted a reaffirmation of two erroneous premises: (1) that communism, rather than indigenous Arab nationalism, lay at the root of the turbulent condition of the Middle East; and (2) that communism could be contained by military means. If one accepted these premises, one might perhaps say that a declaration of "so far and no further" might serve to prevent Soviet miscalculation and a consequent overt aggression, such as had occurred in Korea, but such a declaration could provide no defense whatever against the more evident danger of political penetration. The Truman Doctrine had not prevented the bloodless communization of Czechoslovakia. The Eisenhower Doctrine seemed unlikely to save Syria or any other Middle Eastern country from a similar fate. Lebanon was the only country to welcome the Eisenhower Doctrine. Syria had already refused to accept economic assistance from the United States because of American support of Israel's right to exist.

Before the Eisenhower Doctrine was enacted into law by Congress on March 9, 1957, the United States was presented with two more opportunities to reconsider its Middle East policy. The first of these opportunities related to an approach to peace through multilateral assistance to economic development of the whole Middle Eastern region.

1. In December 1956 a group of independent Middle East experts in Britain published a plan for a United Nations Middle

East Development Authority. The basic assumption of this group was that there could be no security from expropriation of foreign-owned oil installations or from sabotage of pipelines controlled by private oil companies unless the foreign development of oil resources acquired the firm backing of Middle Eastern public opinion and recognized international law.

The proposal was to create a United Nations Regional Development Authority, authorized to place a levy upon all oil shipments from Middle Eastern ports and to take over and operate all pipelines, charging an additional levy to cover operating costs and transit rights. The proceeds of the two levies would then be applied toward an approved program for the economic development of the entire area.

The authors claimed that by this plan the oil producers and the oil consumers would acquire greatly increased and internationally guaranteed security. They would, admittedly, pay more for Middle East oil than they had been paying, "but not so much as it will certainly cost them if Middle East conditions continue as anarchic as they must otherwise become." The Middle East countries would have a stake in oil revenues sufficient to give them a strong vested interest in uninterrupted production and marketing. Since the collective revenues would be channeled through the United Nations, all the Middle East countries would have a reasonable assurance that these funds would be equitably shared and applied where they would most benefit the area as a whole, instead of the profits from oil being monopolized by those countries in whose territories the oil deposits happened to lie.

The writer strongly endorsed this plan in his previously mentioned article in the February 7, 1956, issue of *The Reporter*, adding the suggestion that the United States should not only sponsor the creation of the Middle East Development Authority but should offer to channel through it all of its contributions to Middle East economic development, on condition that the Soviet Union would do likewise. Were the Soviet Union to agree to such a proposal, all political overtones would be removed from American and Soviet assistance to the economic development of the area. If the offer were made by the United States and rejected by Moscow, the expansionist aims of the Soviet Union would be clearly exposed and its influence throughout the area diminished.

The proposal received some support in the Congress, but none whatever from the Eisenhower administration.

2. On February 12, 1957, a note was addressed by Moscow to Washington, London and Paris suggesting precisely what the Western powers should have suggested six months earlier, namely, a mutual hands-off agreement with respect to the Middle East. The six points of the proposal were:

1. The preservation of peace in the Near and Middle East by settling questions at issue exclusively by peaceful means.

2. Non-interference in the internal affairs of the countries of the Near and Middle East.

3. Refusal to undertake any attempts to draw these countries into military alignments with the participation of the great powers.

4. Liquidation of foreign bases and the withdrawal of foreign troops from the territories of the countries of the Near and Middle East.

5. Joint refusal to supply arms to countries of the Near and Middle East.

6. Assistance to the economic development of the countries of the Near and Middle East without putting forward any political, military or other conditions incompatible with the dignity and sovereignty of these countries.

Points 1, 2, 5 and 6 constituted a succinct statement of what should have been the American objectives, if the American purpose was to assure the full and free development of the area without seeking to dominate it. Point 6 put precisely the question to Washington which the writer had suggested that Washington put to Moscow; a rejection of Point 6 would imply that the United States did seek to dominate the Middle East.

On the other hand, points 3 and 4 were clearly unacceptable because they called for one-sided concessions on the part of the West. The Soviet Union had no bases in the Middle East; it had no military alliances and no troops except perhaps a few technical advisors. Britain and the United States, however, had both bases and alliances in the Middle East, and Britain had a few troops in the Persian Gulf area. The obvious *quid pro quo* for a Western military withdrawal from the Middle East would have been a Soviet withdrawal from Central Europe, but the time for the United States to make that proposal had been in October 1956.

In a letter to the *Washington Post* and a number of leading newspapers across the country, the writer said in part:

> For us to reject the Soviet proposal out of hand—which is probably what the Kremlin wants us to do—would be the height of folly. What we should do is to accept in principle the proposed neutralization of the Middle East, stating, however, that we shall be willing to discuss the dissolution of military pacts, the withdrawal of troops and the relinquishment of bases only in the context of a corresponding Soviet withdrawal from Eastern Europe. Any other answer will leave us in a wholly invidious position in the eyes of the peoples of the Middle East.

The letter was endorsed and placed in the *Congressional Record* by prominent Republican as well as Democratic leaders in the Congress, but the President's press secretary, James Hagerty, brushed off the Soviet overture as "insincere propaganda designed to make trouble for the Eisenhower Doctrine."

Obsessive preoccupation with physical defense against the assumed danger of physical invasion continued to cause a neglect of the historical, social, political and economic factors affecting the attitudes of the Middle Eastern peoples. Concern for concessions and military alliances led to overemphasis upon relations with Middle East governments, rather than with the peoples of the area. The American policymakers failed to understand that there was a growing conflict between the old, feudal order and the slow awakening of the people—a revolt not only against foreign influence but against exploitation by indigenous potentates or anti-democratic military cliques.

Syria furnished a good example. With Egypt separated from Israel by the interposition of the United Nations forces, Syria had become the chief troublemaker against Israel and also, because of its unstable internal condition, the chief target of Moscow's attentions. The Ba'ath Party was dominated by a clique of army officers almost all of whom were members of an extremist Shiah Moslem sect (the followers of 'Ali). Opposed to this numerically small but powerful clique were the conservative "notables." In a free election the army-dominated Ba'athist clique would probably not have obtained more than 10 percent of the popular vote. Yet it gained control of the government and on February 1, 1958, formed a union with Egypt in which the two countries were united under the name of the United Arab Republic.

Washington was alarmed by what appeared to be an increase of Nasser's power and was inclined to attribute the new union to Moscow's machinations. Quite possibly Moscow had encouraged the Ba'ath army clique to take over power, but it had almost certainly had little or nothing to do with the creation of the U.A.R. As a matter of fact, Nasser was moving away from too close an association with the Soviet Union. He had outlawed the Egyptian Communist Party, jailed its leaders and made it quite clear that, while he welcomed Soviet support against Western imperialism, he had no intention of becoming a Soviet satellite.

In a move intended to counter the extension of Nasser's power over Syria, the Hashemite kingdoms of Jordan and Iraq joined in what they called "The Arab Federation," which was proclaimed on February 14. Three weeks later, Yemen signed a federation agreement with the U.A.R.

Lebanon declared on March 25 that it would join neither the U.A.R. nor the Arab Federation, although its government was faced with considerable pro-Nasser agitation.

On April 18 Sa'udi Arabia likewise announced that it would join neither the U.A.R. nor the Hashemites.

The stage was now set for a new Middle East crisis.

On May 12 an armed rebellion erupted in Beirut against the pro-Western government of Camille Chamoun, that had welcomed the Eisenhower Doctrine. The rebels cut the oil pipelines belonging to the Iraq Petroleum Company. The Lebanese government accused the United Arab Republic of having instigated and of aiding the rebellion. Nasser denied the charge.

During June the United States and Britain completed

arrangements to reinforce Iraq, Jordan and Lebanon with fighter planes. The Security Council created a U.N. Observation Group (UNOGIL) to "ensure that there is no illegal infiltration of personnel or supply of arms or other material across the Lebanese border." And on June 24 Moscow charged the West with preparing for armed intervention in internal Lebanese affairs and declared that it would not stand by in the event of such intervention.

On July 14 the pro-Western government of Iraq was overthrown by an army revolution. King Feisal and Premier Nuri-as-Said, Britain's faithful friend, were slain and their bodies dragged through the streets. Brigadier Abdul Karim el-Kassim became head of a government which declared: "We have liberated the country from the domination of a corrupt group which was installed by imperialism."

The next day the United States landed 5,000 Marines in Lebanon, informing the United Nations of its action, taken at the request of the Lebanese government under the Eisenhower Doctrine. Two days later, at King Hussein's request, the British airlifted 2,000 troops to Jordan, backed by American jet aircraft. Moscow recognized the new government of Iraq, threatened to intervene if it were attacked and denounced the Anglo-American landings. West Germany objected to the withdrawal of American contingents for use in the Middle East. Austria protested against the troops being flown over its territory. Greece protested against the use of Cyprus as a staging base. An emergency session of the United Nations General Assembly ordered the withdrawal of United States and British forces and called upon all members "to act strictly in accordance with the principles of mutual respect for each other's territorial integrity and sovereignty."

The Lebanon crisis had occurred at a time when American prestige in the world had already reached a new low because, in October of 1957, the Soviet Union had launched its first Sputnik and announced the test of its first intercontinental ballistic missile. This, for the first time, made the United States directly vulnerable to nuclear attack and raised doubts throughout the world as to whether the United States would, if necessary to carry out its far-flung commitments, expose its own cities to nuclear retaliation. American prestige was not enhanced by the outcome of the Lebanese crisis, the results of which might be summarized as follows:

1. The overthrow in Iraq of the one strongly pro-Western Arab government and Iraq's withdrawal from the CENTO alliance.

2. The replacement of the Western-inclined Chamoun government of Lebanon by a neutralist regime.

3. The withdrawal of Jordan from its federation with Iraq and the increased insecurity of the sole surviving Hashemite kingdom.

4. The strengthening of Nasser's claim to leadership in the Arab world.

5. The exposure of Israel to increased pressure from the Arab states, especially from Nasser-controlled Syria.

In addition, the outcome of the crisis inevitably raised apprehensions in Turkey and Iran as to the value of the CENTO alliance. Dulles attempted to provide reassurance by agreeing to have the United States join the CENTO military committee, but not the alliance proper.

To all intents and purposes, the record of the Eisenhower administration in the Middle East was now closed. Dulles was afflicted by abdominal cancer; during the remaining months of his life, he would be preoccupied with matters other than those concerning the Middle East.*

By 1958 the French-Algerian war had degenerated into a brutal conflict in which 400,000 of the best French troops with every kind of modern equipment proved incapable of dealing with the Arab rebellion. (Among American voices raised against France in its attempt to suppress the Algerian revolt had been that of a young Massachusetts Senator, John F. Kennedy, whose outspoken criticism in 1954 had aroused the indignation of the French government.) As the war continued, terrorism and the torture of prisoners became almost daily occurrences, disgusting an increasing number of French citizens, who demanded an end to *la sale guerre*, but a succession of weak governments at Paris had become the prisoners of the generals

---

* Dulles died in May 1959 and was buried in Arlington National Cemetery.

and colonels who refused to accept the humiliation of another defeat such as France had suffered at the hands of Germany and in Indo-China. In May 1958, as result of a near-revolt of the generals and the French colons in Algeria, Charles de Gaulle was called out of his retirement, at Colombey-les-deux-Eglises, by crowds marching through the streets of Paris and Algiers shouting: *"Algérie française! De Gaulle au pouvoir!"* The Fourth French Republic was overthrown and De Gaulle reoccupied the position as Chief of State which he had relinquished in 1946. For the first time since the days of Clemenceau, France had a Strong Man at the helm. In what direction he would lead remained to be seen.

De Gaulle had come to power to keep Algeria French. After sixteen more months of war, he had the strength and courage to proclaim the Algerian people's right to self-determination and to suppress a revolt of the "ultras" among the army officers. The proclamation of Algeria's right to self-determination was made on September 16, 1959. The Evian Agreements of March 18, 1962, determined the means for applying it, and on July 1, 1962, France recognized the new Algerian state.

So far as the Middle East was concerned, the successful revolt of the Arab Maghreb had several important effects: it strengthened Arab nationalism in the other Arab states; it left a residue of French resentment against Nasser because of his aid to the Algerian rebels; and it cooled off French support of Israel.

19

A Deceptive Lull Erupts into Another War—1967

After the Lebanon crisis of 1958, comparative peace settled over the Middle East, except for the continuing war in Algeria. This was due less to an improvement of the situation in the Middle East than to the preoccupation of the non-Middle Eastern powers with crises in other parts of the world.

Prime Minister Macmillan, who had succeeded Eden, was busy picking up the pieces of the all-but-shattered Anglo-American alliance and endeavoring to bring about a relaxation of tensions over Berlin.

De Gaulle was engaged in the difficult task of liquidating the Algerian war.

Eisenhower, during his last months in office, was making a sincere effort to reach an understanding with Khrushchev, an effort nullified by the shooting down of an American spy plane over the Soviet Union and the consequent disruption of the Summit Meeting at Paris in May 1960.

The time which Khrushchev could give to foreign affairs was devoted, first, to visiting the United States and then, after the Paris fiasco, to vilifying the United States at the 20th session of the General Assembly of the United Nations.

The Cuban revolution and disarmament were in the forefront of discussion. No one had much time for the Middle East.*

* For a résumé of the disarmament discussions and the events of

In November 1960 John F. Kennedy was elected President of the United States.

In a deceptively tranquil Middle East, the years 1959 and 1960 were marked by almost continuous border clashes between Israel and Syria. A Syrian guerrilla organization, similar to the Egyptian Fedayeen (who were now restrained by the interposition of the UNEF), conducted raids into Israel from bases in Syria and Jordan. Israeli reprisals were, as before, conducted by regular shock troops and, as before, the Security Council usually condemned these governmental operations while failing to hold the Syrian or Jordanian governments responsible for the guerrilla activities conducted from their territory and presumably by their nationals.

Three times—on March 17 and August 31, 1959, and again on November 10, 1960—Israel complained to the Security Council against the seizure by the U.A.R. of Israeli cargo from non-Israeli ships passing through the Suez Canal. Nevertheless, the procedure continued.

Throughout 1959 and 1960 various organs of the United Nations fruitlessly sought to find a solution to the refugee problem. Israel maintained that there could be no solution without the establishment of peace, while the Arab states refused to discuss peace between themselves and Israel unless the Palestinian refugees were repatriated. Meanwhile, the problem steadily increased in dimensions due to the high birth-rate among the refugees, while Israel's capacity to absorb them diminished through the influx of over 800,000 new immigrants, nearly half of them from Arab states. In August 1961 the Palestine Conciliation Commission appointed an American, Dr. Joseph Johnson, as its special emissary to make an on-the-spot study of the problem.

In January 1961 at Casablanca, Guinea, Ghana, Mali, the U.A.R., Algeria, Morocco and Libya adopted a resolution naming Israel as "an instrument of imperialism and neo-colonialism in the Middle East and Africa." This action was in part inspired by the fact that Israel had been developing the port of Eilat and

---

1959–1960, see J. P. Warburg, *Disarmament, The Challenge of the 1960s* (Doubleday, New York, 1961); also *The United States in the Postwar World*, pp. 115–127.

was beginning to engage in trade with African states as well as to assist some of them in technological and economic development.

On September 29, 1961, Syrian army officers led a revolt against Egyptian domination and a new government declared Syria's independence, thus dissolving the union. This was a sharp blow to Nasser's ambitions. The merger of the two countries had been premature. Their economies were wholly disparate, and Ba'athist socialism had not been easily compatible with the totalitarian socialism of the Egyptian regime. Moreover, the Syrian socialists had been subject to somewhat greater Soviet influence than suited the more cautious Egyptian president.

Dr. Johnson delivered his report on the refugee problem to the United Nations General Assembly on November 22. He saw no prospect of an early peace settlement and reported that there were many indications "that no progress can be made on the Palestine Arab refugee question apart from, or in advance of an over-all settlement. . . .The reintegration of the Palestine refugees, whether by repatriation, resettlement or both, with compensation where appropriate, into a useful life in the Near East will depend upon the rate of economic development."

In December a Special Political Committee in the United Nations debated the problem of the refugees. Fourteen Latin American and African nations introduced a resolution calling upon the Arab and Israeli governments "to undertake direct negotiations with a view to finding a solution for all the questions in dispute between them, including the question of the refugees." Israel favored the resolution. The Arab states opposed it and the resolution failed of passage.

Three other events took place in 1962:

Israel accused the Syrians of sniping at Israeli fishermen on Lake Tiberias and retaliated by bombing Syrian territory. Once again, the Security Council condemned Israel's but not Syria's action.

Israel extended recognition to Algeria when that country obtained its independence, but the Algerian government declared that its attitude toward Israel would be "exactly like that of the other Arab states."

The Imam of Yemen was assassinated and the rebel, Abdullah al-Salal, declared a republic. The new Imam, Mohamad al-Badr, fled to the mountains to continue resistance, supported by Sa'udi Arabia. The United States somewhat prematurely recognized the Republic and would shortly find itself in the company of Nasser and opposed to Sa'udi Arabia. (During the next two years, Nasser sent some 70,000 Egyptian troops to aid the Republicans.)

During his first two years in office, President Kennedy was preoccupied with domestic affairs, with Cuba and with the Soviet threat to Berlin. It was not until after the Cuban missile crisis, in the autumn of 1962, that he was able to begin giving a new direction to American foreign policy.

One important result of the Cuban crisis was that the United States withdrew its nuclear missiles from Turkey as evidence of its intention to seek better relations with the Soviet Union. This had not been a condition for the withdrawal of Soviet missiles from Cuba, but if a détente was to be reached with the Soviet Union, it seemed desirable to remove missiles which threatened its important southern territory adjacent to Turkey. Furthermore, the missiles, because of their vulnerability, could serve no purpose other than that of a first strike. The withdrawal helped to prepare the climate in which Kennedy was able, in the following year, to negotiate with Russia a partial ban on nuclear testing. The effect of the withdrawal upon Turkey was somewhat problematical; it probably did not add to the enthusiasm for what was left of the CENTO alliance on the part of either Turkey or Iran.

Kennedy's assassination in November 1963 cut short what had appeared to be a new era in international relations—an era in which it seemed that the Cold War would be succeeded by some degree of cooperation toward the maintenance of world peace, at least so far as the Soviet Union was concerned. This did not apply to China. The growing rift between the two great Communist empires had developed into open hostility and there appeared to be a chance that, in Asia, the United States and the Soviet Union might pursue parallel courses in containing possible Chinese expansionist aggression.

For a short time—until after the 1964 elections—it seemed as though President Johnson would continue the conciliatory efforts of his predecessor. During the first year of his incumbency the new President devoted himself primarily to the completion of the domestic programs inaugurated by Kennedy and did so with outstanding success. In foreign affairs he pledged himself to continue the new direction taken by Kennedy and won an overwhelming victory in the 1964 election largely because he appeared to the American people as a man of peace.

In 1965 all this changed. Having denounced his Republican opponent's warlike utterances with respect to Vietnam* and promised not to send American troops into combat on the Asian mainland, President Johnson reversed his course, adopting almost exactly the policy in Vietnam advocated by his opponent and rejected by the American electorate. The steady escalation of the war, the continuous increase in the American forces sent into combat and the extension of the war to North Vietnam by means of air attacks wholly altered the international posture of the United States.

The bombing of North Vietnam—a "socialist sister republic"—eliminated any possibility of obtaining Soviet cooperation in bringing the war to an end. Moreover, it alienated the majority of nations friendly to the United States. The Johnson administration's almost exclusive preoccupation with Southeast Asia caused Western Europe to feel neglected, arousing apprehension that American military power would be so heavily engaged in Vietnam as to make questionable any American guarantee of European security. This was grist to the mill of Charles de Gaulle, who, ever since the Cuban missile crisis of 1962, had been warning the European countries that they might be involved in a major war by their alliance with a United States that did not consult them, and who urged the European nations to make themselves independent of American hegemony. Worse yet, the deepening military commitment to the war in Southeast Asia constituted an open invitation to Moscow to make trouble for the United States in other

* For a discussion of these developments, see Warburg, *The United States in the Postwar World*, Chapter 10, pp. 154–197, as well as the Appendix and Postscript to *Western Intruders*, pp. 209–220.

parts of the world.

The Middle East was ripe for each an enterprise, so ripe, in fact, that Moscow's intervention was scarcely needed.

Syria, rather than Egypt, had increasingly been the instigator of trouble ever since the debacle of 1956. Nasser had somewhat reluctantly created the U.A.R. because, at the time, Syria had been hard-pressed between communists and reactionary "notables." He had responded to the rupture of the union in 1961 with vigorous measures to tighten his control in Egypt, including the expropriation of Syrian and Lebanese citizens of Egypt and the reorganization of the single mass political party. Then in 1963 the secessionist regime in Syria was overthrown by Ba'athi leaders who again wished to gain Nasser's support but not at the price of Syrian subordination to Egypt. A series of talks held at Cairo was inconclusive, with Nasser publicly criticizing the Syrian regime.

In 1964 an Arab summit meeting was called, ostensibly to deal with the fact that Israel was about to complete its diversion of part of the water of the Jordan. The Syrians wanted to oppose the completion of this project by force, knowing that their own strategic position would protect them while Egypt would have to bear the brunt of an Israeli counterattack. Nasser was already embroiled with Sa'udi Arabia in Yemen, where he had sent a substantial Egyptian force to support the Liberation Front against the Royalist government supported by Sa'udi Arabia. He apparently now suspected that Syria, Sa'udi Arabia and Jordan were plotting to destroy Egypt by getting it into another war with Israel. At the conference Nasser managed to obtain the rejection of Syria's demand for the use of force against Israel and an agreement, instead, to divert the waters of the Jordan at their sources in Syria and Lebanon. The conference also agreed to establish the Palestine Liberation Organization (PLO) as a political entity representing the Palestinian refugees.

From what records are available, it would appear that Nasser was willing to risk a diversion of the Jordan headwaters chiefly in order to relieve himself of Syrian pressure. However, Syria and Lebanon delayed starting the diversion project and Syria continued its overt criticism of Nasser. By 1965 Nasser was

ready to scuttle the diversion project. In August of that year
the Egyptian president broke up a Moslem Brotherhood plot
against his regime, which may have been supported by Syria
and Jordan. At another Arab summit conference in September, a truce among the feuding Arab states relegated into the
background any thought of war with Israel, much to the disappointment of Syria and the PLO.

On February 23, 1966, an even more radical group of Ba'ath-
ists seized power in Syria and encouraged the terrorist activities of the PLO. The new regime decided to proceed with the
diversion project. On June 6 Ahmad Shukairy, head of the
PLO, placed his armed terrorists under Syrian command. This
was an ominous development. As the PLO activities increased
in frequency and destructiveness, Israeli retaliation became
sharper. On July 14 Israel's air force retaliated for a particularly
strong terrorist raid by destroying the recently begun Syrian
water diversion works. The Syrians, in turn, increased their
shelling from the Golan Heights of the Israeli settlements in the
Jordan Valley, and PLO commandos began to operate from
Lebanon and Jordan. On August 15 another air battle took
place between Syrian and Israeli planes and, finally, Israel
launched a massive reprisal upon the Jordanian village of El
Samu. It was interesting that Nasser tried to play down this
affair, while the Syrians used it to incite the Jordanians to revolt against King Hussein.

Early in 1967 there was another air battle in which Israeli
planes pursued five Syrian aircraft into Syrian airspace and destroyed them not far from Damascus. In May Syria accused
Israel of planning a major offensive action; United Nations observers could find no evidence of any preparation for such a
move. It should be noted that up to this point Nasser had given
no support to Syria and had made no move of his own against
Israel. What happened next is not easy to understand.

Whether to divert Israel from starting a war by attacking
Syria or for other reasons of his own, Nasser demanded on
May 17 that the United Nations withdraw its peace-keeping
force from Egyptian soil, thus opening the Sinai Peninsula, including Sharm el Sheikh, to Egyptian occupation.

Secretary-General Thant complied with this request with

what seemed to most observers undue haste. Although the General Assembly was in session and had "peace-keeping" on its agenda, and although it was the General Assembly that had created UNEF, the Secretary-General acted without consulting either it or the Security Council. (In later defending his action, U Thant claimed that he had had no choice since UNEF had occupied its positions in Egypt at Egyptian request and since Israel had consistently refused to have United Nations forces stationed on its soil. Moreover, the Secretary-General said that both Yugoslavia and India had wished to withdraw their contingents—clearly a betrayal of their neutral role, which the Secretary-General seemed to accept without question.) The effect of this action was disastrous so far as United Nations prestige as a peace-keeping instrument was concerned because of the stationing of the UNEF between Egypt and Israel had been by far its most successful operation in this field.

No sooner were the UNEF forces withdrawn than Egyptian troops moved into the Sinai Peninsula, in some cases practically shouldering out the U.N. Blue Helmets. Nasser's next move was to declare the Gulf of Aqaba closed to Israeli shipping and to mine the Strait of Tiran.

Israel's free use of the Gulf had not only been assured as part of the 1956–1957 armistice agreements; it had been specifically guaranteed by the United States. On February 11, 1957, Secretary of State Dulles had given an aide-memoire to Israel's then ambassador to Washington, Abba Eban, reading as follows:

> The United States considers that the Gulf of Aqaba comprehends international waters and that no nation has the right to prevent free and innocent passage in the Gulf and through the Straits giving access thereto.*

The aide-memoire added, according to *The New York Times*, that the United States was "prepared to exercise the right of free and innocent passage and to join with others to secure recognition of these rights."

Israel's then Foreign Minister, Mrs. Golda Meir (formerly Myerson), had said that any violation of Israel's right to use

* Quoted in *The New York Times*, May 31, 1967.

the Gulf of Aqaba would be considered a *casus belli.*

Since 1957 the port of Eilat had become of great importance to Israel's economic life; 90 percent of Israel's oil came in through the Gulf and a flourishing trade with eastern and southern nations had made Israel an important factor in the economic development of many of them.

Nasser's action in May 1967 was, therefore, an act of extreme provocation, all the more so as it was coupled with the massing of Egyptian troops in the Sinai Peninsula. He may have thought that Soviet support would enable him to carry out this plan without arousing Israel to armed action, and it is possible that Moscow may have encouraged this belief, confident that the United States was so heavily engaged in Vietnam that it would take no action and would seek to restrain Israel. The fact that a squadron of ten Soviet warships passed through the Turkish Straits and on May 30 anchored in Egyptian ports "to pay a friendly visit" may have encouraged this belief.

So far as the United States was concerned, the Soviet calculation—if such was the Soviet calculation—proved almost entirely correct. President Johnson strongly urged Israel to refrain from overt action while he tried to unite the major maritime nations in a demand that the Gulf be reopened or, if necessary, in forcing the Straits open. Israel's Foreign Minister, Abba Eban, flew to Washington to see President Johnson and gained the impression that the United States would definitely live up to its commitments. With this assurance, Israel withheld action for almost two weeks, waiting in a state of partial mobilization while Egypt forces massed in Sinai, while the Cairo radio blared forth that the day had come for Israel's destruction and while King Hussein of Jordan came to Cairo in order to place his Arab Legion under Egyptian command—an act for which he was to pay with the loss of half of his kingdom.

President Johnson's somewhat feeble efforts to muster intervention by the maritime nations produced only negative or lukewarm reactions. Actually, with the powerful Sixth Fleet in the Mediterranean, the United States needed no support from other nations, but the Congress was in no mood to sanction American involvement. To all intents and purposes, the United States was paralyzed by its ill-considered commitment in Vietnam.

Premier Eshkol was having a difficult time in restraining his armed forces. A large part of the Israeli public was impatient under the nervous tension and the economic strain of partial mobilization. People clamored for him to relinquish the Defense Ministry to Moshe Dayan, the hero of the 1956 war. On June 1 Eshkol yielded and Dayan assumed office as Minister of Defense, with Major-General Itzhak Rabin under him as Chief of Staff. On June 3 Dayan declared that Israel required no military assistance from any foreign country. (It was fortunate for the United States that this turned out to be true.)

On the morning of June 5 Israel's air force struck at the Egyptian airfields and destroyed most of Egypt's Soviet-supplied airplanes on the ground. Within two days Israel's ground forces cleared the Sinai Peninsula, destroying or capturing most of Egypt's Soviet-supplied armor and artillery, along with vast quantities of supplies. Cairo put out the story that American and British planes had participated in the June 5 attack. The Russians, who had been shadowing the Sixth Fleet, knew that not a single plane had taken off, except for a few which, with prior notice over the "hot line," had gone to the rescue of an American communications vessel mistakenly attacked by Israeli planes and torpedo-boats off the coast of Sinai. (President Johnson and Soviet Premier Kosygin had, at the outbreak of the war, assured each other over the "hot line" that they would not intervene.) Nevertheless, the story put out by Cairo was widely believed in the Arab world and, to some extent, took the early sting out of the crushing defeat.

Jordan, though urged by Israel not to intervene, nevertheless attacked and was soundly defeated on June 6–7, losing the entire territory it had previously held on the west bank of the Jordan. Syria, too, had launched a feeble attack and, as a consequence, lost the Golan Heights from which it had so long shelled the low-lying Israeli settlements. The capture of these strongly fortified heights by Israeli infantry was perhaps its most outstanding accomplishment.

By June 9 the war was practically over.

In the Security Council the Soviet and Arab speakers demanded that Israel be denounced as an aggressor and be forced to withdraw to the 1956 armistice frontiers and to pay reparations. The Russians did their best to turn military defeat into political victory, but the effort ended—for the time being—when the Security Council ordered, and Egypt accepted, a cease-fire without any conditions and without any condemnation of Israel. On June 10 Nasser resigned, accepting full blame for the disaster, but in response to a popular demonstration he withdrew his resignation.

However, the political battle at the United Nations was not over. The Soviet Union demanded an emergency session of the General Assembly. This session, which began on June 17, was attended by Premier Kosygin and Foreign Minister Gromyko.

Both President Johnson and Premier Kosygin were anxious to meet each other, but Kosygin was unwilling to go to Washington and Johnson considered it inappropriate for him to go to New York. A meeting was finally arranged at a halfway point, in the little-known college town of Glassboro, New Jersey. Two days of discussion were friendly but inconclusive. They gave the two leaders a chance to size each other up and to understand although not to reconcile each other's points of view. So far as the Middle East was concerned, one hopeful suggestion was made by Johnson, namely, that the two countries inform each other of any arms shipments into the area.

Returning to the forum of the United Nations, Kosygin repeated his condemnation of the United States' action in Vietnam, reiterating that it stood in the way of any peaceful settlement in the Middle East, and repeating as well his condemnation of Israel as the aggressor and his demand for Israel's withdrawal behind the armistice frontiers.

Israel's case was forcefully presented by Abba Eban, who denied that Israel had been the aggressor and asserted his country's refusal to withdraw from conquered territory except in the context of a peace settlement that would guarantee Israel's security and its right to free use of the Suez Canal and the Gulf of Aqaba. To withdraw on any other terms but these, he said, would simply mean re-establishing the very conditions that had led to the conflict.

The Arab states flatly refused to negotiate with Israel, insisting that Israel had no right to exist.

The United States gave indirect backing to Israel's position by refusing to back the Soviet-Arab demand for withdrawal without a peace settlement, while, at the same time, it reasserted its opposition to any territorial changes in the Middle East by military conquest.

The Emergency Session adjourned without result. Soviet diplomacy proved unable to convert military defeat into political victory. There was clearly no majority in favor of condemning Israel as the aggressor. A notable feature of the discussion was the pro-Arab position taken by India and the scarcely less unfriendly attitude of France toward Israel. Although the United States opposed the condemnation of Israel, its support of Israel was far from wholehearted. The American government was clearly paralyzed by its involvement in Vietnam, where it had neither a national interest nor a commitment of its national honor comparable to its interest in and its commitment to Israel.

Fortunately for the United States—and for the world—Israel, outnumbered and surrounded by its enemies, had achieved an almost miraculous victory—a victory which preserved its own existence, saved the United States from a fearful dilemma and, very likely, saved the world for the time being from the outbreak of a major war. What would the United States have done if the war had gone against Israel? And what would the Soviet Union have done if the United States had intervened to save Israel from extermination?

With the failure of the General Assembly to agree upon any United Nations resolution, the matter automatically reverted to the Security Council before which the Arabs, backed by the Soviet Union and India, once more took up the battle to force Israel to withdraw unconditionally from conquered territory. After almost six weeks of debate, the Security Council finally adopted a British resolution on November 21 which provided for:

> The termination of all claims or states of belligerency and respect for and acknowledgment of the sovereignty, territorial integrity and political independence of every state in the area and their right to live in peace within secure and recognized boundaries, free from threats or acts of force.

This paragraph modified one which preceded it, calling for "the withdrawal of Israeli armed forces from territories of recent conflict," thus leaving open for negotiation what would be the "secure and recognized boundaries" within which the Israeli forces would withdraw.

The resolution further affirmed the necessity for:

a) guaranteeing freedom of navigation through international waterways in the area;
b) for achieving a just settlement of the refugee problem;
c) for guaranteeing the territorial inviolability and political independence of every state in the area, through measures including the establishment of demilitarized zones.

Finally, the resolution requested the Secretary-General to send a special representative to the Middle East to "establish and maintain contacts with the States concerned in order to promote agreement and assist efforts to achieve a peaceful and accepted settlement in accordance with the principles and provisions of the resolution."

Lord Caradon's carefully prepared draft was unanimously approved by the Security Council, the action being the first concerning the Middle East upon which the United States and the Soviet Union voted together during the 1957–1967 period.

The Arab states were not happy with the resolution because it did not call for immediate and unconditional withdrawal. For the same reason, Israel declared that the resolution was one "with which we can live," although it was made clear in Jerusalem that the appointment of a United Nations special emissary would not alter Israel's insistence upon direct negotiations.

On November 23 the Secretary-General announced the appointment of Gunnar Jarring, an experienced Swedish diplomat serving at the time as Sweden's ambassador to Moscow, a duty from which he was promptly released by the Swedish government.

On the same day, President al-Attassi of Syria denounced the Security Council's action and President Nasser of Egypt made a belligerent speech in Cairo, asserting his determination to deny the use of the Suez Canal to Israeli shipping and strongly indicating an unwillingness to make peace.

Clearly, the road to the establishment of peace in the Middle East was going to be long and difficult, requiring magnanimity and restraint on the part of Israel and a painful acceptance of

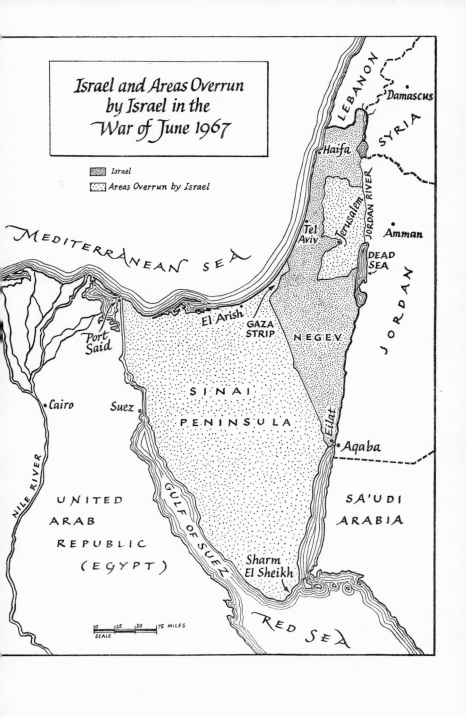

Israel and Areas Overrun
by Israel in the
War of June 1967

Israel
Areas Overrun by Israel

LEBANON
Damascus
SYRIA
Haifa
Tel Aviv
Jerusalem
Amman
JORDAN RIVER
DEAD SEA
NEGEV
JORDAN
MEDITERRANEAN SEA
El Arish
GAZA STRIP
Port Said
Cairo
Suez
SINAI PENINSULA
Eilat
Aqaba
NILE RIVER
GULF OF SUEZ
UNITED ARAB REPUBLIC (EGYPT)
SA'UDI ARABIA
Sharm El Sheikh
RED SEA

0   25   50   75 MILES
SCALE

reality by the Arab states. Peace would require also the strengthening of the United Nations peace-making and peace-keeping capabilities, as well as the cooperation of the great powers, especially the cooperation of the United States and the Soviet Union. The prospects for such cooperation were doubtful so long as the United States continued to pursue a course in Vietnam which alienated the Soviet Union and many if not most of the world's nations.

20

The Aftermath of War

The results of the six-day war of 1967 were superficially similar to but fundamentally different from the results of the 1956 conflict. Both wars left the Arabs stunned, humiliated and intransigent. Both wars left Israel in possession of important parts of enemy territory. Both left the Suez Canal temporarily blocked to all shipping. In both wars Israel was left temporarily in possession of the Sinai Peninsula, but in the 1967 war Israel also captured the important Golan Heights in Syria and part of the headwaters of the Jordan, as well as all of Jerusalem and all of the Jordanian territory west of the river. And whereas the 1956 war left Israel's access to the Gulf of Aqaba dependent upon the United Nations and an American guarantee, the 1967 war left Israel in possession of Sharm el Sheikh and thus in control of the Tiran Strait.

More important, however, were the changed attitudes toward a peace settlement of most of the nations directly or indirectly concerned. Israel's own attitude clearly reflected these changes.

In 1956 Israel had withdrawn from its conquests in compliance with the demands of the United Nations upon three quite definite assumptions: (1) that the United Nations would compel Egypt to open the Suez Canal to Israeli shipping; (2) that the United Nations would occupy the Gaza Strip, from which Egyptian Fedayeen and Palestinian commandos had conducted raids into Israel, as well as Sharm el Sheikh at the entrance to the Gulf of Aqaba; and (3) that the United States would guarantee Israel's free use of the Gulf. The first of these assump-

tions had never been fulfilled in spite of Israel's repeated com-
plaints to the United Nations. The second assumption had been
invalidated when in May 1967 Egypt demanded and the
United Nations agreed to the withdrawal of the UNEF from
Sinai. And the third assumption had proved invalid when
Egypt reoccupied Sharm el Sheikh, closing the Gulf, and the
United States had failed to reopen it.

As the result of this experience, Israel was no longer willing,
in 1967, to rely for its security upon either the United Nations
or the United States.

A further closely related change in Israel's attitude was its
insistence, in 1967, that peace negotiations would have to be
conducted through direct talks between Israel and the Arab
states, instead of through any intermediary. This was due in
part to loss of confidence in any outside mediation and in part
to the fact that the United Nations Conciliation Commission
had made the mistake of attempting to deal with the Arab
states as a whole, instead of following the bilateral pattern
successfully employed by Dr. Bunche in negotiating an armistice in 1949.

Important changes in the Arab world and in the attitudes of
the non-Middle Eastern powers also affected the 1967 posture
of Israel.

The Arab states were even more disunited in 1967 than they
had been in 1957. Nasser was no longer the unquestioned
leader. In 1956 Anglo-French intervention had made him a
hero even though his armies had been swept from the field by
Israel. In 1967 he had no such alibi, although he tried to create
the fiction that British and American planes had participated in
the Israeli attack. The failure of the union with Syria and
Egypt's unsuccessful intervention in Yemen further diminished Nasser's stature. The Syrians, who had constantly urged
him to attack Israel and who were largely responsible for getting him into trouble, had done little or nothing to aid Egypt
once the fighting had begun. The Yemen adventure had earned
Nasser the enmity of Sa'udi Arabia. The Soviet Union was
embarrassed by the military failure of its protégé. King Hussein
felt let down. President Arif of Iraq, whose brother had overthrown the Ba'athist Kassim regime and had subsequently been

killed in a helicopter crash, was more friendly to Cairo than to
Damascus, but he had a strong interest in selling oil to the West
and a Kurdish minority inclined to be sympathetic to Israel.
President Bourguiba of Tunisia scarcely concealed his con-
tempt of Nasser's pretensions to Arab leadership, while Colonel
Boumedienne of Algeria, who tended to side with China in the
Sino-Soviet quarrel, disliked Nasser's reliance upon Moscow.

Even within Egypt, Nasser was far less secure than he had
been ten years earlier. In fact, it was probably the insecurity of
his domestic position that had partly caused his reckless 1967
adventure. Nasser still had his charismatic appeal to the masses,
but he no longer had the full support of the army. This apparently was true even before the defeat caused Nasser to dismiss
his close friend General Abdel Hakim Amer as Chief of Staff,
along with several hundred other officers. Having taken this
action, Nasser found himself forced to suppress an incipient
officers' revolt, led by Amer, whom he had arrested and who
then committed suicide in rather strange circumstances. Nasser
was threatened on the Right by the reactionary Moslem
Brotherhood, which hated his social reforms, and he had failed
to consolidate his mass support on the Left into an effective
political force.

Finally, the 1967 adventure left Egypt close to bankruptcy;
it had lost its chief sources of revenue through the closing of
the Canal, the cessation of tourist traffic and the loss of its oil
wells in the Sinai Peninsula. The latter had produced about 60
percent of Egypt's oil requirements; the remaining 40 percent
came from a relatively new oilfield discovered under the Gulf
of Suez by an American oil company which was permitted to
continue operations in spite of the anti-Western fury that had
caused a severance of diplomatic relations with Britain and the
United States.

For the time being, power if not leadership in the Arab
world had shifted into the hands of the oil-rich feudal states,
whose rulers were more interested in selling oil to the West
than in wiping out Israel. This became very clear at the end
of August, when most of the Arab leaders met at Khartoum at
the invitation of Sudan's President Ismail Al Azhari. (Until now,
the Sudan had played no great part in the political struggles

in the Middle East, partly because Nasser's ambition to achieve
Arab leadership had diverted his attention to the north and east,
and partly because the Sudan was torn by internal conflict
between a Moslem north and a black, part-Christian and part-
animist south.)

The Khartoum Conference produced three important results:

1. Under great pressure, Nasser agreed to withdraw his
troops from Yemen and to cease his support of the Republican
rebels against the Sa'udi-supported Royalist regime. (This undoubtedly displeased Moscow, where the overthrow of the
Imam had been seen as a prelude to the establishment of Soviet
influence in South Arabia after the scheduled British withdrawal.)

2. Over the loud protests of Syrian, Algerian and Palestinian
intransigents, the leadership agreed to seek a "political solution" to the problem of getting Israel to withdraw from conquered territory without recognizing its existence or directly
negotiating with it. This course had been recommended to the
Arabs by Nasser's friend, Tito of Yugoslavia. (Ten years earlier, Tito, Nasser and India's then Prime Minister Nehru had
formed a "neutralist third force"; since then, both India and
Yugoslavia had remained friendly to Egypt and, in consequence, hostile to Israel.)

3. Pending the search for a "political solution" along the
above lines, Sa'udi Arabia, Kuwait and Libya agreed to finance
Egypt, Jordan and, to a small extent, Syria. The three oil-rich
states pledged a grant of $266 million to Egypt and $112 million to Jordan, both to be paid in quarterly installments. This
ended all talk of a continuing oil boycott against the West and
put the three oil-producing states in the driver's seat.

Although Israel denounced the proposed "political solution"
as unacceptable, it did seem to imply the renunciation of another resort to war, at least in the near future—an implication
rendered doubtful by recurring violations of the cease-fire
along the Canal. In October there were two even more disturbing occurrences: the sudden sinking, with considerable loss of
life, of the Israeli destroyer *Eilat* by highly sophisticated missiles fired from two Egyptian missile boats at Port Said; and the

subsequent destruction by Israeli artillery fire of the Egyptian oil refineries at Suez. It was not clearly established whether the *Eilat* was in international waters or whether, as the Egyptians claimed, she had crossed the twelve-mile line during what appeared to have been a routine patrol. Nor was it clear whether Nasser had ordered the attack. However, by publicly praising and decorating the officers who had fired the missiles, Nasser assumed full responsibility for the consequences. These were disastrous. The Israeli reprisal destroyed the installations which processed the oil from the Gulf of Suez, Egypt's sole source of domestic fuel, thereby forcing Egypt either to purchase foreign oil or to transport its own crude oil around the Cape of Good Hope to be processed in foreign refineries.

It was evident that Israel's security situation was now quite different from what it had been in 1957. Due to its possession of the Golan Heights, West Jordan and Sinai down to the west bank of the Canal, Israel was now reasonably secure against invasion although, as the sinking of the *Eilat* showed, it was now vulnerable to missile attack. On the other hand, the retention of enemy territory, particularly West Jordan with its large Arab population, exposed Israel to subversive activity by terrorists from Jordan. This involved the danger of renewed conflict.

On the Arab side, the decisive leadership had now apparently passed from Nasser to Faisal of Sa'udi Arabia, a feudal monarch whose outlook upon Middle Eastern affairs was quite different from that of the non-oil-producing Arab states. It was worth nothing that Sa'udi Arabia and Yemen were the only two Arab states that had never been under any form of Western rule; such hostility as they might feel toward the West would therefore derive not from memories of Western domination or betrayal, but from religious orthodoxy and resentment of the democratizing influence exerted upon the area by the West. (The same factors would operate against Moscow.) Similarly, Sa'udi Arabian hostility to Israel might be expected to derive less from Israel's intrusion into Arab territory than from its non-Moslem intrusion into the Moslem world and from its example of democratic government.

It is important to realize that, in spite of limited revolutions, the condition of the vast majority of the Arab peoples has undergone little change. Many are still nomads. The majority of the remainder consist of urban slum dwellers or peasants who own little land and have been forced to surrender half or more of their crops to absentee landlords and moneylenders. Until Nasser's limited land reform in Egypt, more than 25 million miserable fellahin averaged less than a single acre apiece in the fertile Nile Delta; and since land reform, they are not much better situated because of their rapidly increasing numbers and the limited amount of land available for cultivation. (It has been estimated that the Aswan Dam, when completed, will not add enough arable land to offset the population growth that will have taken place before its completion.)

There is no similar problem of overpopulation in the other Arab states, but the peasants still live under feudal conditions of semi-serfdom. This remains true even in the oil-producing states. The annual per capita income figures tell the story. They show the same figure—$199 per annum—for the people of wealthy Sa'udi Arabia, wealthy Iraq and impoverished Egypt. Because of its commercial development, the Lebanon figure is slightly higher at $349. This compares to Israel's per capita income of $999, and to a figure of $3,399 for each of the small number of people who share in the enormous wealth of Kuwait.*

Quite obviously, these are the preconditions for revolution. This has been wisely recognized in Iran, the non-Arab oil-rich country of the Middle East. Here Muhammad Reza Shah has inaugurated a "white revolution" ("white" as opposed to communist, or "red"). The royal estates have been to a large extent broken up and sold to small holders; other rich landowners have been forced to break up their huge holdings and have been induced to invest the proceeds of expropriation in industries promoted by the government. The medieval conditions of life have been radically changed. Education and health services have been vastly expanded. Rural co-operatives and courts have been fostered; women have been given the vote; industrial development is proceeding rapidly. Iran has set a challenging example for other authoritarian Middle East states. Unlike

* United Nations 1965 income estimates.

the Arab countries, Iran has recognized Israel.

Another factor affecting the future of the Arab world is that "Arab nationalism" has never attained regional dimensions. The British had tried to promote Arab unity under the leadership of Cairo, but Egypt was then the least Arab of the Arab states, and its leadership was unacceptable to most of them, especially to the Hashemite kingdoms and Sa'udi Arabia. Insofar as pan-Arab nationalism has existed at all, it has come into being for two purposes: liberation from foreign rule, which has been achieved; and the destruction of Israel, which has not.

The aim of destroying Israel has been frustrated to the point at which it is no longer a unifying force comparable to the divisive elements existing in an Arab world which is half rich and half poor, a world of states that have achieved sovereign independence but have not freed themselves from foreign influence nor freed their peoples from exploitation and medieval conditions of life. It is perhaps significant that hostility to Israel has been least pronounced in Lebanon, which has raised its people's living standard and achieved a balance between the Moslem and non-Moslem elements in its population, while in neighboring Syria hostility to Israel has been kept virulent by an unrepresentative government controlled by a fanatical clique of army officers.

Egypt, under Nasser, has been the apparent leader of anti-Israel pan-Arabism, but Nasser's fulminations against Israel have probably been inspired less by the sentiments of the Egyptian people than by his ambition to be accepted as the Arab leader by Syria and Iraq. If Nasser succeeds in the difficult task of raising the living standards of his people, it seems quite possible that he will no longer require Israel as a scapegoat. It is tragic that Nasser's ambition to become the leader of the Arab world has led him into disastrous military adventure and diverted him from his laudable efforts at domestic reform and betterment, leaving him, for the time being, dependent upon precisely those Arab leaders who are the most hostile to his relatively progressive ideas. Actually, as a leader in the revolt against medieval feudalsim, Nasser has more in common with Israel than with Sa'udi Arabia's King or the Sheikh of Kuwait.

Much will, of course, depend upon Israel's future policy and upon what sort of a state Israel intends to be. We shall revert to this question in the next chapter.

Much will also depend upon the attitudes and actions of the non-Middle Eastern intruders into the area. These, too, had undergone considerable change between 1956 and 1967.

Britain had practically ceased to be a factor in the Middle East after the Suez debacle. Its alliances had fallen apart. Its colony at Aden was about to be relinquished and its Persian Gulf protectorates were in the process of liquidation. The unsuccessful British attempt to create a South Arabian Federation had demonstrated that any foreign-imposed plan, no matter what its merit, stood little chance of being carried out once foreign military power had been withdrawn. (Britain had encountered the same experience in its withdrawal from its East African possessions.)

France, in 1956 a firm friend of Israel, had by 1967 become an unfriendly neutral. This was due more to De Gaulle's flirtation with the Soviet Union and his growing hostility toward the United States than to a change of heart on the part of the French people. In May 1967 the French President had peremptorily warned Israel against taking pre-emptive action after Egypt had closed the Gulf of Aqaba and mobilized its army in the Sinai Peninsula. When this advice was ignored, De Gaulle took the view that Israel had been the aggressor—a view held by the Arab states and the Soviet Union, but rejected by the majority of the members of the United Nations. Although Israel's air force had been equipped by French manufacturers and was dependent upon them for spare parts, De Gaulle embargoed all arms shipments to the Middle East, including an order for fifty additional planes for which Israel had already paid in part. This action could have had fatal consequences for Israel had it not achieved quick victory. De Gaulle went even further. At his annual press conference in November, he went out of his way to denounce Israel in terms which betrayed his hostility not only toward Israel but toward the entire Jewish people and which awakened memories of the Dreyfus affair, even though his remarks were sharply criticized in much of the French press. The French government lost no time in capitalizing its changed attitude toward Israel by seeking new oil concessions in Iraq and was reported to have offered arms to that Arab state on the grounds that it had not participated in the war! (Iraqi troops had entered Jordan but, because of the speed of Jordan's defeat, had seen no action.)

Between 1956 and 1967 the Soviet Union had moved from seeking to oust the United States from the Middle East to a policy of establishing a power position of its own in the area. Moscow had probably not wanted to precipitate a war in 1967, but it had certainly encouraged Arab belligerence and, after the Arab defeat, had promptly begun to replace the equipment lost by Egypt and Syria.

The strengthening of the Soviet power position in the Middle East and the weakening of the Western position were reflected in the attitudes of both Turkey and Iran. By 1967 both countries had shifted from outright hostility to the Soviet Union toward a more friendly posture—a posture short of neutrality but also short of unqualified allegiance to the West. In Turkey's case, the changed attitude was no doubt in part due to the quarrel with Greece over Cyprus. The maneuvering of the Iranian government was more difficult to fathom but undoubtedly reflected concern over the obvious growth of Soviet influence and the uncertain response of the United States.

While Soviet aims in the Middle East were not clear as 1967 drew to a close, the increase of Soviet influence was very evident. It appeared that, as a condition for replacing Egypt's lost equipment, Moscow had demanded and obtained a voice in the reorganization of its armed forces. Several thousand technicians and instructors were reported to be in Egypt. In Yemen a Republican airman shot down by the Royalists was identified as a Soviet pilot. The Soviet fleet in the Mediterranean was greatly augmented, and the "friendly visits" of Soviet warships to Egyptian and Syrian ports began to take on the look of permanent stationing. Harlan Cleveland, United States ambassador to NATO, stated that, by July 1967, 46 Soviet warships were operating in the Mediterranean, including some of the latest guided-missile cruisers, ten submarines and a number of supply ships.*

* See the NATO Letter of November 1967, published by the Atlantic

Like France, the Soviet Union lost no time in taking advantage of the confusion and demoralization in the Middle East by moving into the oil situation in Iraq. The projected deal between the French state-owned Compagnie des Pétroles and the Iraqi government was quickly followed by a similar Soviet move. The lands included in these two transactions had been part of the original concession granted to the Iraq Petroleum Company by the Hashemite government and then taken away by General Kassim's Law 80. (The Iraq Petroleum Company is owned by five Western oil companies—British Petroleum, Shell, the French Compagnie des Pétroles and the American Mobil Oil and Standard Oil of New Jersey.) To the extent that France and the Soviet Union were helping the Arif government of Iraq to reduce the dominant power of IPC, they were ingratiating themselves with the Arabs, but the deals also served their own purposes.

According to *The Times* of London, the Soviet Union, although one of the world's largest producers of oil, was beginning to face an oil shortage. France needed to diversify its sources of crude oil, for which it was heavily dependent upon Algeria.

Both France and Russia were interested in reducing the position of the Anglo-American oil companies in the Middle East. Although France no longer had any real position of power in the Middle East, it was skillfully playing the role of scavenger, and because of De Gaulle's hostility to the United States and Britain, it was helping the Soviet Union to advance its power position without incurring an imperialist or colonialist label.

Meanwhile, Britain, anxious above all else to get the Suez Canal reopened, was making advances to Nasser.

In these circumstances, the question uppermost in the minds of the Israelis was obviously how the United States would react to the Soviet challenge. Would Washington seek by agreement with Moscow to de-fuse the arms race in the Middle East? Or would it provide Israel with countervailing arma-

---

Council. In the same statement Cleveland estimated that the operating days of the Soviet fleet in the Mediterranean showed an increase of 400 percent over 1963.

ments to restore the balance of military power? Lifting the American embargo upon arms shipments to the Middle East, if it meant supplying arms to Jordan as well as to Israel, could scarcely be called a policy designed to meet Israel's needs. Where else than to the United States could Israel turn? The history of the past twenty years was not reassuring.

The United States, in 1947 the sponsor of Israel's creation, had in 1956 found it necessary to condemn Israel, along with Britain and France, for its invasion of Egypt. When war threatened in 1967 over Egypt's closure of the Gulf of Aqaba, the United States failed to fulfill its guarantee, given ten years earlier, of Israel's free use of the Gulf, and when war actually broke out, the State Department had declared that the United States would be "neutral in word, thought and deed." It was not until after Israel's victory that the American government came to Israel's support at the United Nations, backing Israel's refusal to withdraw from conquered territory without a peace treaty that assured its security.

In contrast to the ambiguous attitude of their government, most Americans were more friendly to Israel than to the Arab states up to the time of the 1967 war. In part this was due to the fact that they had a better understanding of the Jewish cause than of the Arab case against Israel; in part it was due to the traditional American sympathy for the "underdog." After Israel's spectacular victory in June 1967, some of this sympathy was transferred to the Arabs, especially in view of Israel's "hard-nosed" attitude with respect to Jerusalem and the repatriation of some 200,000 newly created Arab refugees.

The atmosphere prevailing in the United States in 1967 was scarcely conducive to the formation of reasoned judgment based upon a full knowledge of fact. The American people were torn by dissension over the war in Vietnam, distracted by internal racial strife and distrustful of the Johnson administration's leadership. There was a widespread feeling, especially among young Americans, that something had gone wrong in the whole social order—that America had lost its sense of direction and that a radical change was required, a change the nature of which few could define. In this climate of anxiety the Middle East crisis appeared to many Americans as "just one more thing to worry about" but not as a subject requiring careful study and concentrated thought.

Yet a careful study of Western Man's behavior in the Middle East is capable of supplying the key to an understanding of much of what has gone wrong and still is wrong in our Western society, for the story traced in this study is a tale of selfish greed, of divisive bigotry and of man's savage inhumanity to man. And are not these the very evils that, in our time, threaten the survival of human civilization? The Middle East is not only a laboratory in which to study the human failings of the past and present; it is the ideal testing ground for the ideas and techniques by which past error may be redeemed.

21

A Look into the Future

Broadly speaking, there are three schools of thought about the future of the world. There are those who regard as more or less permanent a world of many fully sovereign nation-states, dominated by two or perhaps three superpowers—the United States, the Soviet Union and, perhaps, Japan or China. A second school of thought envisions a future world dominated by only one superpower which would preserve a *Pax Americana,* a *Pax Sovietica* or possibly a *Pax Asiatica.* A third school of thought, to which the writer belongs, believes that, in order to survive, the world must eventually be governed as a whole by a universal world organization authorized and empowered by universal consent to enact, administer and enforce world law upon all the world's nations and peoples. In this latter group are people who believe in the almost total submergence of national sovereignty under a world "parliament of man," while others, such as the writer, envision a world government of strictly limited powers delegated to it by the sovereign states primarily for the purpose of preserving peace in spite of ineluctable change. Even such a limited world government cannot be expected to come about until there is a far greater consensus than presently exists between those nations and peoples who are reasonably well satisfied with the *status quo* and those who are dissatisfied and wish to change it.

Most people would agree that today's world is one of bipolar power in which peace hangs precariously upon decisions made and actions taken or not taken in Washington and Moscow. No one knows how long this condition will last, but while it lasts it is of the utmost importance whether the two present super-powers will contend for world supremacy, share world hegemony or cooperate toward strengthening a world organization in which all nations and peoples have a voice in the creation of a world order based upon peace and justice under law. If the United States and the Soviet Union contend for world hegemony, there is little hope for peace in our time; if they attempt to establish a world condominium, they may perhaps for a time preserve peace of a fragile sort, in which discontent on the part of other nations and peoples will almost certainly erupt in rebellion. The best if not the sole hope for enduring peace rests upon the cooperation of the two present super-powers with each other and with all the world's nations and peoples toward the strengthening of the United Nations or the creation of a new world organization capable not only of preserving peace but of mediating disputes and preventing conflicts from erupting into violence.

The past relationship of the United States to supra-national world organization reflects a long-standing inner conflict between parochialism and world-mindedness. No nation has done more to create world organization; no nation has been more reluctant than the United States to participate in it. At the conclusion of World War I, an American President took the initiative in founding the League of Nations only to be repudiated by his own people. Toward the end of World War II, the initiative for founding the United Nations again emanated from Washington. Secretary of State Hull flew to Moscow in 1943 to obtain Stalin's agreement to participate in a new world organization. The United Nations Charter was drafted at Dumbarton Oaks and adopted at San Francisco. But President Roosevelt's world-mindedness was tempered by an overcautious appraisal of the limits of the attainable, and for fear of another repudiation, the Charter was weakened to the point where the powers of the new world organization were incommensurate with the assignment of preserving peace, especially in the then-dawning atomic age.

In the postwar period a succession of American Secretaries of State issued declarations asserting that support of the United

Nations must be "the cornerstone" of American policy. Yet, with few exceptions, the major actions of the United States were undertaken unilaterally or at least outside of the United Nations. This was true of the American interventions in Greece and Turkey, in China, in Vietnam and in the Dominican Republic; it was true of the secret operations conducted in Iran, Cuba and Guatemala.

Soviet obstructionism provided the usual rationalization for American action outside of the United Nations, especially in cases where time was deemed of the essence. But there was a deeper cause. In 1944, when John Foster Dulles participated as the advisor of Governor Dewey of New York in drafting the Charter at Dumbarton Oaks, he expressed this view:

> The plan to impose peace presupposes a political unity of the great powers which has rarely occurred and which, if it prevails, will itself assure peace. While the Security Council can be useful as a forum where controversial matters are discussed, and where public opinion may focus its pressures, the force proposals are little more than scenery.

This was a sharp challenge to Roosevelt's declaration that the Security Council "must have the power to act quickly and decisively to keep the peace, by force if necessary" and that it "must be endowed in advance . . . with authority to act."

From the conviction that the teeth in the Charter would not bite, Dulles did not draw the conclusion that the enforcement powers should be strengthened. On the contrary, he concluded that peace enforcement should be left to regional military organizations. In a book published in 1950, Dulles stated that he himself had drafted Article 51 of the Charter (which permits regional alliances and under which the United States has sponsored NATO, SEATO, CENTO and a number of other alliances).* He related how he considered the United Nations a "town meeting of the world," while laboring to develop regional military alliances "within the Charter but outside the veto." Concerning the veto, Dulles made it clear that he and the Republicans with whom he worked at San Francisco were

* John Foster Dulles, *War and Peace* (Macmillan, New York, 1950).

convinced that the United States must insist upon the right to
veto any enforcement action. (Leading Democrats were
equally insistent upon this right. The veto was not a Soviet
invention.)

The point is that, as early as 1944 and before there was any
sign of a Cold War, there was a strong disinclination on the
part of American policymakers to subordinate any part of
American foreign policy to a world organization. This remains
true today; and nowhere has this disinclination been more
clearly demonstrated than in the Middle East. The ineffective-
ness of the United Nations is due only in part to its Charter,
which could, after all, be amended.* It is due primarily to the
unwillingness of the major powers to use the United Nations as
more than a forum for discussion and propaganda.

One thing is certain. If one believes that the establishment of
enduring peace requires universal national disarmament enforced by supra-national authority, the pursuit of such disarmament will remain the pursuit of a mirage so long as the major
powers are not prepared to establish a limited form of world
government. There are, to be sure, certain limited measures of
arms control which can be taken to reduce the likelihood of
major conflict, but even these cannot be expected to be effective unless all the world's nations, including the People's Republic of China, are brought into agreements such as the contemplated treaty to prevent the proliferation of nuclear
weapons.

So far as the Middle East is concerned, two measures of arms
control would seem essential:

1. An agreement among all the nations capable of supplying
armaments to limit, if not to embargo entirely, all arms shipments into the area after the peace treaties between Israel and
the Arab states shall have gone into effect. Hopefully, these

* For a concrete detailed example of what could be done to strengthen
the United Nations by Charter amendment, if the will to do so existed,
see Grenville Clark and Louis Sohn, *World Peace Through World Law*
(Harvard University Press, Cambridge, 1958).

With the accretion of many mini-states as members, the principle of
"one nation, one vote" is becoming increasingly preposterous. One
answer to the problem could be found through a system of weighted
voting; a simpler answer would be through the creation of a bicameral
legislature similar to the United States Congress.

treaties might provide for a limitation of armaments.

2. Accession by all the nations in the Middle East to the Non-Proliferation Treaty, whereby they would renounce the manufacture or acquisition of nuclear weapons.

If there is any one lesson that the United States government should have learned from sad experience, it is the folly of trying to preserve peace by selling or giving away the weapons of war. Between 1945 and 1967 the United States had doled out over $300 million in military aid to the Arab states and $28 million to Israel. (Israel purchased most of its arms from France, to a large extent with funds privately raised in the United States.) Egypt received something like $500 million in military equipment from the Soviet bloc. Syrian forces received Soviet equipment. The United States provided Sa'udi Arabia with $162 million, Iraq with $47 million, Jordan with $55.5 million. When Jordan invaded Israel in June 1967, American tanks manned by Jordanians clashed with American tanks manned by Israelis. After the cease-fire, Israeli troops found abandoned Jordanian crates of ammunition with each crate bearing a sticker showing two hands clasped across a red, white and blue background—the symbol of American aid.*

It is one thing to arm a dependable ally against a commonly recognized danger; e.g., arming Western Europe against an assumed military threat from the east. It is quite another thing to arm a country like Pakistan or Iraq in the hope of gaining an ally against the Soviet Union when neither country recognizes the existence of a Soviet threat and when each wants arms not to defend itself against communist invasion, but to use against its neighbor: in Pakistan's case, against India; in the case of Iraq, against Israel.

Fortunately, the folly of some of this past policy is gradually being recognized, but the Pentagon still maintains a high-pressure sales organization to distribute American arms abroad. This procedure is defended on the grounds that it helps to cure the deficit in our balance of international payments and by the further argument that if the United States does not supply modern arms to nations that want them, some other arms-sup-

---

* When war erupted in 1962 between India and Pakistan, each side was similarly equipped with American planes and tanks.

plying nation will.

Clearly, what is needed is a policing of the trade in arms by international agreement enforced by a strengthened United Nations. The international trade in narcotics is controlled in this manner. Surely, modern weapons are no less dangerous. A good place to begin would be an Anglo-French-Soviet-American agreement with respect to the Middle East.*

The present situation in the Middle East—and in Southeast Asia—clearly shows the need for strengthening not only the peace-preserving but the peace-making capabilities of the United Nations. The authority and prestige of the world organization as a peace-maker have suffered severely from past failures in the Middle East. If Ambassador Gunnar Jarring succeeds where others have failed, much of the past may be redeemed not only by the establishment of peace after twenty years of belligerence, but through restoring the confidence of Israel and the Arab states in the United Nations.

The greatest need for strengthening the United Nations and the most promising opportunity for doing so lie, however, in another direction, namely, in the field of striking at the causes of conflict rather than aiming merely at the control of violence.

It is a truism to say that the discrepancy between the conditions of life existing in the highly developed and underdeveloped parts of the world is one of the major causes of discontent and potential violence. The United Nations and its specialized agencies have done much in the way of supplying technical knowledge and assistance needed to eliminate those primitive conditions which have for centuries held back the development of two-thirds of the world's population. But, as everyone knows, development requires capital, and this the United Nations has not been in a position to supply. Some of the urgent need for capital has been supplied by the World Bank and its soft-loan subsidiary, but these institutions are limited by the

* Nothing came of the suggestion at the Glassboro meeting between Kosygin and Johnson that the United States and the Soviet Union agree to inform each other of any arms shipments to the Middle East. This was probably because the Soviet Union was determined to replace the armaments lost by Egypt in the June war. Later in the year the United States resumed arms shipments to Israel.

means at their disposal and the restrictions which necessarily govern their operations. Moreover, they are institutions controlled by the industrialized nations in which the countries in need of capital have no proprietary interest. While this may seem logical, the division of the world into those countries which provide capital and those who need it creates a psychological cleavage which is not conductive to peace.

For these and other reasons, many students of world affairs, among them the writer, have long felt that the United Nations should be put in a position to provide capital as well as technical assistance. If this could be accomplished, three major purposes would be served:

1. Aid to economic development would become a function of the whole world community—a function in which donor and recipient nations would cooperate for the good of all and from which competition among donors for political ends of their own would be eliminated.

2. Long-term planning and scheduling of capital investment would become possible; it is not now possible because the flow of aid is dependent upon the annual decisions of governments that supply most of the funds.

3. The prestige of the United Nations would be vastly strengthened.

Ten years ago, in April 1957, the writer first put forward a proposal to establish a United Nations Development Authority so constituted as to give appropriate representation both to the nations supplying it with funds and to those seeking assistance.*

It was proposed that the U.N. Development Authority be constituted somewhat along the lines of the U.N. Security Council, except that there would be no veto. Five permanent seats would be allotted to the industrialized nations as a whole, to be occupied each year by those particular industrialized nations which, in the preceding year, had made the largest contributions of funds. Another five or perhaps six seats would be

---

* The proposal was endorsed by the Commission to Study the Organization of Peace in its Tenth Annual Report. In revised form, it was endorsed by a group of Congressmen in 1959 and published by them in *The Liberal Papers* (Doubleday, New York, 1962).

occupied by annually rotating regional representatives of the non-industrialized beneficiary nations.

In addition to the parent Authority, there would be created five or possibly six regional subsidiaries, among which the Middle East Development Authority mentioned in Chapter 18 would be one. The regional boards would consist of representatives of the nations within the region. Each board would sift the problems and opportunities existing in its area and would assign priorities to the projects which it approved. Each regional board would then, through its annually rotating spokesman on the parent Authority, present its approved projects for consideration.

The fixing of priorities among the projects recommended by the Regional Authorities as well as the actual allocation of funds would be determined by the parent Authority's board. A majority of the five nations holding the permanent seats would be required for the approval of any project or appropriation. Thus, the ultimate control of the funds would rest with the United States and the four other major contributors, of which the Soviet Union would undoubtedly be one, if it elected to participate in the scheme. However, the Soviet Union alone could not obstruct action, since there would be no veto; nor could it in the foreseeable future control a majority as against the other holders of the permanent seats since none of the smaller Soviet-bloc nations would be likely to become major contributors. And if China were to become a member of the United Nations and to earn the right to a permanent seat, there would still be only two Communist votes out of five.

We cannot know, until the proposal is put forward, what the Soviet attitude would be. Moscow's note of February 12, 1957, quoted in Chapter 18, certainly did not rule out the possibility of Soviet cooperation. Should the Soviet Union agree to participate, one of the major facets of the Cold War would be eliminated.

The creation of a United Nations Development Authority as described above *would not require Charter amendment.* It could be put through by a simple two-thirds vote in the General Assembly.

So far as the economic development of the Middle East is

concerned, there is no other land area in the world as richly endowed with natural resources as this region. In no other area are existing natural resources being developed to the extent that they are in the Middle East. The wealth to finance development is there; it flows each day in millions of barrels of "black gold." Unfortunately, it flows at the present time into foreign lands or into the pockets of the greedy, corrupt and selfish few, the native potentates, instead of flowing as it should to the impoverished peoples through the hands of governments responsive to their needs. Nowhere else in the world could peoples, if freed from exploitation, so readily use their own resources to lift themselves out of the Middle Ages into the twentieth century.

In 1963 an idea was brought forward which revolutionized all previous thoughts of world economic development. In an article published in *War/Peace Report* and later elaborated in a book,* John Stoessinger suggested that the United Nations General Assembly should adopt a resolution declaring that the sea-bed beyond the limits of national jurisdictions belonged to all the world's peoples and should be exploited to finance the economic development of the poor nations.

The idea was enthusiastically taken up by the Commission to Study the Organization of Peace and several times included among the recommendations in its annual reports. In July 1967 a "World Peace Through Law" Conference at Geneva, attended by over 2,000 lawyers and judges from more than 100 nations, called upon the United Nations General Assembly to declare that "the non-fishery resources of the high seas outside the territorial waters of any state and the bed of the sea beyond the continental shelf appertain to the United Nations and are subject to its jurisdiction and control."

At the subsequent 1967 session of the General Assembly, Malta's Ambassador, Arvid Pardo, introduced the "sea-bed item" to the agenda. In a three-hour presentation backed by careful research, Mr. Pardo opened the eyes of the delegates to the hitherto unsuspected wealth of resources awaiting exploration and development. Many of the statistics provided came

* John Stoessinger, *Financing the U.N. System* (Brookings Institution, Washington, D.C., 1963).

from John L. Mero's exhaustive study, *The Mineral Resources of the Sea*. Backed with a mass of impressive evidence, the Maltese ambassador showed that the sea-bed held not only vast, already-known resources of oil, but also great quantities of manganese nodules and other minerals constantly being produced in quantities far exceeding possible annual extraction. Mr. Pardo made the startling estimate that within five years of the creation of an international agency and the beginning of exploration, the agency's annual income after all expenses would be "at least $5 billion, to be used directly or through the United Nations development program to further the development of the poor countries."

A considerable number of delegates, among them United States Ambassador Arthur Goldberg, supported the proposal to appoint a special committee to study the matter and to look into the legal as well as the practical aspects. Pardo himself expressed doubt as to whether it would be wise to make the United Nations itself the administrator of the development program. "It is hardly likely," he said, "that those countries that have already developed a technical capability to exploit the ocean floor would agree to an international regime if it were administered by a body where small countries, such as mine, had the same voting power as the United States or the Soviet Union."

The writer's 1957 proposal for the creation of a United Nations Development Authority had been drawn with precisely this difficulty in mind. It therefore seemed appropriate to urge the Commission to Study the Organization of Peace to bring its repeated endorsement of this proposal to the attention of the United Nations *ad hoc* committee.*

During the past decade, ever since the flight of the first Soviet Sputnik, the eyes of the modern scientific world have been turned toward Outer Space. Vast energies and huge sums of money have been spent on the project of sending human beings

* It should perhaps be explained that the CSOP, on whose executive committee the writer has served for some years, is the research affiliate of the American Association for the United Nations. The CSOP was founded by Dr. James Shotwell as an adjunct to the old League of Nations Association.

to the moon, while the urgent needs of this planet were largely neglected. Recognizing the awesome dangers involved in a possible militarization of Outer Space, the nations of the world have agreed upon and signed a treaty to prevent the use of Outer Space for anything but peaceful purposes. Similar dangers would threaten if the ocean floor were to become militarized.

Perhaps, during the next decade, man's ingenuity will be turned at least in part toward the internationalization of the ocean floor and toward unlocking for the benefit of all mankind the treasure house that we now know lies beneath the seven seas of this troubled planet. There could be no greater single step toward organizing our world for enduring peace.

So much for the long-range view.

In the immediate future, peace in the Middle East will depend at least as much upon the cooperation of the United States and the Soviet Union as upon the actions of Israel and its Arab neighbors. The two present superpowers have a recognized common interest in avoiding a nuclear confrontation. They have a parallel if not a common interest in containing China. Were it not for the American intervention in South Vietnam and, above all, the extension of the war into an attack upon communist North Vietnam, the two superpowers would have no serious conflicts of interest in Asia.

The two areas in which American and Soviet interests are in serious conflict are Central Europe and the Middle East. The United States wants Soviet military power out of Germany; the Soviet Union wants the United States out of the Middle East, where its bases and alliances are seen as a threat to Soviet security. As frequently contended by this writer in the past,* these two confrontations could best be resolved in conjunction, but as yet there has been little if any progress in that direction. Nor can there probably be any progress until the Vietnam war is liquidated.

As for the prospects for peace between Israel and its Arab neighbors, it is difficult to quarrel with the statement of Israel's

---

* *Agenda for Action: Toward Peace Through Disengagement* (1957); *The Liberal Papers* (1960), Chapter 2; and *The United States in the Postwar World* (1966), Appendix "B."

position made by Foreign Minister Eban to the United Nations
General Assembly in October 1967:

> "Israel will not return to the political and juridical an-
> archy or the strategic vulnerability from which she has
> emerged. Apart from the cease-fire agreement, we have no
> contractual agreements with our neighbors at this time.
> We must now build not a ramshackle structure based on
> ambiguity and doubt, but a durable edifice of relations em-
> bodied in treaties of peace."

This leaves a number of questions to be answered at the
proper time, such as:

1. What portions of the territory she has conquered will Israel wish to retain or to have demilitarized in the interest of her
national security?

2. What agreements for the limitation and control of armaments will Israel wish to see written into the peace treaties?
And what provisions for inspection and enforcement does Israel contemplate?

3. What concessions, if any, is Israel prepared to make to
world opinion with respect to Jerusalem?

4. What roles, if any, does Israel wish the United Nations
and the great powers to play in underwriting the peace
treaties?

5. Upon what conditions will Israel compensate, repatriate or
cooperate in the resettlement of the Arab refugees from Palestine and West Jordan?

These are perhaps the five most important surface questions
to be answered, but beneath the surface lies a far more important question which will largely determine the nature of the
peace. That question reads:

"What sort of a state does Israel intend to be?"

It is difficult enough at times to understand the nature and
the behavior of one's own country. It is often impossible fully
to understand the nature and behavior of another nation.

In the Israel of today there appear to be a number of conflicting trends, difficult to understand and impossible to evaluate.
We have earlier noted the "hawk-dove" conflict which existed
within the Jewish community in Palestine before Israel became

a state, and which existed in 1956 between Ben-Gurion and Moshe Sharett. Much the same kind of conflict appears to exist today, affecting not only the decisions whether or not force is to be used but the decisions concerning the demands to be made by Israel in the interests of its future security. Questions of security inevitably affect Israel's attitude toward the refugee problem, and this, in turn, affects and is affected by the nature of the society which Israel desires to create.

On June 11, 1967, Israel's Defense Minister, Moshe Dayan, appeared on a nationally televised American broadcast, *Face the Nation*. One of his interlocutors, Sydney Gruson of *The New York Times*, asked General Dayan:

> "Is there any possible way that Israel could absorb the huge number of Arabs whose territory it has gained control of now?"
>
> *Dayan:* "Economically we can; but I think that is not in accord with our aims in the future. It would turn Israel into either a binational or poly-Arab-Jewish state, and we want to have a Jewish state. We can absorb them, but then it won't be the same country."
>
> *Gruson:* "And it is necessary in your opinion to maintain this as a Jewish state and a purely Jewish state?"
>
> *Dayan:* "Absolutely—absolutely. We want a Jewish state like the French have a French state."

Allowing for the fact that this sort of colloquy does not lend itself to carefully considered exposition and for the further fact that the interview took place almost immediately after the heady Israeli victory, it nevertheless raised some disturbing questions.

What did General Dayan mean by "a purely Jewish state"? Ever since its creation, Israel had contained a considerable number of Arabs who had gradually become full citizens. And when the General spoke of "a Jewish state, like the French have a French state," he was surely aware that France has absorbed and granted citizenship to immigrants of many races, religions and national origins, including Jews and Moslems. One could fully understand that the people of Israel did not want the Arabs to become a majority or even a powerful minority in their state, but did it follow that the majority must be 100 percent Jewish? And, if so, Jewish by what definition? Chaim Weizmann had said that a Jew was any person who declared himself to be a Jew. However, according to the basic laws of Israel, a Jew is anyone born of a Jewish mother. But what determines the "Jewishness" of a woman? Race? Surely, Israel has not adopted the Hitler-Rosenberg thesis that there is such a thing as a Jewish race. If not race, then what? Religion? But Israel is a secular state in which, despite a disproportionately politically powerful Orthodox theocracy, the majority of citizens are apparently non-religious. The theocracy decrees that no Jewish man may marry a Gentile woman within the state of Israel, and that a Jew who has married a Gentile woman in some other country may not be buried in the soil of Israel with his wife and children.

As the king in Rodgers' and Hammerstein's play *The King and I* remarked: "It is a puzzlement."

A similar "puzzlement" applies to the Israeli Law of Return which declares that any Jew, no matter where resident or what his present citizenship, is automatically also a citizen of Israel. The persistent Zionist campaign for the "ingathering" of all Jews implies the belief that all Jews, wherever they may be, are under some sort of moral obligation to emigrate to Israel or, if they do not wish to do so, to assist others in returning to Israel. Also implied in this propaganda for the "ingathering" has been a warning that what has happened to the Jews of Europe may someday happen to the Jews who remain in other countries.*

From the Israeli point of view, the campaign for the "ingathering" is understandable on the grounds that the country needs more people to aid in its development—especially people with specialized knowledge and skills—although, prior to the war of 1967, there was substantial unemployment in Israel. Since Israel's victory, the pleas for greater immigration carry the implication that Israel expects to retain substantial parts of the

---

* The writer rejects this pessimistic view and believes that there is not only a future for the Jews of the diaspora but that they will have increasing opportunities to contribute to the cultural, scientific, and artistic development of the countries in which they live. This may not be true in the case of the Jews in the Soviet Union, who, if they were free to do so, might well wish to emigrate to Israel.

21. A Look into the Future

235

territory it has conquered. This may or may not be the case; whether or not it is true, it is evident that Israel can absorb only a limited number of Arabs so long as their presence constitutes a threat to the state's internal security. Apart from the Arab minority, Israel already has an internal demographic problem about which little is said: more than one-third of Israel's Jewish majority consists of Middle Eastern or African Jews, some of them quite dark-skinned, who are looked down upon by some of the dominant European element and who are, in fact, in some respects more like the Arabs among whom they have lived for centuries than like the sophisticated Jews from the West. The fact that the aging European elite finds its dominance threatened by the oriental influx and, perhaps even more, by the rapidly growing native-born Sabra population probably accounts at least in part for the urgent call for greater immigration from the West.

For an American, it is difficult to understand why this much-desired Western influx should necessarily be 100 percent Jewish, why the immigration of a certain number of non-Jews should not be desirable, so long as such non-Jewish immigrants were willing to become loyal citizens of Israel. Inevitably, one recalls the vast benefits that accrued to the United States from heterogeneous immigration in the eighteenth and early nineteenth centuries.

The proclaimed desire to build a "purely Jewish" state, the insistent demand for more Jewish immigrants, even in times of unemployment, and the Israeli government's acquiescence in the imposition of illiberal laws and restrictions by a bigoted theocracy—these are disturbing features that carry overtones of something very like racism in reverse. Fortunately, the dangers inherent in quasi-racism, religious bigotry and chauvinistic nationalism are well recognized in Israel—more clearly perhaps than they are recognized by some of Israel's most ardent supporters in the United States.*

* Not long ago, the writer aroused a considerable controversy in the American Jewish community by pointing out that some of the funds raised annually for charitable purposes by the United Jewish Appeal were being used to support political parties in Israel, among them the avowedly expansionist *Herut* Party of Jabotinsky followers led by Menachem Begin, former head of the Irgun terrorists.

In the long run, Israel and its Arab neighbors face a choice between two kinds of peace:

One is a peace of reconciliation based upon Israel's full integration in the Middle Eastern community of nations. This requires not only Israel's desire to integrate, but a realization on the part of the Arab states that Israel has much to offer as a welcome member of the Middle Eastern community. One might expect such an attitude to materialize most readily in the more progressive Arab states and least readily in the more theocratic feudal countries.

The alternative is a peace based upon Israel's turning its face toward the West and becoming a Mediterranean rather than a Middle Eastern nation, linked, like Greece, to the European community. Such a peace will be acceptable to the Arab states only if they are convinced that an Israel so oriented will not be a tool of the West, lending itself to continued Western exploitation of the Middle East.

At present, the choice is not open to Israel nor to the Arab states. Nor will it be open so long as the United States pursues its present policy. This American policy—if such it can be called—is based upon two primary considerations: (1) the safeguarding of the American oil interests; and (2) the prevention, without major war, of Soviet domination of the Middle East. In conjunction, these two aims ally the United States with the feudal, oil-producing states against the oil-poor Arab countries struggling toward social and economic progress—the latter backed by the Soviet Union for political purposes of its own. Since Israel is heavily dependent upon private American subsidy and upon American diplomatic support—and since the United States does not dare to use its own military power in the Middle East—the present American policy, in effect, makes Israel the supplier of the military muscle required to hold down social revolution in the Middle East.

The present American policy not only causes the United States to appear as the enemy of progressive change, while the Soviet Union poses as its friend; it also casts Israel, the most progressive state in the Middle East, in the unnatural role of providing the chief military support for the politico-economic *status quo.*

This American policy will, if continued, force Israel willy-nilly into a Mediterranean rather than a Middle Eastern orientation. Thus oriented, Israel may perhaps be able to negotiate peace terms with its Arab neighbors that fulfill its security requirements, but it will not be able to avoid remaining an outpost of the West and a thorn in the flesh of the Arab world.

The alternative American policy—one that would leave Israel free to determine its orientation—has been suggested earlier in this study. This would be a policy of fostering and aiding regional social and economic development by bringing about an equitable sharing of the region's oil, water and other resources among all the peoples of the area. Such a policy would cast Israel in the role of setting an example in the area's development and of becoming the supplier of technical knowledge, technological skill and experience in democratic government. In such a role, one can imagine Israel and the Arab states not merely signing peace treaties but actually laying the foundations for enduring peace in the area.

For the time being, the present American policy may perhaps protect the interests of the international oil cartel and the feudal rulers of the oil-rich Arab states. In the long run, one suspects that this policy can at most delay the overthrow of the feudal potentates and the expropriation of foreign-owned oil properties by revolutionary governments.

It is difficult to ascertain who in the United States makes its Middle East policy. As previously pointed out, that policy is the product of a number of conflicting interests and pressure groups among which the oil lobby is perhaps the most powerful. But in recent years the oil interests have become less an independent pressure group than an important part of that military-industrial complex against the rising power of which President Eisenhower warned in his valedictory address to the American people. This complex has become more than a pressure group. It has all but usurped the power that rightfully belongs, in a pluralistic society, to the process of accommodation between and among a variety of interests. The State Department has become subservient to the military-industrial complex; so, to some extent, have the media of communication. And the complex has a vested interest, not in war, but in the perpetuation of a condition that is neither war nor peace.

To say this is not to say that the military, the arms makers and the merchandizers of strategic goods, such as oil, are evil men. Nor is it to say that they have purposefully sought power over the formation of American foreign policy. It would be nearer to the truth to say that power has drifted into their hands through the abdication of power by the American people and the officials of their elected government. But there are signs of an awakening on the part of the American people. The Executive Branch and the Congress are beginning to feel the pressure of the potentially greatest pressure group of all—the growing mass of American citizens who demand that their country's resources be devoted, not to war in distant lands, but to the work of peace at home and abroad.

So long as the war in Vietnam continues, there will be little hope of Soviet-American cooperation toward the establishment of peace in the Middle East. In the absence of such cooperation there is likely to be a vicious circle of Arab terrorism and Israeli reprisal, exacerbating tensions and preventing progress toward negotiated peace.

Fortunately as this book goes to press there is a growing realization among Americans that the intervention in Vietnam has become a massive and increasingly senseless misadventure demanding a wholly unwarranted sacrifice of human life, of material resources and of the nation's reputation—a misadventure in which the American people have found themselves imprisoned by the irrational compulsion on the part of their leaders to reinforce error rather than to admit misjudgment and miscalculation.

Fear that there may be no limit to what a desperate leadership might do to escape from admitting its mistakes has reawakened the long-dormant democratic processes of discussion and debate and a demand for a reappraisal of the nation's true interests, of its proper responsibilities at home and abroad, and of the resources and power available to meet them. The reawakening of the American people holds promise of bringing about either a change of policy or a change of leadership. Upon the outcome depends to a large extent the hope of peace not only in Southeast Asia and the Middle East but in the whole of an anxious world.

BIBLIOGRAPHY

Antonius, George. *The Arab Awakening*. London: Hamish Hamilton, 1938.

Campbell, John C. *Defense of the Middle East*. New York: Harper, 1958.

Carmichael, Joel. *The Shaping of the Arabs*. New York: Macmillan, 1967.

Churchill, Winston S. *The Grand Alliance*. Boston: Houghton Mifflin, 1950.

Crossman, R. H. S. *A Nation Reborn*. New York: Atheneum, 1960.

———. *Palestine Mission*. London: Hamish Hamilton, 1950.

Crum, Bartley C. *Behind the Silken Curtain*. New York: Simon & Schuster, 1947.

Dayan, Moshe. *Diary of the Suez Campaign*. New York: Schocken, 1966.

Dimont, Max I. *The Jews, God and History*. New York: Simon & Schuster, 1962.

Dunner, Joseph. *The Republic of Israel*. New York: McGraw-Hill, 1950.

Eban, Abba. *The Voice of Israel*. New York: Horizon, 1957.

Faris, N. A., and T. H. Husayn. *The Crescent in Crisis*. Lawrence, Kan.: University of Kansas Press, 1955.

Frank, Gerold. *The Deed*. New York: Simon & Schuster, 1965.

Frank, Waldo. *Bridgehead*. New York: Braziller, 1957.

Gabbay, Rony E. *A Political Study of the Arab-Jewish Conflict*. Paris: Minard, 1959.

Glubb, John. *A Soldier with the Arabs*. New York: Harper, 1957.

Halasz, Nicholas. *Captain Dreyfus*. New York: Simon & Schuster, 1955.

Hirschmann, Ira. *The Embers Still Burn*. New York: Simon & Schuster, 1949.

Hurewitz, J. C. *Middle East Dilemmas*. New York: Harper, 1953.

———. *The Struggle for Palestine*. New York: Norton, 1950.

Joseph, Dov. *The Faithful City*. New York: Simon & Schuster, 1960.

Kerr, Malcolm. *The Arab Cold War.* New York: Oxford University Press, 1967.

Kimche, Jon and David. *A Clash of Destinies.* New York: Praeger, 1960.

Koestler, Arthur. *Promise and Fulfillment.* New York: Macmillan, 1949.

Lawrence, T. E. *The Seven Pillars of Wisdom.* New York: Doubleday, 1947.

Lowdermilk, Walter Clay. *Palestine: Land of Promise.* New York: Harper, 1944.

Morris, James. *The Hashemite Kings.* New York: Pantheon, 1959.

Nutting, Anthony. *No End of a Lesson.* New York: Clarkson N. Potter, 1967.

Parkes, James W. *End of an Exile.* London: Valentine Mitchell, 1954.

———. *History of Palestine.* New York: Oxford University Press, 1949.

Pearlman, Moshe. *The Trial of Adolph Eichmann.* New York: Simon & Schuster, 1963.

———. *The Zealots of Masada.* New York: Scribner, 1967.

Peretz, Don. *Israel and the Palestine Arabs.* Washington, D.C.: Middle East Institute, 1958.

Rosenberg, James N. *Unfinished Business.* New Rochelle, N.Y.: Vincent Marasia Press, 1967.

Seale, Patrick. *The Struggle for Syria.* New York: Oxford University Press, 1967.

Seder, Irving. *Behind the Egyptian Sphinx.* Philadelphia: Chilton, 1960.

Sheean, Vincent. *Personal History.* New York: Doubleday, Doran, 1935.

Sherwood, Robert E. *Roosevelt and Hopkins.* New York: Harper, 1948.

Steinberg, Milton. *A Partisan Guide to the Jewish Problem.* New York: Bobbs-Merrill, 1945.

Sykes, Christopher. *Crossroads to Israel.* Cleveland: World, 1965.

Thomas, Hugh. *Suez.* New York: Harper and Row, 1967.

Truman, Harry S. *Memoirs.* New York: Doubleday, 1950.

Weizmann, Chaim. *Trial and Error.* New York: Harper, 1949.

Wilber, Donald N. *Iran, Past and Present.* Princeton, N.J.: Princeton University Press, 1958.

INDEX

JAMES P. WARBURG

*James P. Warburg is a writer, lecturer and fre-
quent commentator on world affairs, well known
both here and abroad. In 1932, as one of Wall
Street's youngest bank presidents, he was summoned to Washington by Franklin D. Roosevelt
as a financial adviser. He declined a Cabinet post,
but participated actively in the First Hundred
Days of the New Deal and attended the ill-fated
World Economic Conference in London, after
which he broke for a time with the Roosevelt
Administration. He returned to serve during
World War II as the official in charge of American propaganda policy in the European Theatre.
Since 1945 he has devoted himself to the cause of
world peace. Mr. Warburg's home is in Green-
wich, Connecticut. He is a member of the Coun-
cil on Foreign Relations in New York and of the
Commission to Study the Organization of Peace.
A former director of the American Academy of
Political and Social Science, he is now a trustee
of the Institute for Policy Studies in Washington.*

Atlantic Ocean

FRANCE

AUSTRIA
HUNGARY
ROMAN

ITALY
YUGOSLAVIA

BULGAR

PORTUGAL
SPAIN

GREECE

Mediterranean Sea

MOROCCO

TUNISIA

ALGERIA

LIBYA

MALI

NIGER

CHAD

The Middle East

Map by Morgan